Victorious Mom, Victorious Daughter

Daily Devotional to Joyfully Share Your Life!

Holly LaChappell

xulon
PRESS

Copyright © 2013 by Holly LaChappell

Victorious Mom, Victorious Daughter
Daily Devotional to Joyfully Share Your Life!
by Holly LaChappell

Printed in the United States of America

ISBN 9781628710526

All rights reserved solely by the author. The author guarantees all contents are original and do not infringe upon the legal rights of any other person or work. No part of this book may be reproduced in any form without the permission of the author. The views expressed in this book are not necessarily those of the publisher.

Unless otherwise indicated, Bible quotations are taken from The Holy Bible, New Internatonal Version (NIV). Copyright © 1973 by Zondervan.

www.xulonpress.com

Introduction

Note to Readers:

In our highly-connected technological world, we are not really so connected emotionally! As my daughters have grown up, moved away to go to college and begun their own lives, I have had a great desire to connect on a deeper level. Phone and text conversations are great, but how are you feeling, really? I can read your tone, but I cannot see your body language, unless we are facetiming or Skyping!

This is why I embarked to write this devotional book. I want to know my daughters' thoughts. Not as a way of being invasive, but as a way of growing and staying positively connected to them and point them to an intimate, loving relationship with Jesus. Whether they are near or far, *Victorious Mom, Victorious Daughter* is a devotional book that that will connect you with your Daughter, Mother, Girlfriend, Grandma, Granddaughter, Daughter in law, Aunt or Niece in a positive and enriching way! In the sisterhood of women, it's our shared experiences in Christ that binds us together in His love for us.

You can determine how often you will check in with one another: once a week or every day! **Choose at least one "Let's Talk" and "Let's Go!" application to discuss weekly.** As parents and friends, it is so comforting to know that no matter how far apart you might live you are reading God's same powerful Word daily! It's in our love relationship with Jesus that we grow closer to His heart. He in turn, works through us as we linger in His presence and meditate on His word throughout the day.

Be blessed and encouraged as He makes you strong and victorious together! "Through the victories you gave, his glory is great; you have bestowed on him splendor and majesty" (Ps. 21:5). May your relationship in Christ grow deeper as you cherish Him and your sharing time together! "No eye has seen and no ear has heard, and no mind has imagined what God has prepared for those who love Him" (1 Cor. 2:9 NLT).

Acknowledgments

To my Savior Jesus who truly teaches me how to be in wonderful relationships with my precious Mom, girlfriends and Tapestry sisters.
You have truly woven a beautiful golden thread of love and support around my heart!

To my adorable and smart daughters, Olivia and Juliet.
Thank you for all of your charming wit, love and laughter.

To my most favorite men: my husband Jeff and son Blake.
I love you all and am blessed by your generous support!

January

"There are two lasting bequests we can give our children:
One is roots. The other is wings."
~ Hodding Carter, Jr.

January 1

Victorious Action: Thanking God for the Special Women in Your Life!

"I always thank my God for you because of His grace given you in Christ Jesus. For in Him you have been enriched in every way—with all kinds of speech and with all knowledge God thus confirming our testimony about Christ among you" (1 Cor.1:4-7).

Let's Talk: Mom, daughter, sister, girlfriend, grandma, daughter in law, aunt and niece. I am so grateful for YOU! God has bestowed upon you every kind knowledge and wonderful grace. You have freely and generously shared your love and words of encouragement with me. Your day by day routines and gestures of life have shown me love. You have pointed me to the Word when I needed advice. You have given me grace when I have made a mess of myself. You are a beautiful example of our Savior shining through you. Thank you for teaching me how to study the Word, ride a bike, craft, knit, can preserves, bake goodies, garden flowers and vegetables and run the long races of life with grace and beauty. Most of all, thank you for your loving prayers and support! I love you!

Let's Glorify: God, thank you for this special woman in my life. She has made me the person I am today. She has woven me with loving thoughts and prayers, always pointing me to you, Jesus. I am so grateful for these precious women! They are precious gifts from you God, the Giver of all great gifts. Thank you and how I praise you for these wonderful ladies! In Jesus' name, I pray. Amen.

Let's Go! Who in your life have been a life encourager and supporter to you? Write them a Thank you card and tell them how much they mean to you.

January 2

Victorious Action: Be a Woman Who Follows After Jesus!

"Soon afterward Jesus began a tour of the nearby towns and villages, preaching and announcing the Good News about the Kingdom of God. He took his twelve disciples with Him, along with some women who had been cured of evil spirits and diseases. Among them were Mary Magdalene, from whom He had cast out seven demons; Joanna, the wife of Chuza, Herod's business manager; Susanna; and many others who were contributing from their own resources to support Jesus and his disciples" (Luke 8:1-3 NLT).

Let's Talk: Joanna was healed and saved by Jesus during the time her husband Chuza served under Herod. The bible doesn't say exactly what Jesus healed her of, but most likely it was a disease that could not be cured by the doctors of her day. As a result of Jesus' healing upon Joanna, she followed Him and ministered out of her own financial resources. She knew Jesus and His disciples did not have a lot of means and she gave out of her plenty with generous grace. Joanna also had the opportunity to witness Jesus' healing touch and love to those in Herod's household. Surely this was something that was very risky for her to do. The bible records Joanna's faithful care of Jesus and the disciples as they preached through towns and villages. She followed Jesus to the cross, watched Him be crucified and then die. She was one of the last to leave Him at the cross and at the resurrection, she was among the ladies who heard the angels speak the astonishing news, "He isn't here! He is risen from the dead" (Luke 24:6 NLT).

Let's Glorify: God, thank you for Joanna's faithful service given to Jesus during His ministry. She gave her all to Jesus with deep thanks and reverence for all He had done for her! Jesus, I want to serve you and honor you like Joanna did. Help me to remember your suffering and dying for me. I am set free today and forevermore! As a result, I will share your goodness and salvation with others. In your saving name, I pray. Amen.

Let's Go! What example do you show the world that you follow lovingly after Jesus? Discuss with your mom, daughter or girlfriend. Would you like to have lived in Jesus' day? Why or why not?

January 3

Victorious Action: Come and Rest!

Matt. 11: 28-30 tells each of us: "Come to me, all you who are weary and burdened, and I will give you rest. Take my yoke upon you and learn from me, for I am gentle and humble in heart, and you will find rest for your souls. For my yoke is easy and my burden is light."

Let's Talk: "Come," Jesus gently whispers as He woos me unto Him. Come and be refreshed. Come and see what is on my heart. Come and be fully restored and healed. This is the way you were made to be, since I formed you in your mother's womb. Stop resisting my gentle lead. Rest, relax. "I've got this," He whispers to my weary soul. "Zugos" is the Greek word for yoke. A yoke serves to couple two things together. Jesus takes your yoke (your burdens and your weariness) upon Himself as you submit to His loving and gentle authority. He joins and links you together in Him though the power of the magnificent Holy Spirit living within.

Let's Glorify: Dear Gentle Jesus, thank you that I can come to you at any moment of the day and find you! Lord, I do need you and so humbly I ask that you would guide and direct me today. Lord, I surrender my plans for your perfect plan and provision. As I stop and reflect on you, I find rest for my soul. I am forever grateful. Amen.

Let's Go! Recall a time of your favorite vacation as a family. Was it restful? Pray for someone in your life that needs Jesus' gentle leading and restorative healing today. Send them a card, email or text of encouragement.

January 4

Victorious Action: Dream His Dreams for You!

1 Cor. 2:9 shares graciously about your dreams and aspirations: "What no eye has seen, what no ear has heard, and what no human mind has conceived the things God has prepared for those who love Him."

Let's Talk: What dreams do you have for your life? Have you achieved all of your dreams? Have you noticed when you are pursuing your dream, you are motivated in a forward motion by hope, purpose and passion? I sure have! You are energized by the Holy Spirit's guidance. You serve and move towards your life dream with joy, knowing God is helping you! Your dream was fashioned in your heart by Almighty God before you were born! So live boldly! Your fulfillment of your dream honors God and blesses others! Praise God for such a great purpose!

Let's Glorify: Dear God, Thank you for the special dreams you have put in my heart! Help me to realize in your power and creativity, your dreams will come to fruition in my life. "God, you not only love me very much, but you also have put your hand upon me for something special" (1 Thess. 1:4 MSG). That is exciting! In advance, I want to give you all the praise, honor and glory. In Jesus' name, I pray. Amen.

Let's Go! Together, if possible visit a place that symbolizes a dream God has given you. Journal and photograph your experience with great gratitude to the Giver of all good gifts!

January 5

Victorious Action: Know God's Everlasting Embrace!

Dt. 33:27 tells you a beautiful promise: "The eternal God is your refuge, and underneath are the everlasting arms."

Let's Talk: God has Everlasting arms which are holding you up, everyday! Do you really know this in your heart of hearts? God's embrace is a forever kind of hug! He never lets go and He never stops thinking about you. There is no God like Him! He is your refuge, your strength, your great Protector and Provider. El Olam means The Everlasting God. His everlasting arms will hold you up, even in your greatest trial. He will bring you into triumph as you lean into His warm and soothing embrace!

Let's Glorify: Lord God, You are my holy Abba Daddy. Thank you for holding onto me when my world seems as if it is going to spin off its axis. Thank you for whispering to my heart, "I have you and I will never let you go." I know this is a promise you will always keep! I love you. In Jesus' name, I pray. Amen.

Let's Go! Look for His precious assurances in the Word, the Bible. Commit one of your favorite verses to memory this week. Recite it to one another.

January 6

Victorious Action: Be a Beautiful Fragrance Maker!

"Be imitators of God, therefore as dearly loved children and live a life of love, just as Christ loved us and gave Himself up for us as a fragrant offering and sacrifice to God" (Eph. 5:1-2).

Let's Talk: You and I are dearly loved children of the Most High God! Doesn't that just make you smile? He asks you to imitate Him and carry His love to others. How do you do this? Look at Jesus' example. He was obedient out of His love to His Father God. He was also grateful for their relationship, so He carried His message to our world. Out of your loving obedience to Jesus, you can share His Good News of love and Salvation to your world, too.

Let's Glorify: Dear God, I want to be a fragrant offering going up to you. Lord, help me to rely on the love that you already have for me. Please help me to share your love and Great News to our dying world. Let me make a difference as I live victoriously in you. In Jesus' precious name, I pray. Amen.

Let's Go! What is your favorite perfume? Discuss a way you have recently shared Jesus' love and life with another. Pray God will bring someone today to you that you can share His Great News with!

January 7

Victorious Action: Receive His Gift!

"For God's gifts and His call are irrevocable" (Rom. 11:29).

Let's Talk: My life is full of wonderful gifts of love, beauty and friendship. You, Lord give these gifts to me. My salvation is sure and the greatest gift even given to man: Jesus Christ's life poured out on the cross. His blood frees me from my sin and I am forgiven! His love transforms my brokenness and heals my heart. Yes, His gift is the most precious gift ever given. It will not be taken away! I am set free indeed!

Let's Glorify: Dear Savior Jesus, I praise you and thank you! Your precious gift is irreversible. And, you are irresistible love. I thank you Lord Jesus for your free gift! Thank you for healing my brokenness. Let me help others with the help I have received from you. I love you. I pray this all to your glory. Amen.

Let's Go! Who in your world needs to hear about Jesus' saving love and grace? Share with them how Jesus has set you free. Discuss when you became a believer with your mom, daughter or special friend.

January 8

Victorious Action: Hold Onto our Only True Hope!

"Let us hold unswervingly to the hope we profess, for He who promised is faithful" (Heb. 10:23).

Let's Talk: Who is truly faithful in your life? Is it your spouse, your child, a parent, a friend? Even these loved ones will let you down at times. Our God is ever present, an ever faithful confidant. He can be called on in the middle of the night when you are sleepless. He knows the decisions you need to make. He sees you in your distress and in your sorrow. Jesus is praying right now for you and interceding on your behalf. Be comforted. Be loved and encouraged. He is faithful. He will help you. Just **A. S. K!** (Ask-Seek-Knock!)

Let's Glorify: Lord Jesus, you tell us: "Ask and it will be given to you; seek and you will find; knock and the door will be opened to you. (Matt. 7:7) You are my only true hope, Lord! Thank you for being ever faithful, even when I give up on myself. Thank you for opening the doors of opportunities to me. I love you. In Jesus' name, I pray. Amen.

Let's Go! What area of your life is God asking you to ask Him, seek Him and keep knocking? Will you lay down your skepticism, your pride and worry so you can have His will be done in your life? He is our ONLY true source of true hope today and tomorrow! Discuss with your mom, daughter or special friend.

January 9

Victorious Action: Having an Intimate Personal Relationship with Jesus!

"Having loved His own who were in the world, He loved them to the end" (John 13:1). "Jesus knew that the Father had put all things under His power, and that He had come from God and was returning to God; so He got up from the meal, took off His outer clothing, and wrapped a towel around His waist. After that, He poured water into a basin and began to wash His disciples' feet, drying them with the towel that was wrapped around Him" (John 13:3-5).

Let's Talk: Intimacy is defined as a close or warm friendship or understanding; personal relationship, an act or expression serving as a token of familiarity, affection, or the like. Jesus had a close fellowship with His disciples. In the intimate setting of the Upper Room Discourse Jesus' actions share His devoted love to His followers, who were family to Him. He shares this with you as well, because you are family to Him.

Let's Glorify: Dear Lord, thank you for your example of washing your family's feet in loving service. You loved them to the very end as scriptures said, even in the long and hard moments. You deeply cared for your followers even though you knew soon you were going to the cross. Help me God to keep on serving and loving my family, even when I am tired and frazzled. Thank you that your grace is sufficient for me. In Jesus' name, I pray. Amen.

Let's Go! Whose feet do you need to wash today in loving service to Jesus? If possible, plan on going to get pedicures together.

January 10

Victorious Action: Joy! <u>J</u>esus <u>O</u>mnipresent in <u>Y</u>ou!

"Surely you have granted him eternal blessings and made him glad with the joy of your presence." "For the king trusts in the Lord; through the **unfailing love** of the Most High he will not be shaken" (Ps. 21:6-7 emphasis mine).

Let's Talk: Jesus, your Presence is sweeter than life! How can I describe what that means to me? Even though my words are not adequate, being in an intimate and close relationship with you is like visiting with my best friend. You know what is on my heart before I even start to express it. You can finish my sentences and know exactly what to say to soothe my anxieties and fears. No wonder there is true peace and joy in your presence! You are true joy within, because you never leave your beloved! <u>J</u>esus <u>O</u>mnipresent in <u>Y</u>ou = **J.O.Y.**

Let's Glorify: Dear Jesus, thank you that you are truly a Man of Joy! When you see me and think of me, you delight in how I try to please you and serve you. And, even when I sin and want to do life in my stubborn way, you still love me and will never leave nor forsake me! I can rest in your blessed love. Your love is a fact and not a feeling! How I love you and appreciate you. Amen.

Let's Go! How can you share Jesus' unfailing love with somebody else today? Will you believe that Jesus loves you with a never ending and unfailing love? Discuss it over coffee.

January 11

Victorious Action: Speak with Kindness!

"When she speaks, her words are wise, and she gives instructions with kindness" (Prov. 31:26 NLT).

Let's Talk: Hey mom, thank you for your wise instruction! It only took me until I was a grown up to figure out you truly did know what you were talking about! Hey daughter, thank you for being kind to me, even when I didn't know what I was talking about, I made you clean your room, finish everything on your plate and change the hamster's cage!

Let's Glorify: Dear Lord, thank you that you are a patient God and you do not repay me as my sins deserve. You sing gently over me, "as you lead me along with your ropes of kindness and love. You lifted the yoke from my neck, and you stooped to feed me" (Hosea 11:4 NLT). How can I not thank you and speak of your kindness? Let me freely pass your kindness to others today. In Jesus' name, I pray. Amen.

Let's Go! Think of a time when someone's kindness really meant a lot to you. Pray for an opportunity to share that same kind of kindness today.

January 12

Victorious Action: Love with a Pure Heart!

"The goal of this command is love, which comes from a pure heart, and a good conscience and a sincere faith" (1 Tim. 1:5).

Let's Talk: Loving with a pure heart is not always easy! When you are wondering about your own love and motives towards others, especially your family, ask God to cleanse your mind. Pray and ask Him to help you to have a faith that is genuine and authentic in Him alone, not worrying about what others think, say or do. Ask Him to remind you what a beautiful witness you'd like to be for your family and friends!

Let's Glorify: Dear Lord, you are my holy God and you ask me be holy, too. Lord, I cannot do this on my own! I need your sanctification process daily to be worked out in my life. This occurs as I pray, read your word, obey and walk in your loving and merciful grace. Thank you that you never stop working in me! Please forgive me now. In Jesus' name, I pray. Amen.

Let's Go! Do a word study on sanctification. What does it mean to be sanctified? Have a conversation over tea and scones.

January 13

Victorious Action: Keeping His Covenant Laws!

"This is the covenant I will make with them after that time, says the Lord. I will put my laws in their hearts, and I will write them on their minds" (Heb. 10:16).

Let's Talk: A covenant is a special promise God gives to His followers. It is an agreement between God and the ancient Israelites, in which God promised to protect them if they kept His law and were faithful to Him. Today, God doesn't leave us to our own strategies. He places His laws in our hearts, so we will know which way to turn when it is time to make decisions. He engraves His thoughts on your mind as you study the Word. He loves you so much that He has engraved your name on the palms of His hand! You are always before His eyes! (Isa. 49:16, ERV)

Let's Glorify: Lord God, you promise to keep your promises to us. I am so grateful I can count on you at all times! Thank you I am always in your thoughts! Please remind me to remember this precious promise of what **Emmanuel** means: you are always with me! In Jesus' name, I pray. Amen.

Let's Go! Find a picture of you growing up. Discuss what you remember about the time the photograph was taken. What joys or sorrows did you experience during this time? (Kleenex alert!)

January 14

Victorious Action: God Does Not Change His Mind!

"He who is the Glory of Israel does not lie or change His mind; for He is not a human being, that He should change his mind" (1 Sam. 15:29).

Let's Talk: Aren't you glad, God doesn't change His mind like shifting sands or the blowing of the wind? I sure am glad! God does not lie and can be trusted 100% of the time! His ways are truly not our ways. His ways are much higher and greater than our ways. "May you be blessed by the Lord, who made heaven and earth" (Ps. 115:15). Has there been a time when you have changed your mind? How did it turn out?

Let's Glorify: Father God, I am so grateful you are completely trustworthy and faithful to me. I am yours and you are mine. You are everything to me. Your wisdom is always accurate and I can trust that you will lead me down the right and true paths for my life when I ask for guidance. Lord, remind me to ask for guidance every day. As I do so, Lord I want to surrender my will for your perfect and pure will. I love you. In Jesus' name, I pray. Amen.

Let's Go! Pray for your children and grandchildren to seek God's guidance for their lives every day. Do you have a favorite bible story your mom shared with you growing up?

January 15

Victorious Action: Draw Near!

"Let us draw near to God with a sincere heart in full assurance of faith, having our hearts sprinkled to cleanse us from a guilty conscience and having our bodies washed with pure water" (Heb. 10:22).

Let's Talk: What makes you feel guilty? God is described as the spring of living water, being the source of life and salvation to those who come to Him. His pure water can be fresh and bubbling out of you because of the Holy Spirit living within you. He can cleanse you of any and all guilt you are feeling right now! Ask Him to forgive you. Ask Him to remove any guilt, shame or condemnation. Walk freely in His love today.

Let's Glorify: Lord, I want to be near to you right now, fully aware of your presence, for where you are there is precious peace. Holy Spirit, help me to internalize with your grace, the washing of my sins. You are pure and cleansing water. Thank you, Lord Jesus. I receive your forgiveness right now. Amen.

Let's Go! What are some of the funny things you did as a kid still have not told your mom (or daughter) about? Is there someone in your life you need to give the cleansing water of forgiveness to today? Do not delay! Shower them with mercy and grace just as Jesus has done for you!

January 16

Victorious Action: Keeping Your Problems Small and God BIG!

"For our present troubles are small and won't last very long. Yet they produce for us a glory that vastly outweighs them and will last forever" (2 Cor. 4:17).

Let's Talk: Praise the Lord! Our problems set against the backdrop of our Big and Almighty God are small in comparison to Him and His awesome power! He IS greater! God knows the timing of each fiery trial you will go through and how close the fire will get to you. You might get singed but not scorched! He has you in a loving control burn. Once His work is finished the heat's intensity will die down. You will come forth as purified gold.

Let's Glorify: Lord, I thank you for you know the intensity of the fiery trial I am going through. Thank you for being ever so close especially in those heated times when all I seem to feel is the flames of the fire. Lord, help me to have faith and an unending trust in you. Let my attitude say, this trial will bring you all the praise, honor and glory until you take me home to be with you in heaven! In Jesus' powerful name, I pray. Amen.

Let's Go! How have you experienced a glory of blessedness in your fiery trial? Has your blessedness outweighed and overwhelmingly exceeded your troubles? Share with each other.

January 17

Victorious Action: Spur Each Other On!

"And let us consider how we may spur one another on toward love and good deeds" (Heb.10:24).

Let's Talk: You can be an inspiration to those around you! Encourage each other to show love! How you might ask? By holding onto the faith you have in Jesus! Other believers need a great godly example to emulate. Jesus is our true example and you are the hands and feet of our Lord and Savior! "Let us draw near with true hearts and fullest confidence, knowing that our inmost souls have been purified by the sprinkling of His blood just as our bodies are cleansed by the washing of clean water. In this confidence let us hold on to the hope that we profess without the slightest hesitation—for He is utterly dependable—and let us think of one another and how we can encourage each other to love and do good deeds" (Heb. 10:23-24 PHILLIPS, emphasis mine).

Let's Glorify: Jesus, thank you for your examples of love throughout the bible. You cared for the least of people: the hurting, the sick, the blind and the lame. You turned people who were steeped in their sin and healed their hearts and revealed their hidden motives. You do the same for me. Thank you for cleansing my soul of my sins. I am eternally grateful. Let me do good deeds out of a heart filled with deep love of you. In your precious name, I pray. Amen.

Let's Go! Encourage each other to show love! What are some helpful deeds and noble activities you can get involved with and share Jesus' saving love?

January 18

Victorious Action: Quality and Quantity Time!

"Their work will be shown for what it is, because the Day will bring it to light. It will be revealed with fire, and the fire will test the quality of each person's work" (1Cor. 3:13).

Let's Talk: I want my work and my time spent doing it, to count for your glory, Lord. I want my work to stand the test of time under fire! What job or career have you done that has been tested by the quality of your work? What employment has lasted and which ones have been burnt up? Why do you think this has happened?

Let's Glorify: Dear Jesus, you tell me the fires of testing will critically appraise the character and worth of the work I have done throughout my lifetime. I want my life's work to stand for the goodness and love you have poured out into my life. Wherever I am found working and serving you please let your light shine through me all to your glory and deep grace. In your holy name, I pray. Amen.

Let's Go! Do you volunteer anywhere? Where can you shine His light onto others? If possible, plan a volunteering time you can do together.

January 19

Victorious Action: Renown: Celebrating God's Fame!

"Ah, Sovereign Lord, you have made the heavens and the earth by your great power and outstretched arm. Nothing is too hard for you. You show love to thousands but bring the punishment for the parents' sins into the laps of their children after them" (Jer. 32: 17-18).

Let's Talk: Nothing is too hard for the Lord! He is loving and gracious. When you ask for forgiveness for your sins, He wipes your guilt away. You can be so grateful your sins do not have to be handed down to your children!

Let's Glorify: Sovereign Lord, thank you for your out stretched arm which is always reaching towards me! Let me firmly grasp your arm of love, forgiveness and new life! Forgive me now Lord so my children will not be hindered in their walk. Help them to walk in your holy ways so their children will be blessed. May we live all to your glory today and forever more. In Jesus' name, I pray. Amen.

Let's Go! How have you stopped the generational sins from being handed down to your family? Was there a time as your mom (or daughter) I kept a promise that really meant a lot to you? Or did I break a promise? Share how these experiences affected you. Extend His loving arm of forgiveness and hope to one another today.

January 20

Victorious Action: Rejoice!

"Rejoice in the Lord, you who are righteous, and praise His holy name" (Ps. 97:12).

Let's Talk: You are called to consistently rejoice in the Lord in all circumstances! You are also to give thanks at the remembrance of His holiness. He is a reverent God. Jesus gave His Father reverent submission and fulfilled all that He was asked to do, down to the last detail. This is why God celebrates Jesus! You can rejoice and celebrate Jesus today. Praise His holy name and shout for joy! He has made you righteous, upright and blameless!

Let's Glorify: Lord, you are a holy God and Savior! Help me Lord to stay open to you by having a grateful heart. When I do not, my vision narrows and I miss out on all the great things you are creating in my life! Jesus, let me look at what I have in you and not what I think I am lacking. It's in your precious name, I pray. Amen.

Let's Go! How are you rejoicing in the Lord today? When is it hardest for you to rejoice? When is it easiest for you to rejoice in God? Sing a song together praising His goodness to you!

January 21

Victorious Action: Recognizing His Sovereignty!

Hab. 3:19 shares, "The Sovereign Lord is my strength; He makes my feet like the feet of a deer, He enables me to tread on the heights."

Let's Talk: Adonai signifies Lord or Master. Elohim is another name for God. The high places in your life are the mountainous problems and steep hills of challenges that loom so large in front of your eyes and trembling heart. Adonai will make sure your feet will not slip as you keep your gaze upon Him. **Elohim Adonai the conqueror** will lead you upon the high places singing Psalms of praises! He is Sovereign! As you pray, remember and recognize His sovereignty today!

Let's Glorify: Elohim Adonai, thank you for being my sovereign Lord. As my good, loving and faithful Master who owns and cares for me, you see me and will not let me stumble. Thank you for leading me through the rocky challenges today holds. Let me look into your face knowing you will help me be more than a conqueror with your help and guidance. How I praise you! In Jesus' name, I pray. Amen.

Let's Go! What mountains are you facing today? With God's help, how have you gotten over these mountain ranges? Share how you have seen His conquering power made real through some really hard situations in your lives.

January 22

Victorious Action: Trust in the Lord!

"The Lord will keep you from all harm. He will watch over your life; the Lord will watch over your coming and going both now and forevermore" (Ps. 121: 7-8).

Let's Talk: God, the Eternal One will keep you safe from all of life's evils, from your first breath to the last breath you breathe, from this day and forever (Ps. 121:7-8 VOICE). Do you believe this? How freeing it is to know God never sleeps and never grows weary. He is faithful and He is watching over you, even in this moment! You can count on Him at all times.

Let's Glorify: God, thank you for guarding me today, tomorrow and always. I pray for your protection over my family as well. You are my sentinel and my Hightower. Holy Spirit, you are my very breath giving me life and encouragement. I praise you for your deliverance over evil. Thank you for breathing Jesus' life into me. In the holy name of Jesus, I pray. Amen.

Let's Go! Where do you need God's holy breath of the Holy Spirit breathed into your life? Chat about it with your mom, daughter or friend.

January 23

Victorious Action: Working Together!

"Two people are better off than one, for they can help each other succeed" (Eccles. 4:9 NLT).

Let's Talk: The CEV bible says it this way: "You are better off to have a friend than to be all alone, because then you will get more enjoyment out of what you earn." It is true you were made by our Creator God to be in community and relationship with others. As we cooperate with each other in any task large or small, we are strengthened, and rewarded as we learn about each other and our self! We learn what we like, what we abhor and what is fun!

Let's Glorify: Lord, thank you for my girlfriend, my daughter and my mom. These women are such a blessing and a gift to me. Let us learn more about each other as we share our successes, failures, our hobbies and our lives. Let us accept each other as we truly are, not trying to change each other but choosing to love each other unconditionally. Thank you for placing this dear woman in my life! In Jesus' name, I pray and ask these things. Amen.

Let's Go! Share what you love about each other today. Have your picture taken together and frame it. Make sure you both have a copy!

January 24

Victorious Action: Know His Voice!

"I am the good shepherd; I know my own sheep, and they know me, just as my Father knows me and I know the Father. So I sacrifice my life for the sheep. I have other sheep, too, that are not in this sheepfold. I must bring them also. They will listen to my voice, and there will be one flock with one shepherd" (Jn. 10: 14-16 NLT).

Let's Talk: Jesus you are my good Shepherd. I recognize you have laid down your life for me. I in return, surrender my life and take up my cross in a loving and satisfying relationship with you. You tell us your sheep know your voice and there are those who are not yet of your sheep pen. Lord, knock on their hearts so millions more will come to know you and your voice.

Let's Glorify: Jesus I pray for the "not yet" who have not yet invited you to be the Lord of their lives. I pray I can in some small way be a part in bringing people to the saving grace of your precious love and life! Lord, let be open to the Holy Spirit to speak love and life into others' lives. In your saving name, I pray. Amen.

Let's Go! When did you accept Jesus to be the Lord and Savior of your life? What questions do you have about Jesus? (Email me please if you have any questions or ask a pastor or bible study leader) **Holly@HeartForTheCross.com**

January 25

Victorious Action: Watch!

"On my charge I stand, and I station myself on a bulwark, and I watch to see what He doth speak against me, and what I do reply to my reproof" (Hab. 2:1 YLT).

Let's Talk: Waiting for God's answers is certainly not easy! It is however possible as you station yourself solidly upon Him. He is your Hightower, your rampart and wall. Nothing comes against you that He doesn't know about or allow. God knows how to shape and build your character. God knows how to transform and mold you into the very image of Jesus. Waiting is indeed part of this process. In the meantime, you need to be gentle with yourself. You also need to be patient.

Let's Glorify: Lord God, help me to rest in you at all times. Lord, if I am to be reprimanded for my behavior or deeds, let it be so under your covering of unfailing love. Forgive me please. Help me to stand strong in the waiting times. May all the glory, honor and praise be yours, for you know how long this time will be to cause fruition of my character. Help me to abide in you as I wait peacefully. In the holy name of Jesus, I pray. Amen.

Let's Go! Are you in a waiting season right now? What has been the longest waiting season you have experienced? What did God teach you about Himself during this time?

January 26

Victorious Action: Prayer!

"Now when Daniel learned that the decree had been published, he went home to his upstairs room where the windows opened toward Jerusalem. Three times a day he got down on his knees and prayed, giving thanks to his God, just as he had done before" (Dan. 6:10).

Let's Talk: The charge against Daniel by his conspirators was he worshipped God and not King Darius. The conspirators did not like Daniel's favor with the king. The conspirators returned to press the matter further. They reminded King Darius he could not get out of edict which was established by him. In fact, a king's edict cannot be revoked, changed, or ignored. Daniel did not let their words stop or intimidate him for praying as he had done before.

Let's Glorify: Lord of Heaven, thank you that you had a different ending to Daniel's story. You tamed and shut the lion's mouths when Daniel was thrown into their den. Lord, thank you when people rise against me you too close their mouths. Thank you that I can rely on your love and protection. In Jesus' name, I pray. Amen.

Let's Go! When is a time you had to rely on the love of the Lord to get you through a really hard situation in regards to other people? Daniel's story is a great reminder that people regardless of their position who insult God or try to render God irrelevant are destined to fall and fail.

January 27

Victorious Action: He Knows Your Ways!

"You have searched me, Lord, and you know me. You know when I sit and when I rise; you perceive my thoughts from afar" (Ps. 139:1-2).

Let's Talk: God knows **everything** about you. He understands your needs, your wants and dreams. He hears you when you cry and He sees you when you are lonely. His arm is not too short to reach down and help you as you cry out to Him. He even hears the silent tears of your heart. He knows what your favorite color is and what kind of dessert you crave! God knows all the details of your life and cares about each one of them.

Let's Glorify: Lord God, Abba Daddy. Thank you for knowing all my ways. Because you know me so well, you cause good things to come to fruition. You know what is truly best for me and my life. My heart can rest today and always, believing this fact about you! I love you, Abba. In your name, I pray. Amen.

Let's Go! What thoughts do you need to turn over to Abba Daddy today? Share as freely as you can with each other.

January 28

Victorious Action: Zealous for God!

"Before a word is on my tongue you, Lord, know it completely" (Ps. 139:4).

Let's Talk: The words on your tongue are formed in your heart first! God knows the thoughts of your heart and what is dear to you and not so dear to you! Out of the overflow of the heart the mouth speaks! So, whatever is in your heart (mind, emotions, will) will come out eventually through your mouth. Spending time with Jesus is time well spent. He shapes our affections and cleanses you of your sins. As you move and have your being in Him, He shapes your thoughts and therefore your actions, all to His glory!

Let's Glorify: Jesus, thank you that your reassuring presence is all around me—even in me! I want to carve out a quiet time with you every day. I want to meditate on you throughout the day, knowing you are as close to me as I am to myself. Lord, I want to glorify you in my heart feelings and outward actions. Thank you for being my Savior. In your precious name, I pray. Amen.

Let's Go! What are some words you have spoken lately that you wished you had not? Do you have any words from your past you'd like to ask forgiveness for? Share with each other.

January 29

Victorious Action: Banner of Love!

"He brought me to the banqueting house, and His banner over me was love" (Song of Songs 2:4 NKJV).

Let's Talk: Jehovah Nissi means the Lord is my banner. His love and care for you is waving as a protecting and comforting banner over your head all the time. As a believer, you can look around at all that God has done for you. It should be obvious how much He loves you! You are invited to sit with Jesus as His beloved bride of the church. His flag always waves in strong support and love for you!

Let's Glorify: Lord God, thank you that you look at me with love. You see me through the lens of looking at your Son Jesus. Thank you for the coming time when I will sit at your banquet table with Jesus as His bride, the church. Thank you for your flag of love waving over my head continuously. You promise never to depart me. In your Almighty name, I pray, Amen.

Let's Go! How has God declared His love for you? How do you show His love for one another?

January 30

Victorious: Crown of Beauty and Joy!

Isaiah 61:3 shares, God has graciously "bestowed on them a crown of beauty instead of ashes, the oil of joy instead of mourning, and a garment of praise instead of a spirit of despair."

Let's Talk: God takes your spirit of heaviness, turning it into a spirit of joy and praise! Our Almighty God does this so that we might be called trees of righteousness, planted by the Lord, that He might be glorified" (Is. 61:3 KJV). It is such a wonder God Himself plants you so you will grow like mighty oak trees: strong, and magnificent, distinguished for uprightness. He gives you justice and right standing with Himself.

Let's Glorify: Lord, how I needed this promise today! You are my King and I am your beloved daughter. You give me a crown to wear! You have picked me up out of the ash pile, turning my discouragement and fear into joy and gratefulness. I praise you my magnificent Lord! In Jesus' name, I pray. Amen.

Let's Go! Do you realize that you are a beloved daughter of the Most High God planted to grow strongly in Him? Did you know you are distinguished for uprightness? Uprightness means honor, respectability, worthiness and righteousness. **Wear His crown well today!**

January 31

Victorious Action: Taking Away the Devoted Things!

"There are devoted things among you, O Israel; you will be unable to stand before your enemies until you take away the devoted things from among you" (Josh. 7:13 NLT)

Let's Talk: Joshua spoke to the Israelites about the subject of sanctification in Joshua 7:13. He said, "There are devoted things among you, O Israel; you will be unable to stand before your enemies until you take away the devoted things from among you." Ohhh! We want to stand strong and yet. . . there are things, hobbies, addictions, people, pleasures that we are MORE devoted to, then being HOLY and right before God. Do you have any "devoted things" today, He is asking you to give UP entirely over to Him?

Let's Glorify: Lord, you are holy and you call me to be holy. Point out to me if I am giving devotion to people, things, vacations or anything else besides you. God, I want to live wholly devoted to you. Forgive me Lord. In Jesus' name, I pray. Amen.

Let's Go! Someday you will meet with the Lord your God, face-to-face. Discuss what you believe a devotion (an idol) you have or had with each other. Commit to praying for each other in this area.

February

Dear daughter,
>
> I am so glad God gave you to me!
>
> He has wonderful plans for your life.
>
> I will cherish your nose kisses, hugs and laughter
>
> in my heart forever.
>
> Love you, Mom

February 1

Victorious Action: Exalting the One!

Phil. 2:9-11 shares, "Therefore God exalted Him to the highest place and gave Him the name that is above every name, that at the name of Jesus every knee should bow, in heaven and on earth and under the earth, and every tongue acknowledge that Jesus Christ is Lord, to the glory of God the Father."

Let's Talk: There is no Name above Jesus! No other God has died and risen from the dead! No other God could heal the lame, the deaf, and the blind and save you from an eternal death separated from the Trinity. This is the best news ever! God has exalted His only Son Jesus to the highest place next to Himself. Jesus obeyed His Father sacrificing Himself upon the cross. We will all acknowledge someday that Jesus is absolutely Lord over all. We will all humbly bow before Him.

Let's Glorify: Lord Jesus, thank you for being my God, my Savior, my Healer and friend. I want to exalt you in my life, lifting you up in word, action and deed. I look forward to the day when I will humbly bow before you. So, today I humbly bow my wants and desires to your holy and perfect plans. In your precious name, I pray. Amen.

Let's Go! How do you exalt (praise and elevate) Jesus in your life? Are you willing to humbly bow and give up your wants and desires to Jesus' holy and perfect plans, just as He did to His Father?

February 2

Victorious Action: Living in Grace!

"Therefore, since we are surrounded by such a great cloud of witnesses, let us throw off everything that hinders and the sin that so easily entangles. And let us run with perseverance the race marked out for us, fixing our eyes on Jesus, the pioneer and perfecter of faith" (Heb. 12:1-2).

Let's Talk: Are you running this life with perseverance? Climbing that hill is going to take a clear focus on Jesus, the only One that can help you run up it! One fall afternoon I was running the hills in my neighborhood. I came to the top and noticed the street at the top was named Grace Court. It was fitting, I thought as I huffed and puffed up the third hill of the afternoon. It made me pause and reflect how **everyone in the race of their life, needs Grace Court**. You need God's undeserved kind grace, mercy and favor poured into you every day so you can get through life. So do I. So, the next time someone accidently cuts you off in traffic, cuts in line at the movies or has more than fifteen items in the Fast Checkout line in the grocery store, in your mind's eye, remember the street sign: *Grace Court*. *Grace:* God's freely given gift of mercy, kindness, favor and pardon. You and I can do nothing to deserve grace!

Let's Glorify: God, thank you so much for extending grace to me. I see Jesus as the perfect model of grace because His sacrifice on the cross gives me pardon of my sins. He didn't deserve to die; these were my sins, not His. He has blessed me with kindness and favor and I had the blessing of opening up His gift of salvation! Lord, how I thank you for your kindness and love. I know I do not deserve it, but because you are extending

February

your grace and love, I gratefully receive it. In Jesus' precious love and grace, I pray. Amen.

Let's Go! Who do you need to extend grace to today? Maybe it's you! Have a conversation about God's grace and when you have especially needed it!

February 3

Victorious Action: Being a Friend of Jesus!

"I no longer call you servants, because a servant does not know his master's business. Instead, I have called you friends, for everything that I learned from my Father I have made known to you" (Jn. 15:15).

Let's Talk: Jesus was speaking to His beloved disciples in the Upper Room right before He was going to be crucified for our sins. As His beloved disciples and friends, you and I have the privilege of reading Jesus' teachings in the Word. He also speaks to us gently through the Holy Spirit all revealed through the Father's teachings. How blessed we are!

Let's Glorify: Lord Jesus, you call me friend! I am so blessed by your kindness. What a privilege to be considered your friend. Lord, I want to speak to you and have a wonderful relationship as my best friend, conversing heart to heart. Thank you for sticking closer to me than a brother. Thank you my friend, Jesus. In your name, I pray. Amen.

Let's Go! Who is your best friend and why? What do you love about them? Share with each other.

February 4

Victorious Action: Practice Hospitality!

"One day Elisha went to the town of Shunem. A wealthy woman lived there, and she urged him to come to her home for a meal. After that, whenever he passed that way, he would stop there for something to eat. She said to her husband, "I am sure this man who stops in from time to time is a holy man of God. Let's build a small room for him on the roof and furnish it with a bed, a table, a chair, and a lamp. Then he will have a place to stay whenever he comes by" (2 Kings 4:8-9 NLT).

Let's Talk: The Shunammite woman undoubtedly saw Elisha the prophet waiting to be asked to stay for a visit. In Biblical times, it was a customary act when a guest came to a town at the end of a day. The weary traveler would wait at the town center or at the city gates waiting for an invitation for the night. If an invitation did not come, they would stay the night outside. The hosts would not only provide food, but a place to sleep and protection from robbery and harm. The Shunammite woman must have let Elisha know to look her up every time he passed through Shunem, because the verse says "he would stop there for something to eat" (vs. 8). He must have been a frequent visitor because this hospitable woman and her husband made him his own room on their rooftop.

Let's Glorify: Lord, thank you for the Shunammite woman's example of hospitality. Her kind concern made a difference in this prophet's life. Lord, let me make a difference in other's lives by opening up my home, my heart and sharing my belongings and meals with others you send my way. Thank you for opening up your table of fellowship with me. Let me express kindness and generous love in all that I do. In Jesus' name, I pray. Amen.

Let's Go! Who are you opening up your table of fellowship to? Could you invite some friends or neighbors who do not know Jesus over for a fun evening of pizza and games?

February 5

Victorious Action: God Calls Things What They Will Become!

"I have made you a father of many nations. He is our father in the sight of God, in whom he believed—the *God who gives life to the dead* and *calls into being things that were not*" (Rom. 4:17, italics mine).

Let's Talk: Abraham believed God when He said that things were true even though they had not happened yet. Abraham believed God and what the Lord shared with Him by faith. As a result, Abraham was a father to many nations and his descendants were as numerous as the stars in the sky. Where do you need to have faith to believe God? God will give the dead area of your life a new transformation by breathing His powerful breath into it!

Let's Glorify: El Elyon, my Most High God, you can do anything! You give life to the dead and you call things that are not into what you deem them to be. Lord, take the dead parts of my anxious heart and breathe your holy breath into it! Make me fully alive and aware of you. In your Almighty name, I pray. Amen.

Let's Go! Do you have any dead areas in your life that you need the Most High God's breath to bring it back to life? Where do you need **CPR**? (**C**hrist's **P**recious **R**estoration!) Do you believe God can do anything? **When God becomes bigger than your fears and doubts you will start to believe and rest in Him.**

February 6

Victorious Action: Have a Happy Face!

"A warm, smiling face reveals a joy-filled heart, but heartache crushes the spirit and darkens the appearance" (Prov. 15:13 VOICE).

Let's Talk: Have you ever noticed how someone's smiling face is lit up with light and joy? Do you wonder if they have always been this way? I bet if you asked them, they can tell you about some pretty horrible things that have happened in their lives. *But you secretly wonder, you are smiling still. They might not be able to describe what has happened to them, but I can.* It's called grace and transformation. Jesus upholds us with His righteous right arm. He gives us free grace; unearned and undeserved. He transforms the bruised and hurt parts of our hearts and gives us a new heart when we open ourselves up to Him.

Let's Glorify: Lord, please make me new! I give you my heartaches, my challenges and the things that are causing me discouragement today. Brighten my heart Lord and give me your precious joy as I live and move in you. I desire a close and intimate relationship with you Jesus, the Lover of my soul. Let my face reveal the joy I feel in your home; my heart. In your name, I pray. Amen.

Let's Go! Remember a time you felt great joy as a child and now as an adult. Why did you have such great joy? Describe in detail to each other.

February 7

Victorious Action: Having a Joyful Attitude!

"Surely you have granted her unending blessings and made her glad with the joy of your presence" (Ps. 21:6).

Let's Talk: I tend to have a joyful attitude when I know I have truly been in His presence. What about the times when life is not going so well? Can we still be joyful? Yes, I believe so! Staying close to Jesus' heart, in prayer and worship helps combat our stress when we are going through turmoil. Praising Him in advance of the desired outcomes we are praying for gives us the right perspective. We give up control and give God His rightful place in our lives.

Let's Glorify: Lord Jesus, I surrender this trial I am going through today to you. I want to stay obedient to you and what you have asked me to do with a willing, cheerful heart. Lord, I delight in your Word today. It brings me joy, guidance and great hope. How I praise you! Thank you for being a happy and joyful Savior. In your name, I pray. Amen.

Let's Go! Where do you need to give up control and trust God so you can experience joy in His presence? Talk about it.

February 8

Victorious Action: Knowledge is From the Lord!

"For the earth will be filled with the knowledge of the glory of the Lord, as the waters cover the sea" (Hab. 2:14).

Let's Talk: Two-thirds of our earth's surface is covered in water. God's knowledge is covering even more than all the water! The whole earth is filled with the knowledge that our Eternal God is glorious and powerful. Jesus Christ is seen as expressing the full nature and purposes of God, so believers may be certain that, through Christ, **they know God as He really is.** You are being brought to into fullness of who God is as you read the Word. Believers are also brought to complete fullness of His joy when we go home to live in heaven.

Let's Glorify: Thank you Lord God, that true wisdom and real power belong to you. From you I learn to how live and also what to live for. Thank you for your Word, which guides, directs and gives me understanding for my life. Thank you for the Bible's course correction in my life. In Jesus' name, I pray. Amen.

Let's Go! What area of your life are you seeking God's knowledge? What do you remember your Mom teaching you as a young child?

February 9

Victorious Action: His Light Shines on the Godly!

"Light shines in the darkness for the godly. They are generous, compassionate, and righteous" (Ps. 112: 4 NLT).

Let's Talk: As a follower of Jesus, you are to shine His light in those dark places of life, school, work and social situations. His light is a light of joy, kindness, peace, mercy and compassion. You do not have to be afraid of the dark places in life. Jesus will always shine His light of peace and confidence into you. His light is peaceful, calming and radiant!

Let's Glorify: Dear Lord, I pray my daughter (mom) is generous, compassionate and righteous because she is living a life of being a woman after your own heart! Thank you for your light, the Holy Spirit living within her. Praise you for your guidance and precious peace. In Jesus' name, I pray. Amen.

Let's Go! Choose to volunteer together (if possible) at a Homeless shelter or Food pantry, sharing the love, light and compassion of our Savior Jesus. Share your experiences with one another.

February 10

Victorious Action: All In!

Jesus replied, "You must love the Lord your God with all your heart, all your soul, and all your mind. This is the first and greatest commandment. A second is equally important: 'Love your neighbor as yourself'" (Matt. 22: 37-39 NLT).

Let's Talk: Jesus binds us together in love for Himself because He first gave love to us. When I am walking side by side Him in prayer and meditation, surrendering my life, He shows me I am indeed loving Him with all that I am. Knowing my walk is secure in Him, He then asks me to extend a helping hand to others.

Let's Glorify: Jesus, I desire to be ALL IN for you, not holding anything back, giving all that I am! I know this happens in my life, when I am in relationship with you. It is not me striving so hard but giving up the reigns and letting you live through me, which makes all the difference. I can stop trying so hard to be religious (following the law) and instead know you intimately. As I learn to know you better, I can love and care for my neighbor better. In your holy name, I pray. Amen.

Let's Go! Introduce yourself to the new neighbors on your block. Bring them cookies or a veggie tray and invite them to your church!

February 11

Victorious Action: Jesus Radiates God's Love!

Heb. 1:3 is astonishing! "The Son is the radiance of God's glory and the exact representation of His being, sustaining all things by His powerful word. After He had provided purification for sins, He sat down at the right hand of the Majesty in heaven."

Let's Talk: Jesus as God's only Son is the sparkle in God's eye! Jesus brings great joy to His Abba Father! Jesus is the exact image of God the Father. Jesus sustains you and me by His Word, the bible. He is sitting at the right hand of the Majestic Father, praying and interceding for you. Jesus did all of this because He loves you and wants to be in a close relationship with you!

Let's Glorify: Thank you, Jesus for being everything I need. Your joy is contagious! Lord, please fill me with your joy in this moment. I am elated you love me and care for me even now. Thank you for taking away my sins and purifying me in the process. All glory, praise and honor are yours. In your name, I pray. Amen.

Let's Go! Growing up, what gave you great joy? Share with your mom, daughter or special friend.

February 12

Victorious Action: God Delights in You!

"For the Lord your God is living among you. He is a mighty savior. He will take delight in you with gladness. With His love, He will calm all your fears. He will rejoice over you with joyful songs" (Zeph. 3:17 NLT).

Let's Talk: It is so amazing to realize our God is living among us through the Holy Spirit's power within! He is our true Knight in shining armor, one who can always be counted upon all times, especially when your heart needs calming. Did you hear the birds singing joyfully today? He is rejoicing over you right now! Did you see the beautiful sunset? He is reminding you of His precious care. Even at the end of the day He is still with you!

Let's Glorify: Dear God, thank you that you live inside of me because of the Miracle of the Holy Spirit. I am so happy that you actually delight in me and you love me. I want to rejoice in you and praise you all the days of my life. Thank you for hearing me, caring for me and seeing all that I had to do today. How I love you. In Jesus' name, I pray. Amen.

Let's Go! What is your favorite song and why? Discuss it with your mom, daughter or friend.

February 13

Victorious Action: Radical Life Changer!

"You didn't think, did you, that just by pointing your finger at others you would distract God from seeing all your misdoings and from coming down on you hard? Or did you think that because He's such a nice God, He'd let you off the hook? Better think this one through from the beginning. God is kind, but He's not soft. In kindness, He takes us firmly by the hand and leads us into a radical life-change" (Rom. 2:3-4 MSG).

Let's Talk: God has a way in quickly showing you where you need to let His light of healing in, doesn't He? It does seem easier to point out the log in someone else's eye instead of getting real and honest about the plank in your own eye! As the verses above say, God is kind, but He's not soft! He is all about radically changing our lives! Are you ready for a radical life-change?

Let's Glorify: God, thank you for kindly pointing out in me what needs changing in my heart and life. I love that you do not condemn me when I need to work on something in my heart. You gently probe, guide and instruct. You always give me the better way to live. Thank you for caring that much about me. In your Son's healing name, I pray. Amen.

Let's Go! As your Mom, (or daughter) I am sorry for the times I had a huge chunk of wood in my eye and didn't hear your opinion! Please forgive me today.

February 14

Victorious Action: The Language of Love!

"For the king trusts in the Lord; through the unfailing love of the Most High he will not be shaken" (Ps. 21:7).

Let's Talk: What helps you feel the most loved? Is it feeling safe and protected? Is it small gifts of appreciation? Or is it words of affirmation? Is it the gift of time or service? Do you know what your Family's love languages are? (Words of affirmation, physical touch, quality time, acts of service, receiving gifts) A person's primary love language is communicated best through one of the above languages. When we give a person what they need, they are filled emotionally and you are helping satisfy their need for love. As a result they feel honored and valued.

Let's Glorify: Jesus, thank you for knowing exactly what my love languages are. You know how to reach me and help me feel secure. Realizing my identity is rooted in your sacrificial love gives me great comfort and security. I do not have to perform to earn your love. I just need to open up my heart to you and receive your amazing love! How I praise you! In your loving name, I pray. Amen.

Let's Go! Discuss what your love languages are as well as your families. How might you be trying to earn Jesus' love instead of receiving it?

February 15

Victorious Action: God You Reign!

Gideon said, "I most certainly will not rule over you, nor will my son. God will reign over you" (Judg. 8:23 MSG).

Let's Talk: In Judges 8:22 "The Israelites said to Gideon, "Rule over us—you, your son and your grandson—because you have saved us from the hand of Midian." The Midianites were fierce warriors. Many times the Israelites trembled in fear, hiding from them in caves. They also hid their crops because these fighters would raid their homes, taking their food. So, when Gideon heard the Lord calling him to fight against the Midianites, he was not confidant that he was the man for the job! God called Gideon "Courage." Do you know that Gideon grew into his name? He did save his people from the Midianites. "Thus Midian was subdued before the Israelites and did not raise its head again. During Gideon's lifetime, the land had peace forty years" (Judg. 8:28).

Let's Glorify: Lord, let me grow into the name you are calling me today. Let me see with eyes of courage the path you have set before, knowing if you call me, you will equip me. God, I want you to reign in my life. I do not want anything to have the opportunity to reign in my life except you. Help me to be mindful that I do not reign over anyone else's life either! All to your glory, I pray. Amen.

Let's Go! Are you allowing yourself to reign in another's life? Do you have any small gods you might be giving more attention and adoration to? Even our children we can turn into "little gods" if we are not careful!

February 16

Victorious Action: Consecrate Yourself!

Joshua told the people, "Consecrate yourselves, for tomorrow the Lord will do amazing things among you" (Josh. 3:5).

Let's Talk: Consecration implies purification, or to purify oneself. In the very next verse, Joshua told the priests to "Take up the Ark of the Covenant and pass on ahead of the people." And as the priests stepped into the flood stage river, God caused the water to 'stand in a heap' so all the Israelites could safely cross the Jordan. (Josh. 3:16) God wants to do amazing things among you as well! Consecration is done by faith, *before* God acts.

Let's Glorify: God of heaven, help me to be obedient so I will desire to consecrate myself daily before you. I know there are great things you want to do in my life, if I will surrender my life and wait for your direction and perfect timing. It's in your Son's holy name, I pray. Amen.

Let's Go! What area is God asking you to give up to Him? Where is He asking you to be purified so He may do wonderful things among you?

February 17

Victorious Action: A New Song

"Sing a new song to the Lord. He has done wonderful things. By the power of His right hand and His holy arm He has saved His people" (Ps. 98:1 NIRV).

Let's Talk: My shame is gone for you have poured into me a new song; a song of salvation and freedom! You have freed me from my sins and my past. You have given me a new life that is wrapped around you. Thank you for the wonderful ways you have redeemed me!

Let's Glorify: Lord, where would I be today without you? I would be completely lost in my sins, living a life of shame and blame. Thank you for loving me and caring what happens to me. Thank you for transforming me and making me new in you. Thank you for speaking words of life, love and truth into my heart. In Jesus' transforming name, I pray. Amen.

Let's Go! What has God saved you from? Are you singing a new song in Him as a result? Sing a song you both know together.

February 18

Victorious Action: God is My Sustainer!

"And God Almighty bless thee, and make thee fruitful, and multiply thee, that thou mayest be a multitude of people" (Gen. 28:3 KJV).

Let's Talk: "El Shaddai" refers to God as a God who completely nourishes, satisfies, and supplies His people with all their needs as a mother would her very own child. Connected with the word for God, "El" denotes a God who freely gives nourishment and blessing. He truly is our sustainer! You can cry out to Him at any moment of the day and night. He will hear you. He will answer your needs in His special way.

Let's Glorify: Dear El Shaddai, thank you for being such a wonderful sustainer. Where would I be without you? You cover all my needs and fill my heart with a joyful contentment as I rely on you! I praise you! In your name, I pray. Amen.

Let's Go! Where do you need God to be your El Shaddai right now? How has God shown Himself to be faithful to you in the past? Chat about His faithfulness to you.

February 19

Victorious Action: Weeping in the Night Brings Morning Joy!

"Weeping may endure for a night, but joy comes in the morning" (Ps. 30:5 NKJV).

Let's Talk: Jesus wept for his dear friend Lazarus when he died. Jesus had compassion and empathy for Lazarus' sisters Mary and Martha in their grief. Jesus is praying for you right this moment in your despair, confusion and grief. I am so glad the Scriptures say our weeping might endure and continue on through the night, but in the new day there is joy! You have joy in Jesus, knowing He will never leave you nor forsake you! He will hold your hand and your heart during the really hard and emotionally wrenching trials you go through. For this, you can sing for joy!

Let's Glorify: Jesus, thank you that you understand my grieving heart and my despair. Thank you for a new day. Even though it is hard to be in pain, I thank you. You have suffered and understand my pain. I have great hope in you because you have overcome the grave. You are alive and one day I will get to see you face to face! What a day that will be! What joy! I praise you and thank you for the cross that brings me everlasting life. In your name, I pray. Amen.

Let's Go! When you see Jesus face-to-face for the first time, what is that one thing you are longing to ask Him? Share with each other.

February 20

Victorious Action: Desiring His Will!

"I desire to do your will, my God; your law is within my heart" (Ps. 40:8).

Let's Talk: As much as you and I want to be relationship with Jesus, He wants us to be in relationship with Him even more! Jesus tells us over and over again, "I love you. I gave myself up for you and I long for you to be in relationship with me." Desiring His will is easier when we are in relationship with Him and have the word etched on our minds and hearts.

Let's Glorify: Lord Jesus, I am grateful you love me so! Help me to make time to pray, read and memorize scripture so your thoughts are upon and in me. Thank you for being my Jehovah Shammah (The Lord Is There) every moment of the day. Lord, give me a willingness to pour into my family every day so erosion doesn't occur! In Jesus' name, I pray. Amen.

Let's Go! Day by day routines and gestures of life show our love to our families. What are the daily routines and gestures do you do to demonstrate your love to your families?

February 21

Victorious Action: Jesus, My Shepherd!

"The Lord is near to all who call on Him, to all who call on Him in truth" (Ps. 145:18).

Let's Talk: Jesus says, "I love you. I gave myself up for you and I long for you to be in a near and close relationship with me." Do I accept His amazing truths? Or do I try to live life with my own agenda instead? He is a gentle Shepherd, our Jehovah-Raah. He will lead you beside cool waters and help you to rest in green meadows if you will slow down and allow Him to do so.

Let's Glorify: Lord, my Shepherd, how I need to draw near to you today. I need your cooling and restorative touch to my body and spirit. Thank you Lord for being there for me, listening to my sincere prayers for help. Help me to rest and move in you today. In Jesus name, I pray and thank. Amen.

Let's Go! What part of the day do you mostly need to call on Jesus? Share with each other.

February 22

Victorious Action: Caring for Your Family!

"For God is not unjust. He will not forget how hard you have worked for Him and how you have shown your love to Him by caring for other believers, as you still do" (Heb. 6:10 NLT).

Let's Talk: God notices your gentle care for your family, dear daughter. In those moments, when it seems your little children will never grow up or this day will never end, just know God sees you and your selfless work. He sees your insecurities and your fears. Keep caring for and loving others, because He has a blessing in store for you! Ask Him for strength. He is your helper and shield!

Let's Glorify: Lord God, thank you for noticing me in those really long and hard days. Lord bless me and my children, please. (Ps. 115:14) Lord, thank you for your care and unfailing love. How I love you! I will praise you even now through the trials of this day. In Jesus' unfailing strength, I pray. Amen.

Let's Go! Discuss your growing up time with your mom or daughter or a treasured friend. Talk about what you liked about being your mom's daughter or what you liked about raising your daughter.

February 23

Victorious Action: Make a Decision!

"Rise up; this matter is in your hands. We will support you, so take courage and do it" (Ezra 10:4).

Let's Talk: There are times when you know you have to take a stand and make a decision! You know it; the matter is in your hands and in your lap! **Pray and ask God what you should do first!** Do not take a poll and ask everyone you know what you should do. No! Take courage and move forward. He will help you and strengthen your feeble hands!

Let's Glorify: Lord, there are times when I really do not know what to do! So, I am on my knees seeking your face in this matter. God, I do not want to move ahead of you, so please show me when it is the right time to act on what you are asking me to do. Lord, keep me from polling others as I wait upon you. Please confirm your leadings and help me to hear your voice. Let me know I have your mind and favor in this decision. In Jesus' name, I pray. Amen.

Let's Go: What are some of the hardest decisions you have had to make? Did you remember to seek the Lord's guidance first?

February 24

Victorious Action: Wholehearted Devotion!

"For the eyes of the Lord range throughout the earth to strengthen those whose hearts are fully committed to Him" (2 Chron. 16:9a).

Let's Talk: King Asa during the time this scripture was written was not seeking the Lord's counsel whether or not to go to war. In 2 Chronicles 16:7, the seer Hanani came to King Asa and told him, "Because you have put your trust in the king of Aram instead of in the Lord your God, you missed your chance to destroy the army of the king of Aram." Then the seer told him, in 2 Chronicles 16:9a "For the eyes of the Lord range throughout the earth to strengthen those whose hearts are fully committed to him. You have done a foolish thing, and from now on you will be at war." King Asa ended up dying with a severe foot disease. He didn't ask for God's guidance only his physicians, the Scriptures say.

Let's Glorify: Lord, how I mess up my life when I do not ask for your help and guidance! God, you tell us you are looking for believers who have a wholehearted commitment to you. Lord, I want to be a woman of wholehearted commitment to you alone! You will strengthen me and my heart to do what you are calling me to do when I have an "all in" heart commitment. Let it be so. In Jesus' name, I pray. Amen.

Let's Go! Do you have any areas in your life that are not whole-heartedly committed to the Lord and His ways? If so, why do you think this is?

February 25

Victorious Action: Purified in Your Trials!

"These trials will show that your faith is genuine. It is being tested as fire tests and purifies gold" (1 Pet. 1:7a NLT).

Let's Talk: Testing 1, 2, 3! Isn't it a wonder we do not grow when everything is going smoothly in our lives? Your faith is tested under extreme pressure and the heat of the situation. God always promises to help you, deliver you and give you peace. Your job is to first trust Him and wait on His outcomes! Ask Him what He is teaching you in these moments. Pray His will be done in spite of your reactions! In time your life will come forth as shiny and refined as purified gold because you trusted Him in your tests.

Let's Glorify: Dear Lord, I want to trust you right in this moment and rely on the love you have for me. Help me to look at you and not the problem I am in. Father forgive me of my part and help me to move forward in you. I desire for all the praise, honor and glory to be given to you while I wait patiently in you. In your Son's name, I pray. Amen.

Let's Go! What is something positive you can do while you are in your testing season?

February 26

Victorious Action: From Strength to Strength!

"The king rejoices in your strength, Lord. How great is his joy in the victories you give" (Ps. 21:1).

Let's Talk: Lord, you are my strength and my hope! In Ps. 84:7 you tell me, I go from **strength to strength!** Victory happens as I meditate on your truths of love all day long. You bless me with your loving presence as I linger in you. I have overwhelming victory because of Jesus' victory in His life and death.

Let's Glorify: Dear Lord, Thank you for your unfailing love! You give me victory as I abide in you and wait on your timing. What joy is found as I remain peaceful in you. I am ever grateful for your work accomplished on the cross. In your holy name, I pray. Amen.

Let's Go! Thank you for always encouraging me to look toward the Lord for my strength and hope on my down days. Write a prayer of encouragement and thanks to your mom, daughter or special women in your life.

February 27

Victorious Action: Apple of His Eye!

"Keep me as the apple of your eye; hide me in the shadow of your wings from the wicked who are out to destroy me, from my mortal enemies who surround me" (Ps. 17:8-9).

Let's Talk: The pupil is the most sensitive part of the body. Just try to get an eyelash out of it. It feels as if it is as large as a rock in your eye! God notices the tiniest thing that is happening to you, even now. The God's Word Translation says, "Guard me as if I were the pupil in your eye" (vs.8). You cannot get much closer than that to God's eyes and view. He sees you and He protects you. What grace and favor you have in Him, our Abba Daddy!

Let's Glorify: Dear Lord, my Abba Daddy. Thank you for keeping me safe physically, emotionally and spiritually. It is amazing to me that I am the apple of your eye! You are always thinking about me with great love and delight! How I want to please you and love you back! I can rest and have peace in your never ending love! I love you, God. In Jesus' name, I pray. Amen.

Let's Go! How has God protected you and kept you as the apple of His eye?

February 28

Victorious Action: A New Path!

"But forget all that—it is nothing compared to what I am going to do. **For I am about to do something new**. See, I have already begun! Do you not see it? I will make a pathway through the wilderness. I will create rivers in the dry wasteland" (Isa. 43:18-19 NLT, emphasis mine).

Let's Talk: These scriptures tell us to be alert, be present and pay attention! God is about to do something brand-new! **It's bursting out!** Don't you see it? He can make rivers gush in the dry areas of your life. He makes new paths for you to journey on through the trials of your life. He can make a way when there seems to be no way in sight! He can transform your relationships, your children and even you!

Let's Glorify: Lord, help me to be ready and alert for you want to do something new in my life today! Help me not to miss out on your wonderful presence in my life because I am focused with my eyes downcast on my problems. Let my heart and eyes be lifted up to you in praise and positive expectancy! In Jesus' name, I pray. Amen.

Let's Go! Where is God making a new path in your journey called life? Where do you need Him to "burst through?" Discuss with each other.

March

March winds gust and I can hardly tell
Where the sail begins and my Mom's hair blows.
I loved spending time with my Mom, flying kites,
baking cookies and painting our toes.
Mostly I just loved her smile and hugs.

March 1

Victorious Action: Believing Jesus is Alive!

"After Jesus rose from the dead early on Sunday morning, the first person who saw Him was Mary Magdalene, the woman from whom He had cast out seven demons. She went to the disciples, who were grieving and weeping, and told them what had happened. But when she told them that Jesus was alive and she had seen him, they didn't believe her" (Mark 16:9-11 NLT, emphasis mine).

Let's Talk: Mary Magdalene was a woman who had utter devotion to her Savior and healer. She is mentioned fourteen times in the gospels. Time and time again we see Mary serving and helping Jesus and the disciples. She gave of her own means: her money, food and time to support them. What is striking is in eight of the fourteen passages Mary is named in connection with other women, and her name is at the top of the list, implying that she occupied the place at the front in service given by godly females. Through the years biblically, Mary has gotten a reputation for being a prostitute. According to biblical scholars there is no evidence to confirm this. She is referred to as having "seven demons." Her condition most likely was worse than the rest. The moment Jesus laid eyes on the cringing and deranged woman, He saw in her the caring and supportive woman who would be a great blessing to His own heart and to others. It is no wonder she was the first person to see Jesus after He had resurrected!

Let's Glorify: Jesus, you take the broken parts of me and restore me completely. You have done so many miracles in my life emotionally, spiritually and physically. How can I not want to devote myself to you and your loving kindness? Lord, let me serve you as I serve others with pure motives, all to your glory! When others do not believe you are alive, let me not get discouraged. I will remember what you have healed in my life! Thank you, my Jehovah Rophe, my healer. In Jesus' name, I pray. Amen.

Let's Go! What has Jesus healed in your life spiritually, emotionally or physically? Share with your mom, daughter or friend. Give Him all the glory!

March 2

Victorious Action: Strengthened Peace!

"The Lord gives strength to His people; the Lord blesses His people with peace" (Ps. 29:11).

Let's Talk: God does give you strength to face all the trials you must go through every day. He gives you His precious peace as a blessing when you rest and trust in Him and His loving mercy. **P.E.A.C.E.** is something you can meditate upon in an unsettled moment:

P-Precious protector and provider
E-Everlasting love
A-Almighty God
C- Consistently caring and compassionate
E-Emmanuel emanates His love and light in me.

Let's Glorify: Lord, I praise you and thank you for your precious peace which surpasses all understanding. In the deepest part of me, where you dwell, I can rest and know you are with me, caring for my deepest hurts, disappointments and joys! I love you. In Jesus' precious name, I pray. Amen.

Let's Go! How has Jesus been your peace in your darkest moments and greatest joys? Share with each other.

March 3

Victorious Action: Seasoned with Salt!

"Let your conversation be always full of grace, seasoned with salt, so that you may know how to answer everyone" (Col. 4:6).

Let's Talk: There are certain people I just love being around! They are cheerful, happy and encouraging! They don't just puff me up, but speak life and breathe love into me. They speak with words that are flavored just right, to affirm where you are in life. They are such gems to us! These friends are priceless. In Biblical days, a pact of friendship was sealed with the gift of salt and the agreement between God and His people was termed a "covenant of salt" (Num. 18:19; 2 Chron. 13:5). Salt was symbolic of loyalty and eternity. In the Sermon on the Mount the Lord implies the wholesomeness and vitality of the Christian when He calls her "the salt of the earth" (Matt 5:13).

Let's Glorify: Lord Jesus, help me to season my words to be encouraging and calming to others. I want to be an encourager and a life breather into others' lives! This happens as you increase in my life and I decrease giving you first place in my heart. Let me be sweet and savory to my friends, my family and strangers alike because I have spent time with you today. In your precious name, I pray. Amen.

Let's Go! Who has been a life breather of encouragement to you recently? Is there something in your life that makes you sour instead of savory? Discuss this with your mom, daughter or girlfriend.

March 4

Victorious Action: Receiving His Help and Comfort!

"Praise be to the God and Father of our Lord Jesus Christ, the Father of compassion and the God of all comfort, who comforts us in all our troubles, so that we can comfort those in any trouble with the comfort we ourselves have received from God" (2 Cor. 1:3-4).

Let's Talk: How important it is to receive and remember the comfort and help from God! He blesses us in our need and we can certainly pass His grace and compassion unto others immediately in the form of a hug, a prayer, a smile, a nod, even a gentle pat on the back.

Let's Glorify: Lord, I remember the time you sent a dear friend to pray for me and with me when I was in a really hard spot in my life. Help me to remember their sweet, loving compassion sent by you and to pass your loving kindness along. We are better together when we are strengthened in you. Thank you for being our God of all comfort. In Jesus' name, I pray. Amen.

Let's Go! Where have you been the hands and feet of Jesus lately? Have you ever helped someone and then found later, they were there helping you in your trouble?

March 5

Victorious Action: Burst Through!

"So David went to Baal-perazim and defeated the Philistines there. "The Lord did it!" David exclaimed. "He **burst through** my enemies like a raging flood!" So he named that place Baal-perazim which means "the Lord who bursts through" (2 Sam. 5:20 NLT).

Let's Talk: David had just been anointed as the King of Israel. The longstanding enemies of David, the Philistines mobilized all their forces to capture him. David prayed to God and asked Him, "Should I go out to fight the Philistines? The Lord replied, "Yes, go ahead. I will certainly hand them over to you" (2 Sam. 5:19 NLT). Do you have a long standing enemy or foe? It could be a person, a challenge, an attitude or an addiction. Pray and ask God to help you! Ask Him what you should do! Certainly, as you seek His face, **He will burst through** and give you aid.

Let's Glorify: Lord, thank you as I seek you in prayer that you are going to give me a "burst through" of your help and aid in your perfect timing! Lord, protect me from my enemies. Help me to rely on you as I give up my addictions and attitudes. I am only able to be healed as I have total dependence in you. In Jesus' name, I pray. Amen.

Let's Go! Where do you need **God's burst through** to light your path today? Will you seek Him and ask for help? Pray together and lift each other's troubles up to Jesus.

March 6

Victorious Action: Be Courageous!

"This is my command—be strong and courageous! Do not be afraid or discouraged. For the Lord your God is with you wherever you go" (Josh. 1:9 NLT).

Let's Talk: Joshua, Moses aide had just taken over for the deceased Moses. He was charged by God to lead the Israelites across the Jordan River into the land He was giving them. God promised Joshua what He had promised Moses: "No one will be able to stand against you as long as you live. For I will be with you as I was with Moses. I will not fail you or abandon you" (Josh. 1: 3,5 NLT). Joshua had a divine message and great encouragement to do God's will fully. The Father tells you the same message today! **He will not fail you!** He will equip you and energize you as you seek to do the Lord's work, all to His glory!

Let's Talk: Lord God, thank you promise to be with me always; you will never abandon me nor fail me. At all times, I can look to you and know in my heart of hearts you will help me bring to completion the jobs you are giving to me to do. Thank you for the precious Holy Spirit who will energize me to cross the finish line of each day. Amen.

Let's Go! What job or career has been the hardest for you to have a sense of achievement in? Have you ever failed at a job? Talk about it with your mom, daughter or girlfriend.

March 7

Victorious Action: Knowing You are Safe!

"He has made my mouth like a sharp sword. He has hidden me in the shadow of His hand. He has made me a shining arrow, keeping me in His secret place" (Isa. 49:2 NLV).

Let's Talk: Isaiah was a prophet that served under four kings. He prophesied for 44 years! God spoke through Isaiah, his words sharp and penetrating as a sword, warning the people of God's truths. When his job got tough, Isaiah knew God the Warrior, was holding him close to His heart. In fact so close, Isaiah was an arrow in His quiver, guarded jealously by God, "Qanna." Qanna is the Lord's name which means jealous or zealous. God holds you close too in the shadow of His hand. You are safe and protected by the Holy One of Israel.

Let's Glorify: God, Holy One of Israel, how I thank you for guarding me closely in the shadow of your hand. You are a jealous God, wanting all my praise for yourself and no one else. You keep me in the secret place of your loving heart. I am forever safe and grateful. Thank you. In your name, I pray. Amen.

Let's Go! How has God, the Holy One of Israel, Qanna hidden and protected you in the shadow of His hand? Were you ever jealous of a friend growing up and did not want to share her? Talk about it with your mom, daughter or friend.

March 8

Victorious Action: Living in Freedom!

I will say to the prisoners, "Come out in freedom, and to those in darkness, Come into the light. They will be my sheep, grazing in green pastures and on hills that were previously bare" (Isa. 49:9 NLT).

Let's Talk: How God longs to give you freedom out of the darkness in all areas of your life! He is whispering quietly to your heart: **"Come into the light."** Your job is to be willing to turn over the thoughts, the circumstances and the things you do in self-reliance instead of asking Him for help. These are the things you believe give you purpose and satisfaction. Are you performing over receiving His loving grace instead? Come to your Jehovah Shalom. He will provide for you as a Shepherd provides for His sheep. He will give you sweet peace and rest.

Let's Glorify: Lord, thank you as I lift my eyes up to you, you give me freedom from the prison I have put myself in. You give me the light of truth illuminating my situation. You give me peace of mind, comfort and security. You are my refuge and strength, always. Lord, forgive me when I start to perform instead of moving in your loving grace instead. Thank you for being my caring and protective Shepherd. In Jesus' name, I pray. Amen.

Let's Go! How have you performed in your life instead of relying on the Shepherd's loving care and grace? How did that work out for you?

March 9

Victorious Action: Sing for Joy!

"Sing for joy, O heavens! Rejoice, O earth! Burst into song, O mountains! For the Lord has comforted His people and will have compassion on them in their suffering" (Isa. 49:13 NLT).

Let's Talk: Singing for joy can be so difficult in the most wrenching moments of our lives! On those occasions of despair, when we choose to look up to Him, we see His light and His beauty all around us as His creation rejoices at the work of His creative hand! If we can only start to praise and worship Him, for always being there for us, ever faithful, ever loving, we find our hearts and attitude begin to change. Oh how we need Him every hour of every day. Our Savior Jesus knows this about His people. He will comfort you in your suffering anguish.

Let's Glorify: Jesus, thank you for your loving compassion no matter what I am going through! Even in those moments when I feel as if I cannot lift my head, you lift it up, holding me close to your heart. It is your love I adore. I am so grateful for your presence even now. How I praise you and worship you! In your name, I pray. Amen.

Let's Go! How has God's beautiful creation ministered to your heart? Share pictures of a trip you have been on, noting God's beautiful handiwork.

March 10

Victorious Action: Steadfast Heart!

"My heart, O God, is steadfast; I will sing and make music with all my soul" (Ps 108:1).

Let's Talk: When I start feeling super frustrated and overwhelmed, God tells me to check the engine light! His engine within me is the Holy Spirit driving me gently with grace, love, mercy and energy. He wells up within me giving me joy in a worship song, the beauty of the day or running into a dear friend. We chat and laugh for a moment. My mood starts to change and my heart is once again steadfast within because He has never left me.

Let's Glorify: Thank you, God for answering my heart today! Lord, I need to take a deep breath, breathing you and your calmness in. Praise you Jesus; in my moment of frustration and overwhelmness, you are always there with me, ready to bring me back to the center of your love and peace. I can sing a song of praise to you with all my soul and heart. In your love, I pray. Amen.

Let's Go! What song really lifts your spirit and helps you to worship the Lord? Chat about your favorite songs.

March 11

Victorious Action: Healing Our Broken Heart!

"He heals the brokenhearted and binds up their wounds" (Psalm 147:3).

Let's Talk: The more broken you and I are, the more He will come in and transform us. But, we have to be broken and surrendered enough to let our guard down and allow God to work through our pain and suffering. Isn't it true, the more you have experienced heartache, the more experience in life you have to offer to someone else in the way of giving compassion, grace and care? Recently, I took up the art of mosaicking. As I wiped away the dark charcoal gray grout, God whispered to my heart, **"I pick you up, and clean you off.** I make something beautiful out of your shards! I put you back together. I create something beautiful out of your failures, your heartaches, your sorrows and questions!" The jewels below the grout started to sparkle as I wiped away the grout. Our lives sparkle when we let God remove our short comings, our sins and angry attitudes. Praise Him! Let Him do it. Trust Him to do it.

Let's Glorify: Lord Jesus, I want to sparkle for you inside and out. I confess my sins to you right now. Please remove them as far as the east from the west. Show me my brokenness and how it hinders my relationship with you and others. Thank you for the transforming work you are doing in my life daily. I pray to participate fully in what you are doing in me today. Jesus, it's all to your glory, I pray. Amen.

Let's Go! What area in your life is broken? What area(s) has God transformed or is in the process of transforming as you live surrendered before Him? Share honestly with each other.

March 12

Victorious Action: Living in His Mercy and Grace!

"God is sheer mercy and grace; not easily angered, He's rich in love. He doesn't endlessly nag and scold, nor hold grudges forever. He doesn't treat us as our sins deserve, nor pay us back in full for our wrongs" (Ps. 103: 17 MSG).

Let's Talk: The Lord is sheer mercy and grace! I am so glad He is not easily angered as I can surely be! He does not treat us as our wrong doings deserve and while He disciplines us as our parent, we are not disciplined to the full extent because of His deep and rich love!

Let's Glorify: Lord, you are so merciful to me even when I sin. God, help me to extend your loving grace and mercy to others especially my own family. You know me inside and out. You know I am made from dust and would blow apart if it was not for your sustaining love and power. Thank you for your eternal love that is always present to all that have a healthy respect and fear of you. In Jesus' name, I pray. Amen.

Let's Go! Remember a time when you were disciplined for something you did? Did the consequences fit "your crime" or were your parents lenient, extending you grace and mercy you did not deserve?

March 13

Victorious Action: The Lord Knows Your Heart!

"Forgive, and deal with everyone according to all they do, since you know their hearts (for you alone know the human heart)" (2 Chron. 6:30).

Let's Talk: God you formed me in my mother's womb and you know every thought I think or will ever think! God in those moments **when I feel insecure and not good enough,** help me to **rely on your precious, never ending love instead.** When I am afraid or discouraged, Lord I want to remember this is not of you or from you. The enemy is attacking me and playing on my weaknesses. God, help me to know without a shadow of a doubt, I am enough because you are more than enough for me!

Let's Glorify: Lord Jesus, when the "not enough" feelings come, let me know the fact of your unfailing love and **remember my identity is rooted fully in your priceless love.** You tell me I am enough in you, because you are the Sufficient I AM! I am so grateful. Please help me to listen to your still small voice and not what the world or the enemy is trying to tell me or divert me to. In your holy name, I pray. Amen.

Let's Go! The "not enough" feelings can come in many forms. (Being a mom, daughter, sister, friend, aunt, employee, and boss, volunteer, just to name a few) When have you experienced feeling **as if you were not enough?** Ask Jesus to reveal to you why these feelings are coming up at a particular time, if they do. Share with each other these "not enough" times.

March 14

Victorious Action: Believe and Receive His Living Water!

"Whoever believes in me, as Scripture has said, rivers of living water will flow from within them. By this He meant the Spirit, whom those who believed in Him were later to receive. Up to that time the Spirit had not been given, since Jesus had not yet been glorified" (Jn. 7:38-39).

Let's Talk: Oh clear and cool water! How I long to dive in during the hot summer heat! We have the blessed Holy Spirit inside to cool our heated emotions even in this moment. Living water fresh, cool and abundant. Fill me up Jesus, please. Quench my thirst so I will never have to thirst for the world again! Keep your Holy Spirit water fresh within me, please. I do not want to grow stagnant or stale!

Let's Glorify: Thank you, Holy Spirit for living inside me. I am grateful for your everlasting presence. Just as Jesus promised when He went to the Father, we received you as our truth, light and guide. Thank you for the cool refreshment of your living water energizing me, helping me through this life. Thank you for speaking the exact truths the Father gives you to speak to me. In Jesus' holy name, I pray. Amen.

Let's Go! How are you experiencing the Holy Spirit's living water today? Who are you praying for today to receive the Holy Spirit?

March 15

Victorious Action: Patience and Forgiveness!

"A gentle answer turns away wrath, but a harsh word stirs up anger" (Prov. 15:1).

Let's Talk: The Lord sees everything! He sees when I answer kindly, hastily or harshly. The times I answer too quickly or harshly are usually the times I am rushed or spread too thin! At other times, I have not been in the Word as often as I'd like or need. Or, I may be harboring some resentment over something that just happened today or a long time ago.

Let's Glorify: Oh Lord, forgive me of responding bitterly. God, the more time I spend with you, the greater the chance I have to respond kindly. Lord, help me to be patient with those around me, especially my family since they see and hear me the most. Jesus, help me to forgive freely and not take offense so easily. Let my life resemble yours today. Amen.

Let's Talk: Where do you need His loving patience and forgiveness today? Have your actions ever divided your family or brought your family together? Pray together, asking God to strengthen your family's relationships.

March 16

Victorious Action: Needing His Favor to Establish the Work of Your Hands!

"May the favor of the Lord our God rest on us; establish the work of our hands for us—yes, **establish the work of our hands**" (Ps. 90:17, emphasis mine).

Let's Talk: It was the last day of our Ugandan mission's trip with my church. The twelve of us had worked diligently with the 61 junior high kids teaching them how to lead vacation bible school with students their age and younger. *Lord, I wondered. Will they be able to do it? Was our time and energy fruitful here?* God gave me this precise scripture the morning I was praying on my top bunk. I knew He was up to something! A week after we got home to America, we received an email from the children's pastor. The Ugandan Vacation bible school children took the Good News message out to a local village church. 118 children received Jesus that day as their personal Savior! Hallelujah! Yes, He did establish the children and our missionary's work of our hands!

Let's Glorify: Lord Jesus, how I praise you for giving us favor on this trip! Thank you for establishing not only the work of our hands but also these young adults' hands! Lord, thank you that you can do ANYTHING! Thank you for the privilege for being able to serve you and others no matter where we are! In your mighty name, I pray. Amen.

Let's Go! Where do you need to see His favor in your life? Where do you want God to establish the work of your hands?

March 17

Victorious Action: Have a Spirit of Power, Love and Self-Discipline!

"For God has not given us a spirit of fear and timidity, but of power, love, and self-discipline" (2 Tim. 1:7 NLT).

Let's Talk: Fear and timidity are not of the Lord Jesus! He was gentle and yet powerful. He was assertive yet self-disciplined. He calls us to imitate Him. Anything less comes from the enemy of your soul, trying to detour you from what God is calling you to do.

Let's Glorify: Lord Jesus, today I am choosing faith over fear. If you call me to do something, then you will help me bring it to fruition. Faith gives me the green light to go, thwarting the enemy's plans. Thank you for the Holy Spirit who energizes me and gives me the truth of what I am supposed to do! I love you. Amen.

Let's Go! What is God calling you to do that is certainly out of your comfort zone? Will you choose faith over fear? A reckless faith is a wild faith, unhindered by the world because it is locked solidly around God and what He desires for each of us!

March 18

Victorious Action: Be an Encourager!

"So encourage each other and build each other up, just as you are already doing" (1 Thess. 5:11 NLT).

Let's Talk: You are alive in Him! So speak encouraging words to one another. Build up hope so you'll all be together in this and no one left out. Even if you're already an encourager; keep doing it! Everyone needs encouragement daily! Recently I was running a 10K race. There were hundreds of high school volunteers along the course. **Every time** I yelled a *thank you* as I ran past a student, they would respond with an encouraging word! "You're doing great, keep going, good job!" My gratitude invoked a kind response from the volunteers! **I was encouraged every time!** So, keep giving encouraging words. If you feel the urge to be kind then do it. It is exactly what God calls you to do today.

Let's Glorify: Lord, help me to be an encouraging mom, daughter, friend, wife, sister or aunt to not only my family but to all the people you put in my path today. Help me to remember the power of a smile, a kind word and a compliment spoken in front of others. When I encourage someone else, I receive your precious joy! Thank you for your daily loving kindnesses poured out upon me. In Jesus' name, I pray. Amen.

Let's Go! Who will you encourage today? How have you encouraged your mom, daughter or friend lately?

March 19

Victorious Action: Victory in Christ!

"With God we will gain the victory and He will trample down our enemies" (Ps. 108:13).

Let's Talk: It is only in God that you are able to achieve anything courageously. He gives us help to complete the hard tasks in lives. He helps you to give your very best every day. Have you noticed the victory comes through Him as you get still before Him? Each of us has to learn to get quiet and undistracted before Him. He desires to have your undivided and focused attention as you come reverently before Him. Then, with His help you will win the battle!

Let's Glorify: Dear Elohim, you are my Strong Creator. It is only with your help that I am able do mighty and noble things. Please move me in a forward fashion using the gifts and talents you have graciously given. Lord, protect me and my loved ones from the enemy. You are greater and stronger and I do not have to be afraid. How I praise you! In Jesus' name, I pray. Amen.

Let's Go! What is one of the hardest projects you have ever worked on? How did God give you the victory? Did you get quiet and still before Him? If you are having a hard time with this, pray together and ask God for you to be willing to get quiet and still before Him.

March 20

Victorious Action: Patient Prayer Rejoices!

"Rejoice in our confident hope. Be patient in trouble, and keep on praying" (Rom. 12:12 NLT).

Let's Talk: Oh, wouldn't it be great if we could be happy in our hope and wait expectantly in Christ all the time? What if you could learn to stand your ground when you're in trouble, leaning into your Rock and Fortress? If you could stay devoted in prayer and praise, in due time our trial would be over! "Praise the Lord! How joyful are those who fear the Lord and delight in obeying His commands" (Ps. 112:1 NLT). Fun Fact! Ps. 112 is a Hebrew acrostic poem; after the introductory note of praise, each line begins with a successive letter of the Hebrew alphabet.

Let's Glorify: Lord, please help me to give you all the praise, honor and glory as I wait on you to help me through this suffering time. Help me to remember to live in you and live your story for my life. Let me be mindful that I am just passing through this life here on earth. Eternity is going to be awesome! In Jesus, I happily pray. Amen.

Let's Go! What is the easiest for you? Rejoicing, being patient or to keep on praying when you are in a suffering time? Share with each other your thoughts.

March 21

Victorious Action: Let Him Do More Than You Can Imagine!

"Now to Him who is able to do immeasurably more than all we ask or imagine, according to His power that is at work within us, to Him be glory in the church and in Christ Jesus throughout all generations, for ever and ever! Amen" (Eph. 3:20-21).

Let's Talk: It is by God's power at work within you that creates wonders and awe-inspiring great work! He is able to carry out His purpose and do superabundantly; far over and above all that you dare to ask or think! He is amazing and goes beyond our highest prayers, desires, thoughts, hopes, or dreams! God is all knowing and His plans exceed what you might have been asking in the first place. **Lord, let your will be done and help me to pray bigger prayers!**

Let's Glorify: Lord God, you are my Majestic God! You have put the same power in me that raised Jesus from the dead! I have resurrection power in me! Give me renewal Lord to believe that nothing is too hard for you! Help me to remember you are a God of miracles, hope and great love! All glory to you, for ever and ever! In Jesus' name, I pray. Amen.

Let's Go! Has God done more than you can ask or imagine with an event you have worked on? What about in your life? How about in your children or career? Share with each other how great God is!

March 22

Victorious Action: Forgiveness of Yourself and Others!

Gen. 50:17 teaches us to forgive. "This is what you are to say to Joseph: "I ask you to forgive your brothers the sins and the wrongs they committed in treating you so badly. Now please forgive the sins of the servants of the God of your father." When their message came to him, Joseph wept."

Let's Talk: I can have such a hard time serving God and other's when I have bitterness and anger in my heart toward someone! I have to remember by Jesus' wounds we are healed emotionally, spiritually and physically. When we are the hurt, He is our healer! When we are stuck, He uses His solvent called *grace* to get us moving in His direction again. He forgives us freely and asks us to do the same for others. Remember **L.U.B.R.:** **l**oving **u**nconditionally, then **b**less and **r**elease!

Let's Glorify: Lord Jesus, you had every right not to forgive your accusers and murderers. But, you showed us the better way. Forgiveness, love and prayer for others are the keys to emotional freedom. Thank you for your amazing example! I am forgiven and I can freely forgive others. In Jesus' holy name, I pray. Amen.

Let's Go! Hurry and hold every thought captive to the mind of Christ! Don't dilly dally and obsess over your thoughts! Have you noticed, the longer we stay there, the more critical we become of others and ourselves? Who do you need to forgive, bless and release with love to Jesus today?

March 23

Victorious Action: Shining Your Light

"The light shines in the darkness, and the darkness doesn't extinguish the light" (Jn. 1:5 CEB).

Let's Talk: Because of Jesus' light within you, you shine and radiate the difference He is making in your life. People may not understand it, but somehow they know something is different about you. Do not let your light be diminished because someone does not understand your hope and light! Shine brighter still and be a positive light of love, hope and forgiveness!

Let's Glorify: Lord, you tell me in Luke 11:36, "If you are filled with light, with no dark corners, then your whole life will be radiant, as though a floodlight were filling you with light." Thank you for flooding me with your love light of grace and mercy. May I be a candle of hope to those I am around today. In Jesus' name, I pray. Amen.

Let's Go! Where will you shine Jesus' radiant love today? Discuss where you have seen His light radiating in each other.

March 24

Victorious Action: Trusting Our Commander in Chief!

"For I am the Lord your God, who stirs up the sea, causing its waves to roar" (Isa. 51: 15 NLT).

Let's Talk: You are indeed His! He made the beautiful oceans and the rolling, glistening waves. He fashioned you in your mother's body. Certainly, He has you safe, protected and cared for in the shadow of His mighty hand! He can be trusted as our Commander in Chief, the Lord and leader of Heaven's Armies!

Let's Glorify: Lord, you are my Commander in Chief. You have laid the earth's foundations and made them secure. Lord, I am safe and sound in you as you protect me in the shadow of your hand. Thank you, God for caring about me today and always. How I praise thee! In Jesus' name, I pray. Amen.

Let's Go! Are you willing to trust God, the Commander in Chief today with that **one situation** that has you worried? Will you surrender it and turn it over to Him? Pray together releasing your situation into His mighty hands.

March 25

Victorious Action: Believing He IS Doing a Good Work!

"And I am certain that God, who began the good work within you, will continue His work until it is finally finished on the day when Christ Jesus returns" (Phil.1:6 NLT).

Let's Talk: Aren't you glad, God always finishes what He starts? I am! He will not stop in mid-design but will keep perfecting you until the day Jesus our freedom fighter returns to redeem His followers. He will bring each of His believers to full completion in His perfect timing!

Let's Glorify: Jesus, I take great comfort knowing you are not finished with me yet! I appreciate how gentle and kind you are as you grow and transform me unto the likeness of you! Thank you for the good work you are doing in me. Let me cooperate fully. I love you! In your precious name, I pray. Amen.

Let's Go! How is Jesus doing a good work in you? Are you allowing Him to work in others around you?

March 26

Victorious Action: The Desire to Please God!

"For God is working in you, giving you the desire and the power to do what pleases Him" (Phil. 2:13 NLT).

Let's Talk: God is the one who enables you both to want and to actually live out His good purposes and commitments! You do not have to do it alone or in your own strength! Some of us really need to hear this today! God will give you the desire and the energy through the Holy Spirit to finish what He has started. Pray for strength. Pray for creativity. Most of all, pray that He would be glorified with all of your efforts. This focus alone helps me to give my best efforts!

Let's Glorify: God, please help me today with what you have called me to do. I want to go in your strength and energy, not my own. Lord, let me glorify you in word and action. At the end of the day, please remind me to say *thank you for all you have done for me today.* It's in your Son's name I pray, and adore. Amen.

Let's Go! In what area of your life do you need His desires so you can get up and get moving? Do what He asks you to do. Once you have gotten started, plan a fun outing with each other to celebrate your pleasing move in His direction!

March 27

Victorious Action: Let Him Turn Your Darkness into Light!

"I will **lead the blind by ways they have not known**, along unfamiliar paths I will guide them; I will **turn the darkness into light** before them and make the rough places smooth. These are the things I will do; **I will not forsake them**" (Isa. 42:16, emphasis mine).

Let's Talk: He will turn your darkness into light! He will make your rough places smooth. I have found Jesus will use my relationships to help create healing within me. Being vulnerable with each other, letting out our secrets into the healing light and grace of Jesus is freeing! I have found sometimes I ask the wrong question because I am starting with me and my point of view! I need to ask God, starting with Him. It really is a paradigm shift. When you are coming undone, He promises never to leave you. He will lead you in new ways!

Let's Glorify: Lord, thank you for turning my dark, hard and confusing times into something beautiful! I am so glad you help me and turn the rocky places into smooth paths, creating emotional healing in the most unexpected ways! Help me to always start with you, seeking your will first. Thank you for my precious daughters and sisters in Christ, whom I can share my pain with. Thank you God for creating friendships so we can help each other. In your healing grace, I pray. Amen.

Let's Go! How has Jesus turned your dark areas of your life into light? God has meant for us to be in relationship, sharing our hurts and pain with each other. As we do so, praying and asking for help, He creates emotional healing!

March 28

Victorious Action: Attaining the Fullness of Christ!

"To equip His people for works of service, so that the body of Christ may be built up until *we all reach unity in the faith* and *in the knowledge of the Son of God* and *become mature, attaining to the whole measure of the fullness of Christ*" (Eph. 4:12-13, italics mine).

Let's Talk: It is truly God who brings the good things in our life to a true and complete fulfillment of Christ. It is by His hand that He produces in you the desires and actions that please Him. He energizes us to complete wonderful works of service for Him and others. As you do, you are living out the salvation God has given you. You are called to do this with a proper sense of awe and responsibility!

Let's Glorify: Sovereign God, I am amazed by you! You are at work *within me*, leading me forward. You bring your good purposes to completion. Thank you for helping me to spiritually mature. How I praise you and thank you for using me and my life. May it be all to your glory, my Most High God! In Jesus' name, I pray. Amen.

Let's Go! How have you seen God willing you forward to complete His good purposes in you? What is He doing in your life right now? Share what God is doing in your lives.

March 29

Victorious Action: Good Works Are in Order!

"Being confident of this, He who began a good work in you will carry it on to completion until the day of Christ Jesus" (Phil. 1:6).

Let's Talk: Right up till the return of Christ, He will be working on each of us! You are not a finished project, yet! Neither are the people you live with! So grace, peace, long suffering and mercy are needed (probably) every day! Thankfully, your perseverance does not depend on your own efforts! Your perseverant efforts can rely on the grace of God, through the Spirit living inside you!

Let's Glorify: Jesus, I am so glad you never stop working on me! Let me remember to give grace and mercy to others because we are in process with you daily. Help me to rely on your loving grace which is poured out into my heart through the power of the Holy Spirit. Please help me to remember there is great purpose in my life here on earth as I am practicing how to live for heaven. Thank you for your patience today. In Jesus' precious name, I pray. Amen.

Let's Go! What area is God not finished with you yet? How will you exhibit patient with yourself and others today? Talk about this with each other.

March 30

Victorious Action: Serving with a Clear Heart!

"But with you there is forgiveness, so that we can, with reverence, serve you" (Ps. 130:4).

Let's Talk: Fear of the Lord is the beginning of wisdom. There is beautiful forgiveness of all of your sins, so knowing this you can cultivate a respect, worship and adoration of Him. As you do so, your gratitude can grow! Not only do you need to ask God for forgiveness, but you also need to forgive others. **Forgiveness of other's faults is needed if you are going to serve the Lord effectively.** You can serve Jesus and others with a clear head, a pure heart and a sincere faith.

Let's Glorify: Lord Jesus, I want to have a healthy respect of you and your holiness. I want to have reverent submission to your will in my life. Help me to surrender my will for your divinely perfect plans. Please forgive me of all of my sins today as I forgive those who sin against me. Thank you for being my God, my Redeemer and Savior. In Jesus' name, I pray. Amen.

Let's Go! Serving with a clear heart requires a forgiven and forgiving heart. Are you serving the Lord with a healthy reverence and a heart that is absolutely forgiven? Talk about it with your mom, daughter or girlfriend.

March 31

Victorious Action: Give Thanks!

"Give thanks to the Lord, for He is good; His love endures forever" (Ps. 118:1).

Let's Talk: Tell the Lord how thankful you are, because He is kind and always merciful. His love is like a precious ring. It is a circle which never ends: it just goes around and around, never ending, never stopping. Now that is something to be thankful for! **Adopt the attitude of gratitude.**

Let's Glorify: God, I give you a prayer of thanks for the victory you give me today, tomorrow and into eternity. "Thank you your love is eternal" (Ps. 118:1 GNT). When I am having a really anxious moment or am in a bad mood, I can take a breath, look around and say a silent prayer of thanks for what you have given me today. Please remind me how blessed I truly am. In your enduring love, I pray. Amen.

Let's Go! How have you experienced Jesus' love for you? How have you given His love away to your family? Will you **adopt the attitude of gratitude today? Discuss this together.**

April

A daughter is a little girl who grows up to be a friend.

April 1

Victorious Action: Keep His Decrees!

"So that you, your children and their children after them may fear the Lord your God as long as you live by keeping all His decrees and commands that I give you, and so that you may enjoy long life" (Dt. 6:2).

Let's Talk: Leaving a legacy of keeping God's commandments is a gift to your family! Living and being obedient through His loving grace brings you peace. Joshua tells us in Deuteronomy 6:2, to obey not because He is an oppressive God, but obey because He wants you to live peacefully and enjoy a long life. Joshua knew the Israelites needed these solemn words *before* they crossed the Jordan River and inherited the land flowing with milk and honey.

Let's Glorify: Lord God, I want my family and my grandchildren to enjoy a good life of peace, hope and love. The scriptures tell me over and over again to **trust in you alone** and honor you by keeping your commandments. Let it be so in my family. Please help me be a godly witness of your love and light. In Jesus' name, I pray. Amen.

Let's Go! What are the solemn words you are teaching your family about God, the Father? Discuss these words with each other.

April 2

Victorious Action: Reverent Submission to the Lord!

"Reverence for the Eternal is the first lesson of wisdom, and humility always precedes honor" (Prov. 15:33 VOICE).

Let's Talk: Proverbs 15:33 CEV shares, "Showing respect to the Lord will make you wise, and being humble will bring honor to you." I like the fact that as I show the Lord respect by having reverent submission to His will I will become wise! We can all benefit by having more wisdom! Having humility Prov. says, will bring me honor. It is in **embracing humility** that you are lifted up as you bow before Him and His desires for your life. If you seek attention, you will be humbled by your pride and selfish motives.

Let's Glorify: Lord God, I want to give you my reverent submission in all areas of my life. You tell me this is the first lesson of wisdom and humility. Please help me today to remain humble and bowed low in my spirit unto you. Show me Lord, where I am not being submissive in my life. In Jesus name, I pray. Amen.

Let's Go! Where is God, the Eternal One asking you to give Him first place in your life by showing Him reverent submission?

April 3

Victorious Action: Giving Yourself and Your Children to Serve Jesus!

"As evening approached, Joseph, a rich man from Arimathea who had become a follower of Jesus, went to Pilate and asked for Jesus' body. And Pilate issued an order to release it to him. Joseph took the body and wrapped it in a long sheet of clean linen cloth. He placed it in his own new tomb, which had been carved out of the rock. Then he rolled a great stone across the entrance and left. Both Mary Magdalene and the other Mary were sitting across from the tomb and watching" (Matt. 27:57-61 NLT, emphasis mine).

Let's Talk: The other Mary referenced in vs. 61, was the mother to James and Joseph. "James the Little" was one of Jesus' apostles. He was nicknamed this to distinguish him from the other James (disciple) of the same name. Motivated by her gratitude for Jesus and all He had done for her and her son, she served Him with a faithful, true and loving heart. She was there and witnessed where his body was laid after He was crucified. She saw Joseph of Arimathea close up the tomb with a massive rock. Mark 16:1 reports on "Saturday evening, when the Sabbath ended, Mary Magdalene, Mary the mother of James, and Salome went out and purchased burial spices so they could anoint Jesus' body." Of course, she did not need to anoint His body with the preserving spices, because the next day Jesus rose from the grave! Mary was there at the tomb site when the angel gave her the amazing great news. She shows you and I a simple, trusting faith that has witnessed down through the ages of the crucifixion, His resurrection and life!

Let's Glorify: Lord, thank you for Mary's quiet, faithful, simple faith. She trusted you Jesus, that you are indeed the Son of God! Her life witnesses to me today. She served you with a heart full of love and gratitude! As a mother, she gave her son James to you to serve as an apostle. Lord, I give you my children. I pray they will serve you faithfully, passionately and with love. May we show you our gratitude daily out of hearts that are full of joy for all you have done for us! In your resurrected name I pray and ask these things. Amen.

Let's Go! Are you willing to give up yourself and your children to serve and love Jesus? Why or why not?

April 4

Victorious Action: Stand Fast in Your Faith, Holding onto Love!

"Watch, stand fast in the faith, be brave, be strong. Let all that you do be done with love" (1 Cor. 16: 13-14).

Let's Talk: The King James Version says, in 1 Corinthians 16: 14, "Let all your things be done with *charity*" (italics mine). This means to let love prevail in your life, words, and actions. Can you also let love succeed over the troubles of this life? I think so! If at the core of your heart is love for God and you are being cleansed and repenting of your sins all the time, then yes! As you hold onto your faith, watch for His leading and stay courageous in Jesus. You can move and act out of your identity which is based on His precious and pure love.

Let's Glorify: Jesus, I want to move, breathe and walk in your love. Let me give your love to others as freely as possible. Thank you for showing me your love as you walked and guided others on this earth. Thank you for your priceless blood and love poured out on the cross. I love you. In your name, I pray and thank you. Amen.

Let's Go! Where are you in your walk with Jesus? Are you watching for His leadings, standing fast in your faith, being brave or strong? Are you able to love others supernaturally because of the Holy Spirit living inside? Why or why not?

April 5

Victorious Action: Healed by His Wounds!

"But He was pierced for our transgressions, He was crushed for our iniquities; the punishment that brought us peace was on Him, and by His wounds we are healed" (Isa. 53:5).

Let's Talk: He was wounded for your rebellious acts and by Jesus' wounds you are healed! He was whipped and scourged so you could be made whole mentally, spiritually, emotionally and physically. The injuries, the wrong doing, the betrayal He suffered became your beneficial healing. The sufferings of Jesus took away the penalty that you would otherwise owe. **He undoes the effect of your sins!**

Let's Glorify: Jesus, thank you for suffering and taking so much abuse on my behalf. I pray I never take what you did for me for granted. You gave it all and as a result I can live emotionally and spiritually free today. Someday, I will have a new body in heaven and will be made perfect because your body suffered so horribly on earth. I love you. In your precious sacrifice I am made whole. Thank you! In Jesus' name, I pray. Amen.

Let's Go! What area do you need His precious healing and peace today? Talk about how Jesus *undoes the effect of your sins.*

April 6

Victorious Action: True Wisdom is From the Lord!

"There is no wisdom, no insight, no plan that can succeed against the Lord" (Prov. 21:30).

Let's Talk: I am not smart enough to even think I could make a better or wiser plan than the Lord! He made all of creation, including you and I. He made the gorgeous sunsets, the majestic mountains and the beautiful tropical islands. He gives us the beautiful singing of the birds every morning. Certainly, He holds you in the palm of His hand and holds you near His breast.

Let's Glorify: Lord, I trust you with all that I am today and always. Your plans are best for my life! I surrender all that I am to your great and holy character. You can do anything in my life! How I love you! In Jesus' name, I pray. Amen.

Let's Go! What plans are you trying to make for your life without consulting God? Where do you need to trust and surrender your plan for His higher calling?

April 7

Victorious Action: Wholehearted Thanks!

"I give you thanks, O Lord, with all my heart" (Ps. 138:1 NLT).

Let's Talk: My heart can tend to wander for it is restless. It cries out for more! It cries out to be understood. Sometimes I try to fill it up with more of this world, instead of seeking out the true source of real joy and contentment. I desire that my heart, my will, affections and emotions give complete and eternal praise to you Lord all throughout the day! Today I choose to be contented in you alone. Today I choose to walk in your peace for my life.

Let's Glorify: Dear Lord, I give my whole heart to you. Let it be, a heart filled with praise, for I am grateful. Thank you because you have saved me from myself and a life of sin. I look forward to the day when I will live with you forever in my eternal home! Hallelujah! What a sweet day this will be. In Jesus' holy name, I pray. Amen.

Let's Go! How do you best like to praise God? Are you doing this every day? Share your thoughts with each other.

April 8

Victorious Action: Writing His Words on Your Heart!

"My daughter, keep my words and store up my commands within you. Keep my commands and you will live; guard my teachings as the apple of your eye. Bind them on your fingers; write them on the tablet of your heart" (Prov. 7: 1-3).

Let's Talk: God takes His words very seriously. He asks us to pause, linger and ponder His Scriptures. As you regularly meditate on His laws they are etched into the memory of your heart and mind. As you focus on His teachings, they become the clear view of how to live your life!

Let's Glorify: Dear God, thank you for your God breathed words. They are words that are inspired and alive. Thank you as I read them and apply them, your words teach, rebuke, correct and train me for a life that is upright before you (2 Timothy 3:16 VOICE). Thank you for making your instructions clear enough for me to apply to my life. In your Jesus' name, I pray. Amen.

Let's Go! Would you consider wearing a special bracelet, necklace or ring that reminds you to focus on God's Holy Words? Share your favorite verse with each other.

April 9

Victorious Action: He Rescues Me!

"The righteous person faces many troubles, but the Lord comes to the rescue each time" (Ps. 34:19 NLT).

Let's Talk: God will deliver you out of your problems. This is His promise in Ps. 34:19. You may have to face the fiery trial, but you will come through it! Notice it is coming through the trial by God's hand and care that you are rescued! It is not going under or over the problem, but the Lord will save you as you *rely on Him!* You are refined in our fiery trials, but never forsaken!

Let's Glorify: Lord God, thank you for seeing the trials I am in, even today. Thank you I can rest in you and your loving purposes for me. Help me to remember that you will solve this problem and unravel the sticky mess I am in. Thank you for your peace in the midst of my chaotic circumstances. In Jesus' almighty name, I pray. Amen.

Let's Go! Do you believe God can help you in your troubles? Why or why not? Pray together asking God to help you in the midst of your fiery trials. **Pray your faith would increase in Him.**

April 10

Victorious Action: God is Always Awake!

"He will not let you stumble; the one who watches over you will not slumber. Indeed, He who watches over Israel never slumbers or sleeps" (Ps. 121:3-4 NLT).

Let's Talk: Do you ever wake up in the night afraid, wondering what to do next? Pray. Ask God. He is awake and ready to help you and answer your prayers. He will calm your fears and your anxieties. Let Him do so. He is fully alert and awake, caring over you! He is your Abba Father, a near and dear parent to you.

Let's Glorify: Dear God, thank you that you are so attentive to me and my needs. I am so blessed to have you as my Abba Father, ever present, ever caring and ever loving. It is amazing to me; you do not need to slumber! Thank you for being so close to me always. I love you and appreciate you. In your name, I pray. Amen.

Let's Go! What has you awake at night and pacing the floors? Will you give it up to Abba Father?

April 11

Victorious Action: Wanting Only Jesus!

"Then I pray to you, O Lord. I say, "You are my place of refuge. You are all I really want in life" (Ps. 142:5 NLT).

Let's Talk: God is your refuge, your strength, an ever present help in time of trouble! You need to remember to make prayer your first calling and not your last chance! Are you able to say along with David the psalmist, "You O' Lord are **all I really want** in this life?" David penned these words hiding out in a cave, trying to escape his enemies.

Let's Glorify: God, thank you for being my helper, my comforter and my refuge. I can run to you for a safe haven, free from the worries of this world. You calm my fretting heart and soothe my weary soul. Lord, help me to desire only you in this fleeting life. **Show me** what this looks like in my life. In Jesus' name, I pray. Amen.

Let's Go! What do you want more in your life instead of Jesus? Have a conversation about your wants and desires. Pray for your family's wants and desires to be aligned with Jesus' priorities.

April 12

Victorious Action: Search me! Test me!

"Search me, God, and know my heart; test me and know my anxious thoughts. See if there is any offensive way in me, and lead me in the way everlasting" (Ps. 139:23-24).

Let's Talk: Search me. Know my heart. Test me and know my anxious thoughts. I turn these worrisome thoughts over to you now, Lord. Thoughts of *not being good enough*, *not adequate enough* and *what will people think of me* thoughts. God you tell me I am enough. You whisper to my heart, **"Believe what I believe about you."** Words like *forgiven, loved, blessed, enough in Him* spring up in the bubbling cool spring of my mind. His thoughts are precious about you (Ps. 139:17).

Let's Glorify: God, thank you that I am enough in you because **you are the great I AM.** You are more than sufficient for me, my worries and my life. Thank you for handling all my fears today. I ask that you would give me a big dose of faith instead! Thank you for leading me and guiding me on your everlasting path of peace and love today. In Jesus' name, I pray. Amen.

Let's Go! Where have you doubted yourself? God tells you **He is enough** and *therefore you are enough!* Share your insecurities with each other, releasing them to God. Ask Him to strengthen your heart and mind in Him.

April 13

Victorious Action: Living as a Living Sacrifice!

"Therefore, I urge you, brothers and sisters, in view of God's mercy, to offer your bodies as a living sacrifice, holy and pleasing to God—this is your true and proper worship" (Rom. 12:1 NLT).

Let's Talk: Our bodies are to be lived out as a living, holy sacrifice. As a result of Jesus' life giving sacrifice on the cross, you and I live out of the goodness that God has extended us. Our outward actions signify what is coming out of our heart and mind. Because of what Jesus did on the cross, our sacrifice is alive in His resurrection power! His work leads us to life not death! His resurrection steals life from death and makes it possible for those who trust in Him to become a sacrifice and yet live.

Let's Glorify: Lord Jesus, how I praise and thank you for your sacrifice on the cross! Your life poured out makes it possible for me to live a godly life, a living sacrifice in this life. How I live my life in my body, thoughts and mind is how I worship you. Let me be mindful of this fact in what I say, what I eat, what I watch on television and what I think. In the holy name of Jesus, I pray. Amen.

Let's Go! What does offering your body as a living sacrifice look like to you in today's culture? Have a conversation about living holy before the Lord.

April 14

Victorious Action: Your Works are Wonderful! That Includes Me!

"For you created my inmost being; you knit me together in my mother's womb. I praise you because I am fearfully and wonderfully made; your works are wonderful, I know that full well" (Ps. 139:13-14).

Let's Talk: God made you. You are a Masterpiece in His eyes! He fashioned you within your mother. His works are perfect and divinely His. He has a good plan for your life! His fingerprints of love, grace, forgiveness and care are all over you! He made you to be the one-of-a-kind YOU!

Let's Glorify: God, thank you that you knit me together; you formed me with your very own thoughts and hands. I am wonderfully made and beautifully loved by you! How I thank you for this sweet identity! I am no mistake; I am a daughter of the Most High God! In gratefulness and wonder I pray, all to your glory. Amen.

Let's Go! Where have you seen God's fingerprints of love, grace, forgiveness and care on you? Share with you mom, daughter or friend how special and important they are to you.

April 15

Victorious Action: Receive His Blessing!

"You know what I am going to say even before I say it, Lord. You go before me and follow me. You place your hand of blessing on my head" (Ps. 139:4-5 NLT).

Let's Talk: Lord, you are the Eternal One. You know everything I do and everything I'll say even *before* I say it! "You have placed your hand gently on my shoulder," The Voice bible says in Psalms 139:5. I have felt His gentle touch on my shoulder when it was time to make a decision. Maybe you have felt His hand, too guiding and directing you. He does keep you close, hemming you in on all sides! He will help you to act and make good decisions!

Let's Glorify: God, thank you for going before me and promising always to be with me. Lord, I am so glad you care about me and you guide me in your correct ways. Lord, help me to listen to you more carefully today. Help me to seek you *before* I make my decisions. In Jesus' name, I pray. Amen.

Let's Go! How has God "hemmed you in?" Knowing that God knows what you will say even before you say it, can have a beneficial effect upon your speech and character. How has this proven true for you?

April 16

Victorious Action: Answer the Call!

"We live by faith, not by sight" (2 Cor. 5:7).

Let's Talk: It takes courage to live in faith over what you can see, touch and smell. Have you ever felt so sure about something and yet you could not explain why? You just knew it was what you were supposed to do! Perhaps, God has whispered to your heart something He'd like you to do. You know definitely, this is not your big idea! And, it is going to take all the faith you can muster to take that first step of obedience in what He is calling you to do. Your act of faith is sight unseen and yet your faith is seen and revealed by your willingness to please Him!

Let's Glorify: God, help me to *answer the call* of what you are asking me to do! Lord, I do not have to know all the answers but **I do want to respond in faith.** I know it is by faith that I am pleasing to you! Lord, help me and affirm my steps of obedience every step of the way. Shine your radiant light on my next step as I move in faith. In Jesus name, I pray, Amen.

Let's Go! Where is God asking you to *answer His call* in your life? Will you be obedient and surrender your will to His perfect plan? He can be totally trusted! Discuss with your mom, daughter of girlfriend.

April 17

Victorious Action: Be the Fragrance of Christ!

"For we are to God the pleasing aroma of Christ among those who are being saved and those who are perishing" (2 Cor. 2:15).

Let's Talk: "Our offering to God is to be the perfume of Christ that goes out to those who are being saved and to those who are being lost" (2 Cor. 2:15 ERV). He brings knowledge of Christ through you as a sweet fragrance of love and service. You wear a lovely perfume. This happens as you give forgiveness, lend a hand volunteering, give gracious service or even give a kind word and a smile. You smell the best when you are serving obediently in the Holy Spirit's love and power!

Let's Glorify: Jesus, help me to be mindful that not everyone knows and receives you. Lord, let me be a sweet aroma anyway, pointing them to you and your saving grace. Let it be all to your glory. In Jesus' name, I pray. Amen.

Let's Go! What is a practical way you both can extend Christ's pleasing fragrance to other's today? Share with each other.

April 18

Victorious Action: Equipped by the Shepherd!

"Our Lord Jesus, that great Shepherd of the sheep, equip you with everything good for doing His will, and may He work in us what is pleasing to Him, through Jesus Christ, to whom be glory for ever and ever" (Heb. 13:20c-21).

Let's Talk: Jesus equips, trains, prepares and arms you for the job at hand. He will get you ready with **everything** (not just some things) good for doing His will and His Kingdom work. I have found I am not ready for the task just today. Rather, He had already gotten me prepared and ready in the mundane and the ordinary days when I thought nothing too exciting was happening.

Let's Glorify: Lord Jesus, help me not to despise the seemingly small, uneventful days. You are working behind the scenes on my behalf. You are getting me ready for some of your divine work. Help me to trust you while I wait patiently and quietly. In your name, I pray. Amen.

Let's Go! Have you noticed Jesus getting you ready to do His work through the ordinary and mundane days? Have a discussion about some of your most mundane days.

April 19

Victorious Action: Work with All of Your Heart!

"Whatever you do, work at it with all your heart, as working for the Lord, not for human masters, since you know that you will receive an inheritance from the Lord as a reward. It is the Lord Christ you are serving" (Col. 3:23-24).

Let's Talk: These Scriptures create quite a paradigm shift in me! If I seek to glorify my Lord and Savior every day as I serve Him in all that I do, I find this takes the drudgery out of the everyday and ordinary. These scriptures also remind me to seek His favor as I serve people and not try to get glory from people. I can pray and praise while I work committing my efforts and love to the only God who is worthy!

Let's Glorify: Jesus, I want to serve you while I serve others. In those moments when I am not appreciated by my family, my co-workers or friends, I need to desperately remember to work and serve with all my heart, because truly it is you I am working for! I love you and appreciate all that you do for me. In your great name, I pray. Amen.

Let's Go! In your day, when do you need to remember that you are humbly serving the Lord, not human masters? Do you believe you have a future reward of inheritance coming? Discuss this together.

April 20

Victorious Action: Love Your Neighbor!

"Do not seek revenge or bear a grudge against anyone among your people, but love your neighbor as yourself. I am the Lord" (Lev. 19:18).

Let's Talk: Do not take revenge or pay back evil for evil. I have said this so many times to my children as they grew up. I say this to myself: "Do not take offense so easily! Forgive freely as Jesus has forgiven us." It is hard at times isn't it, especially when you feel hurt or slighted. Jesus knows this. He experienced the most brutal of deaths on the cross. He has experienced everything you and I will go through in this life. He understands your feelings and He will help you as you turn your emotions over to Him.

Let's Glorify: Jesus, I want to love my neighbor out of a heart that is full of loving, kind and forgiving thoughts. I can only do this if I fill up on you daily, seeking your ways and releasing my hurts to you. Lord, strengthen me with your love, joy and mercy. In your holy name, I pray. Amen.

Let's Go! Are you holding any grudges today? Would you be willing to give them up to the Lord? Discuss with your mom, daughter or special friend. What holds you back from forgiving someone?

April 21

Victorious Action: Be Transformed!

"Do not conform to the pattern of this world, but be transformed by the renewing of your mind. Then you will be able to test and approve what God's will is—His good, pleasing and perfect will" (Rom. 12:2).

Let's Talk: Transformation happens within as you fix your eyes and mind upon Jesus repeatedly. He teaches, He leads and guides you as you go through your everyday life. Embracing and thanking God for what He is doing in your life is the best thing you can do, realizing you are showing Him how much you trust His authority. The more you follow hard after Jesus, the more you will mature and understand His will for your life. You will want what He wants and not hunger for what the world has to offer...which is fleeting and temporary.

Let's Glorify: Jesus, help me to focus on you alone and not be caught up in what the world says to do. Lord, I embrace what you are doing in my life. **Even when you ask me to do something new and out of my comfort zone, I will trust you.** I look forward to the transforming work you will do in me, maturing my faith. Renew my mind even now. In your name, I pray. Amen.

Let's Glorify: Are you embracing what God is doing in your life? Or are you fighting Him all the way? (Who is winning?) Pray He would renew your mind today.

April 22

Victorious Action: Praising with the Fruit of Our Lips!

"Through Jesus, therefore, let us continually offer to God a sacrifice of praise—the fruit of lips that openly profess His name" (Heb.13:15).

Let's Talk: How many times have you looked in dismay at what you do not have enough of? Instead, how about thanking Jesus for the food you do have to eat and all the bills you were able to pay this month? How about thanking Him for good health? Or thanking Him for the beautiful blue sky and the pine trees? Those might seem like obvious praises. But, are you praising Him for something every day? Acknowledging and confessing His name openly by talking about what He is doing or has done in your life is a beautiful sacrifice of praise.

Let's Glorify: Lord, I want to always have the fruit of grateful lips that openly speak of your goodness, your loving kindness and amazing care! You are so wonderful to me! May I be ever mindful of all that you are doing in my life and my family's lives. In the wonderful name of Jesus, I pray. Amen.

Let's Go! Do you speak with the fruit of lips that **openly profess His name**? Why or why not?

April 23

Victorious Action: God Has Good Plans for You!

"For I know the plans I have for you," declares the Lord, "plans to prosper you and not to harm you, plans to give you hope and a future" (Jer. 29:11).

Let's Talk: Have you ever been in a really bad way and so you are in a really foul mood? Maybe your finances are not so great (again). Perhaps you are really sick. Or, worse yet. Your son or daughters are sick or they have gotten into some trouble. God sees your difficulties. He knows your worrisome patterns. He only makes promises that He will personally keep! He delivers on what He says! He will give you good future plans laced with hope. He knows the plans of your life from the start, to the middle and the ending. He's made those plans and they are to prosper and not harm you. Decide to praise Him no matter what today. It will help lift your bad mood! In those days when you pray, God says, "I will listen" (Jer. 29:12 NLT).

Let's Glorify: Lord God, you are the Master event planner of my life. I know you can be completely trusted! It's my job to praise you, as I look up and give you all the honor you deserve. Help me to focus on your great provision every day with a grateful heart. I am thankful you have good plans for my life! In Jesus' name, I pray. Amen.

Let's Go! Do you trust God to be the Master event planner of your life? Discuss this over a glass of ice tea.

April 24

Victorious Action: Jesus is the Gate to Eternal Life!

"I am the gate; whoever enters through me will be saved. They will come in and go out, and find pasture. The thief comes only to steal and kill and destroy; I have come that they may have life, and have it to the full" (Jn. 10:9-10).

Let's Talk: Jesus is the gate, the Way to eternal life! As we are likened to sheep, He is our true Shepherd. He will guide you home unto His righteous path. The enemy of your soul comes to steal you away from your Shepherd. This is not possible though, because once you have received Jesus as your Lord and Savior, with a whole hearted commitment and devotion, "nothing can separate you from His love and presence." (Rom. 8:38 NLT, paraphrased) Jesus brings you real and abundant life in Him! He asks you to follow Him only. As you do so, your life will be full, joyful and complete.

Let's Glorify: Jesus, you truly are the Way, the Truth and the Life. Thank you for leading me and protecting me from the thief's chaos. Help me to stick closely to you, so I hear your voice guiding me and leading me home. In Jesus' precious name, I pray. Amen.

Let's Go! Are you following after the Shepherd and finding rest for your weary soul? Why or why not? Pray for each other's weary souls!

April 25

Victorious Action: Knowing His Mighty Power and Strength!

"For I can do everything through Christ, who gives me strength" (Phil. 4:13 NLT).

Let's Talk: How many times have you faced a challenge, a situation (public speaking, yikes!) where you had to be courageous? **Did you rely on the Lord and His strength?** Or did you let your emotions and insecurities spin out of control? God does not give us a lack of self-discipline or a spirit of fear. No, this comes from the enemy who does not want you to succeed nor does he want you to shine Jesus' light and love to others. The enemy wants you to shrink back and believe you cannot do whatever God is calling you to do. God says, "I will help you. Rely on me and the love I have for you. Have faith in me and the power I will exercise in your situation!"

Let's Glorify: God, help me to call on your mighty and holy name when I am afraid. I know in my own strength and capabilities I can do nothing. However, in you, "I can do ALL things through Christ who strengthens me!" I am standing on your truth today. Thank you for your willingness to help me in all situations. How I love you and appreciate having the God of the Universe on my side! Amen.

Let's Go! Where are you having a spirit of fear, timidity or lack of self-discipline? Pray for each other's needs and check in next week to see how you are both doing.

April 26

Victorious Action: Run Freely!

"Therefore, since we are surrounded by such a great cloud of witnesses, let us throw off everything that hinders and the sin that so easily entangles. And let us run with perseverance the race marked out for us, fixing our eyes on Jesus, the pioneer and perfecter of faith" (Heb. 12:1-3).

Let's Talk: You have a huge crowd of believers cheering you on! Since this is true, you are to run freely without the baggage of the past and sins of today that holds you from completing the race. It will take time and tons of perseverance. But, it is possible as you focus your eyes and your heart with a single minded focus upon Jesus, your Savior. Your very next breath comes in Him because of Him. Before you know it, you are finished with this particular race, this hard day, or hard situation.

Let's Glorify: Jesus, thank you for being my leader and perfector of my faith. Thank you for **the race called life** that you have set before me. You know exactly what each one of my days will look like. You understand my hurts, my hang ups and you love me anyway. How I thank you and praise you. Knowing you are always with me encourages me to **run with you courageously**. In Jesus' name, I pray and run. Amen.

Let's Go! What action is Jesus calling you to do? Are you running the race of life courageously in Him? Or are you deciding not to participate? Nothing compares to experiencing Jesus first hand in the race of life! Share your thoughts with each other.

April 27

Victorious Action: Be Joyful and Do not Lose Heart!

"For the joy set before Him He endured the cross, scorning its shame, and sat down at the right hand of the throne of God. Consider Him who endured such opposition from sinners, so that you will not grow weary and lose heart" (Heb. 12:2b-3).

Let's Talk: Jesus knew what His life's work was. He knew His identity was secure in His Holy Father. So, He didn't curse His suffering that came at the hand of those He was dying to save. It was a joy set before Him even though people yelled in His face and spit on Him. At the end of His suffering, He went back to His heavenly home to sit at the right hand of His Father. At the end of this life and your suffering is over, you as a follower of Christ, will be with Him forever. You and I are not to lose heart as we look to our Mighty Warrior, Jesus. He is our example to follow.

Let's Glorify: Lord Jesus, thank you for your work on the cross. Thank you that you followed your Father's plan to the last detail. As a result, I get to live eternally with you in heaven. Help me to realize the time and suffering here on earth is so small in comparison to the eternal time I will spend with you and God in my real home. In your powerful name, I pray. Amen.

Let's Go! When have you endured shame or ridicule? Does it help you to read how Jesus handled opposition from those around Him? Talk about this with each other.

April 28

Victorious Action: Standing Strong Wearing God's Armor!

"Finally, be strong in the Lord and in His mighty power. **Put on the full armor of God**, so that you can take your stand against the devil's schemes" (Eph. 6:10-11).

Let's Talk: Sometimes we forget our fights in this world are not against people, but against the devil and his schemes. Our troubles are fashioned in the spiritual realm. This is why we must put on the armor of God each day. "Stand firm then, with the **belt of truth** buckled around your waist, with the **breastplate of righteousness** in place, and with your **feet fitted** with the readiness that comes from the **gospel of peace**. In addition to all this, take up the **shield of faith**, with which you can extinguish all the flaming arrows of the evil one. Take the **helmet of salvation** and the **sword of the Spirit**, which is the word of God" (Eph. 6:13-17, emphasis mine).

Let's Glorify: Lord God, help me to stand strong in you. I need help remembering to put on your armor every day. You promise to help me when I cry out to you. You promise to be with me and for me. I am so grateful for your faithful and protective presence. In Jesus' name, I pray. Amen.

Let's Go! Realizing you are fighting and standing against the dark forces of the enemy in God's mighty power, does this make it easier to stand strong? Knowing there is a spiritual battle going on, does this make it easier for you not to take offense? Discuss with your girlfriend, mom or daughter.

April 29

Victorious Action: Praying All the Time!

"Pray in the Spirit on all occasions with all kinds of prayers and requests. With this in mind, be alert and always keep on praying for all the Lord's people" (Eph. 6:18).

Let's Talk: Keep praying for yourself and others all day long. Pray hard and pray long asking the Holy Spirit to shape your prayers. Pray the Holy Spirit will remind you to keep praying for others and their needs as everyone is in a spiritual battle. We are commanded to pray for one another without ceasing.

Let's Glorify: Dear Jesus, thank you for sending the Holy Spirit to remind me to pray on all occasions. Holy Spirit, let me realize fully when you bring someone to mind I am to stop and pray for them. Thank you for such great privilege to partner with you in prayer. In your name, I pray. Amen.

Let's Go! Share your prayer concerns with each other. Determine a daily time you will pray for each other, lifting up these prayer requests to the Lord.

April 30

Victorious Action: All Grace Abounds from Him!

"God is able to make all grace abound to you, so that in all things at all times, having all that you need, you will abound in every good work" (2 Cor. 9:8).

Let's Talk: God is able to bless you abundantly! He owns everything and He gives to you out of the generosity and loving kindness of His heart. "And God will generously provide all you need. Then you will always have everything you need and plenty left over to share with others" (2 Cor. 9:8 NLT). Are you sharing with others? Ask God to give you His generous heart.

Let's Glorify: God, you are so gracious to me. Thank you for providing for me spiritually, physically and emotionally. Help me to realize you are my Provider, my Jehovah Jireh every day. I want to thank you always with a heart filled with praise and gratitude. Let my attitude overflow in service out of a heart filled with joy! Let me serve others and give myself away with a happy heart remembering all that you have done for me. In Jesus' name I pray, and adore. Amen.

Let's Go! Where do you need God to be your great Provider, your Jehovah Jireh today?

May

"It is not what you do for your children, but what you taught them to do for themselves that will make them successful human beings."
~Ann Landers

May 1

Victorious Action: Loving and Serving God with All Your Heart and Soul!

"And now, Israel, what does the Lord your God ask of you but to fear the Lord your God, to walk in obedience to Him, to love Him, to serve the Lord your God with all your heart and with all your soul" (Dt. 10:12).

Let's Talk: You and I are to live in a way that pleases Him! Loving Him and serving Him as we serve others with all that we are is a great first step. You also need to know God and His voice so you can be obedient. However, listening and being obedient to what God calls you to do seems much harder at times. I think it because you have to surrender something and it feels really BIG! I find it is usually my will, my preferences and attitude. At times, I just plain want to have my own way! As I stop my **mental temper tantrum** and **start to revere God for who He is,** I can let go of my stubbornness and believe He has the best intentions for my life. He truly knows me and what will give me lasting peace and contentment. He is worthy of my trust.

Let's Glorify: Lord God, you are indeed worthy of my trust. Thank you for giving up your only Son so I can truly know you, love you and serve you with all of my heart and soul. Lord, I want to humble myself right now, believing you are all knowing and you know the plans you have for my life. I want to wholeheartedly embrace your will for my life. In Jesus' name, I pray. Amen.

Let's Go! Has God asked you to do something and you are having a "mental temper tantrum" instead of obeying right away? Talk about it with you mom, daughter or girlfriend.

May 2

Victorious Action: Giving as the Widow Did!

Jesus sat down opposite the place where the offerings were put and watched the crowd putting their money into the temple treasury. Many rich people threw in large amounts. But a poor widow came and put in two very small copper coins, worth only a few cents. Calling His disciples to him, Jesus said, "Truly I tell you, this poor widow has put more into the treasury than all the others. They all gave out of their wealth; but she, out of her poverty, put in everything—all she had to live on" (Mark 12:41-44, emphasis mine).

Let's Talk: Jesus notices what you do for others, especially when you give to the poor and to needy charities. This woman, Jesus noticed, "out of her poverty, put in everything—all she had to live on" (vs. 44, emphasis mine). Whether you give generously or carefully; Jesus notices you. Whether you give and serve cheerfully or with reluctance, He sees your heart. He knows what your views are, in giving alms (donations); and whether you do it unto the Lord, or only to be seen by man. Trust God and He will provide for you. Just look at how extravagant God's grace is! Jesus' loving sacrifice on the cross is the evidence of God's love and His physical and eternal spiritual care for you. His abundant provision is another reason to give your tithe and offerings. "The threshing floors will again be piled high with grain, and the presses will overflow with new wine and olive oil" (Joel 2:24 NLT).

Let's Glorify: God, you are a wonderful provider. I want to be a generous giver! Help me to realize there is always someone who needs a smile, my listening ear, a donation, some food or a hug. May I give in poverty

May

or in wealth knowing you will always be there to help me. Encourage me to give with a cheerful heart knowing as I do so, I am serving you. Thank you, Jehovah Jireh! Amen.

Let's Go! Are you giving out of your wealth or out of your poverty? Discuss the last time you gave something away. How did you feel?

May 3

Victorious Action: Produce a Bowl Full of Beautiful Fruit!

"The fruit of the Spirit is love, joy, peace, patience, kindness, goodness, faithfulness, gentleness and self-control. Against such things there is no law" (Gal. 5:22-23a).

Let's Talk: Notice it is the Holy Spirit which produces this beautiful fruit! As you walk with Christ, (who embodies all the fruit of the Spirit) learning and meditating on His ways, reading the bible and praying, the Holy Spirit starts producing the fruit in your life. Your character begins to change and reflect Jesus living within.

Let's Glorify: Lord, please help me to cultivate luscious fruit in my life, all to your glory. I know you will do the work in me and I do not have to strive after it. I will do my part as I draw near and abide in you, my true Vine. Help me to wait patiently when you start **pruning away the sucker shoots, the unnecessary vines,** which represent the extraneous activities in my life. These activities might be good and fun, but they are not always the best use of time. God, help me know how to choose what your best is over what is just fun or good. In Jesus' name, I pray. Amen.

Let's Go! Which fruit of the Spirit is the hardest for you to develop? Ask Jesus to help you cultivate this fruit in your character. Pray for each other to have God's discernment about activities. Pray about whether your activities are His best or just some sucker shoots vying for your attention!

May 4

Victorious Action: Just Be Content Today!

"Every good and perfect gift is from above, coming down from the Father of the heavenly lights, who does not change like shifting shadows" (Jas. 1:17).

Let's Talk: "Just *be content in me* today," I heard Jesus whisper quietly to my heart. I had been struggling with the "what next" in my life and feeling some insecurity and even perhaps some rejection. God gave me such a beautiful and much needed divine hug and kiss when my daughter called the very same morning I heard His whisper. She said, "Mom, I have to tell you some of my friends have been struggling this week. As I tried to encourage them, I heard the words you have been telling me all my life come out of my mouth. Mom, I proud of you and so glad you are my Mom." Well, of course I started to cry! Through my daughter's kind words, I heard such beautiful affirmation and encouragement from God, the Giver of all good gifts! So, **I am choosing to be content** in His loving grace, mercy and kindness today. I know I will experience His joy as I experience His peace.

Let's Glorify: Lord God, thank you so much for your divine hug today through the conversation with my daughter. Jesus, you know exactly what I need at all times. You are a loving God giving away good gifts at the perfect time. I am so grateful to you! I love you. In Jesus' name, I contently pray. Amen.

Let's Go! How has your mom, daughter or friend given you a divine hug or kiss? Share with each other, please. It will help to make each other's day go great and bring a smile to your Heavenly Father's heart!

May 5

Victorious Action: The Humble are Crowned in Victory!

"For the Lord delights in His people; He crowns the humble with victory" (Ps. 149:4 NLT).

Let's Talk: The Lord God takes pleasure in you! He loves you beyond compare and without reservation! **He will give victory as you humble yourself before Him.** He gives His saving grace and mercy to the meek. So, celebrate and praise Him! Tell Him all the things you are most grateful for today! Give up your will for His perfect and pleasing will. Feel your heart and soul filling with a blessed joy and peace even now.

Let's Glorify: Jesus, how grateful I am you give me the victory in this life and eternity as I humble myself before you. You won the battle of sin at the Cross and you extend me the victory to overcome all of life's hurts, obstacles and hang ups. Thank you for your perfect victorious plan of salvation! I love you and am grateful you look at me with a heart of love and delight! In your sweet name, I pray. Amen.

Let's Go! Where do you need Jesus' victory today in your hurts, obstacles or hang ups? Chat with your mom, daughter, sister or friend while you take a walk through nature.

May 6

Victorious Action: He is the Eternal God!

"Acknowledge and take to heart this day that the Lord is God in heaven above and on the earth below. There is no other" (Dt. 4:39).

Let's Talk: Remember and accept He is God! There is no other god. Lay it to your heart and let it root down deeply! Moses reminded the Israelites over and over again to only worship God, the one true God. He reminded them of all the great things God had saved them from time and time again. "You just need to **know with every fiber of your being** that **the Eternal,** and no one else, **is God**" (Deut. 4:39 VOICE, emphasis mine). Turn to Him with your worries. Turn to Him with all of your love and praises! He IS God and He can handle all of your problems!

Let's Glorify: God, you are my Eternal God! Please help me to remember all the times you have provided safety and a way of escape! Lord, I only want to worship you and no other gods. Reveal to me where I have given my heart to another god. I repent right now. You are the only God I want to give my allegiance, love and praise to. In Jesus' name I pray, and ask these things. Amen.

Let's Go! Can you remember all the times when God has kept you safe? Or, recall a time when God pulled you out of a really dangerous situation? Thank Him for His holy and gracious protection.

May 7

Victorious Action: Faith Expresses Itself in Love!

"What is important is faith expressing itself in love" (Gal. 5:6b NLT).

Let's Talk: If I am going to be pleasing to the Lord, I have to respond in faith to what He calls me to do and respond to the TRUTHS He reveals. It's called obedience! Not something I (we) necessarily sign up to do! However, once I start to ponder His love, His goodness, mercy and grace, I have to ask myself, "Why wouldn't I want to have wholehearted obedience and surrender to my Savior Jesus? He has my best (and yours!) interest at heart. He can be absolutely trusted.

Let's Glorify: Lord Jesus, you expressed your love to me and your Father through your loving sacrifice. You thought more of glorifying your Dad then what you'd rather have taken away from you. Lord, I want to express my love and obedience in faith, knowing you've "got me" for the rest of the days and moments of my life. Let me express my love to you by trusting you in faith. I love you. In your name, I pray. Amen.

Let's Go! In what way can you express your love to Jesus today by moving in faith? Is there something He has been asking you to do but you are being resistant because you are afraid?

May 8

Victorious Action: Doing Good unto Others!

"Therefore, as we have opportunity, let us do good to all people, especially to those who belong to the family of believers" (Gal. 6:10 NLT).

Let's Talk: The Amplified Bible says it this way: "Be mindful to be a blessing to all people, especially to those who belong to Christ" (vs. 10). Have you ever wondered about this scripture? Paul knew the gospel would continue to spread if believers stayed united and peaceful with one another. He knew if there was dissension among the flock then the message would fade out or its power would dissipate. Besides, who would want to listen to a bunch of bickering believers? It is the same today. The world waits and watches Christians. *"Are they really different?"* they wonder. Let us be generous, kind and loving to all while we have the opportunity to do so.

Let's Glorify: Lord Jesus, thank you for your servant's heart and beautiful example of helping and caring for others. Lord, let me love others authentically, treating them with love and respect. As I do so, I am giving them a cool cup of refreshment in your name. Thank you for your loving heart towards me. May I express my love to you as I give it away to others. In your holy name, I pray. Amen.

Let's Go! How can you be mindful to be a blessing to the people in your world today? Share your thoughts with each other.

May 9

Victorious Action: Relying on His Love!

"We know how much God loves us, and we have put our trust in his love. God is love, and all who live in love live in God, and God lives in them" (1 Jn. 4:16 NLT).

Let's Talk: God is the complete embodiment of love. You can absolutely rely on the love God has for you. You can rely on His love when you are sick, tired, disappointed, doubting and discouraged. Why? He has proved Himself faithful by sending His Son Jesus to die for your sins while you were still a sinner. You can rely on God's love when your very identity is in question. Put your trust in His love. Ask Him to show you His divine love today. He will give you a divine hug and jewels of affirmation as you seek Him!

Let's Glorify: God, I want to rely on the love that you have for me and my identity. My identity is rooted in your magnificent and everlasting love. Period. Thank you, my identity is not rooted in our ever changing culture, my performance, my looks, my stuff or other's opinions. God, help me to know just how **valuable I am because of Jesus' priceless love and great sacrifice.** In Jesus' name, I pray. Amen.

Let's Go! For your identity, are you relying on God's loving opinion today or the world's fleeting and changing opinions? Talk about the divine hugs and jewels of affirmation you have received from the Lord.

May 10

Victorious Action: Forgiving Others as God Forgives You!

"Bear with each other and forgive one another if any of you has a grievance against someone. Forgive as the Lord forgave you" (Col. 3:13).

Let's Talk: Maybe today is the day you start to forgive that certain someone or situation. God has told you He has canceled all of your debt through the shedding of Jesus' priceless blood on the cross. Why is it then, you and I can refuse to cancel someone else's debt because of the way they have wronged us? Matt. 18:33-34 shares God's thoughts: "shouldn't you have had mercy on your fellow servant just as I had on you?' In anger his master handed him over to the jailers to be tortured, until he should pay back all he owed." Now, you might not get thrown in jail literally, but what about the torture you go through in your minds and spirits, because you obsess and play the scene over and over again? You *hold the key* to *your prison cell*: it's called **forgiveness!**

Let's Glorify: Lord, I want to forgive _____today, right now. Jesus, I bring_____ to the foot of the cross knowing you have freely canceled my debt. With your help, Lord I cancel their debt against me. Thank you for this **forgiveness freedom!** Help me to remember when I get upset and this incident comes up again in my mind that you have given me the gift of forgiveness. Let me remember I am truly set free indeed! In Jesus name, I pray. Amen.

Let's Go! Is there someone or a situation you need to forgive today? Will you be willing to take them to the foot of the cross, where Jesus paid it all, so you could have freedom? Pray together.

May 11

Victorious Action: Listening the First Time!

"God does speak—sometimes one way and sometimes another—even though people may not understand it" (Job 33:14 NCV).

Let's Talk: So, if you are anything like me and human, I find I do not understand God (usually) the first time He is trying to tell me something! "For **God speaks again and again,** though **people do not recognize it**" (Job 33:14 emphasis mine NLT). Am I one of these people? Am I too hurried in my quiet time, to hear the still small whisper in my heart or spoken through the bible passage? **Am I paying attention and focused on you, Lord or am I too busy and distracted to hear you?**

Let's Glorify: Lord, your Word says that sometimes as a people, we do not perceive what you are telling us. God, help me personally, to pay attention to all the cues you are sending me through the bible, prayer, the small voice of the Holy Spirit, divine conversations and even my circumstances. God let me know and sense your slight nudges and even bigger pushes and respond willingly to what you are calling me to do! What a great privilege it is Jesus to have the opportunity to serve you by serving others first. I love you Lord. In Jesus' name, I pray. Amen.

Let's Go! What do you need to change about your quiet time so that you can be more in tune with God and hear his voice? Could it be God is using your circumstances to speak to you? Journal your thoughts and ask God to help you listen better to Him.

May 12

Victorious Action: Knowing the Fullness of His Love!

"And I pray that you, being rooted and established in love, may have power, together with all the saints, to grasp how wide and long and high and deep is the love of Christ, and to know this love that surpasses knowledge—that you may be filled to the measure of all the fullness of God." (Eph. 3:17b-19)

Let's Talk: Sometimes, no matter how hard I try I just cannot fathom how deep, how wide, how long and high God's love is for me! Have you felt this way? I liken it to the beautiful and very blue Lake Tahoe in Northern California. It is such a deep lake and yet the water is very clear. If you ask most people, they'd say no one knows how deep this lake is. They just know it is gorgeous, clear and has always been this way. I feel God's love is this way, too. His love has always been there for me and you because "Christ will make His home in your hearts as you trust in Him." (vs. 17a) His love will always be there for us! I do not have to doubt it and I do not have to question it. His love is beautiful, pure and clear to me.

Let's Glorify: Lord God, how grateful I am that you love me beyond measure! When I stop to realize just how much you love me and that I cannot do anything to earn your love or even lose your love, this gives me great freedom! Then, I start to realize that I can be filled with your fullness of life and power that comes only from you! I am overjoyed by your love! In Jesus' loving name, I pray. Amen.

Let's Go! How have you experienced the love of Christ, though it is too great to understand fully? Share with your mom, daughter or girlfriend.

May 13

Victorious Action: Hearing the Word Speak To You!

"So is my word that goes out from my mouth: It will not return to me empty, but will accomplish what I desire and achieve the purpose for which I sent it" (Isa. 55:11).

Let's Talk: When God speaks through the Bible, He can be trusted. He makes sure the purposes of each word He has said and set forth will come to fruition! His Word will prosper everywhere He sends it. **What He declares creates action!** The Message bible says in Isaiah 55:10-11, "Just as rain and snow descend from the skies and don't go back until they've watered the earth, doing their work of making things grow and blossom, producing seed for farmers and food for the hungry, so will the words that come out of my mouth not come back empty-handed. They'll do the work I sent them to do, they'll complete the assignment I gave them."

Let's Glorify: Lord, how I praise and thank you for keeping your word! You have a specific purpose in everything that you have uttered in the Bible. Thank you for giving me the Word to direct and light my path. Let me read it carefully so I can hear you speaking to me through the Holy Spirit's power. In Jesus' name, I pray. Amen.

Let's Go! Have you ever read the Bible and you just knew God was giving you a direct word to you? Share your thoughts. If not, ask God to personally speak to you through His love letter, the Bible.

May 14

Victorious Action: Knowing You Have Been Ransomed!

"**Do not be afraid,** for I have **ransomed you. I have called you by name; you are mine**" (Isa. 43:1 NLT, emphasis mine).

Let's Talk: *Ransomed* is such a beautiful word which beautifully and powerfully portrays what Jesus has done for ***every believer!*** Ransomed means: redeemed, rescued, restored, released, exchanged, delivered, liberated and set free! Doesn't this list just help you to sigh a huge breathe of relief? Also, thankfully He knows your name! You are His today and forever if you believe and confess He is the Son of God and He died for you sins.

Let's Glorify: Lord Jesus, humbly I thank you for redeeming my past life. I thank you for setting me free from my addictions of people pleasing, worry and anxiety. (Fill in what Jesus has set you free from_____) Lord, thank you for knowing my name. You know me better than I know myself. I look forward to the day when I can hug your neck and praise you face-to-face. In Jesus' name, I pray and love. Amen.

Let's Go! Which of the words for **ransomed** mean the most to you when Jesus set you free from the sins of your past? Have you received Jesus as your Lord and Savior? Do you have any questions about your relationship with Him? If so, please ask your pastor, friend or bible study leader. You are welcome to email me any questions or thoughts as well. **Holly@HeartForTheCross.com**

May 15

Victorious Action: Knowing He is with You in the Rushing Waters!

"When you go through deep waters, I will be with you. When you go through rivers of difficulty, you will not drown. When you walk through the fire of oppression, you will not be burned up; the flames will not consume you" (Isa. 43:2 NLT).

Let's Talk: Where are you today on the journey called life? Are you feeling you are in the deep waters, rivers of difficulties or fires of oppression? God promises as you go through your very hard situation with Him, you will not be set ablaze. You will not be overcome or drown in the rushing waters. He assures you, **"I will be with you. Cling to me. Hold tightly onto me. I will not let you go! Learn from me how much I love you."**

Let's Glorify: Lord, you are my fortress and my steadfast Rock. Thank you for your promise, specifically that you will be with me, no matter what wrenching hardship I am facing! You give me great comfort, peace and supernatural joy even when the waters rush in all around me. How I praise thee! In Jesus' name, I pray and worship you. Amen.

Let's Go! How have you found God to be faithfully with you in the fires of oppression or in the deep waters of life? Have you started to realize that whatever you go through He is FOR YOU and will BE WITH YOU? Talk about how God has brought you through a fiery trial.

May 16

Victorious Action: Love and Serve Others!

"The entire law is summed up in a single command: Love your neighbor as yourself" (Gal. 5:14).

Let's Talk: Loving your neighbor is easy when you like your neighbor. What if you do not particularly care for your neighbor? Pray to change your heart with God's heart thoughts! Your neighbor is anyone you come into contact with on any given day. What are some ways you can love your neighbor? Well, there are words of encouragement and then listening well to their hopes and concerns. There are ways to give physical support: watering their yard while they are away, stacking wood and taking a meal. There is spiritual support: praying silently even while you are listening to their cares and concerns. You can pray after you have left your neighbor asking God how you can really help them. **Then, your love requires action.**

Let's Glorify: Lord, it is easy to love myself because I want to take care of myself and my needs. So, I ask you Jesus, help me to notice the needs of others and compassionately care about what is troubling them. Let me be a generous server not a taker, and a lover of you, not a judgmental hypocrite. I want to be like you, Lord. In Jesus' name, I pray. Amen.

Let's Go! Who are your neighbors? Is there someone God immediately brings to your mind that can benefit from your physical or spiritual help today?

May 17

Victorious Action: Live a Blameless Life!

"Who may worship in your sanctuary, Lord? Who may enter your presence on your holy hill? Those who lead blameless lives and do what is right, speaking the truth from sincere hearts" (Ps. 15:1-2 NLT).

Let's Talk: Who can really come before the Lord and be in His presence? You and I, that's who! We are saved by Jesus' precious blood, redeemed by the Lamb's blood and life! He calls us to lead a blameless life (cleansed and forgiven), speaking the truth from a sincere heart, refusing to gossip. And, keeping a promise even when it hurts (Ps. 15:4).

Let's Glorify: Lord, because of your life poured out, I can receive mercy and forgiveness for my sins and unclean heart. Just by asking for forgiveness with a repentive heart, I am made new. Thank you for making me white as snow! Please help me to refuse to gossip, or speak evil of others. Please help me to keep my promises and commitments to others even when it hurts. Thank you for my Savior's forgiving love. In Jesus' name, I pray. Amen.

Let's Go! Will you refuse to gossip about others? Have you ever had the opportunity to keep a promise even when it hurt and wasn't convenient? What was the result?

May 18

Victorious Action: Disciplining Your Children While There is Still Hope!

"Discipline your children while there is hope. Otherwise you will ruin their lives" (Prov. 19:18 NLT).

Let's Talk: This is such a telling scripture! If I believe the Word, then I truly believe Jesus. He is the Word. These scriptures give a "cause and effect" relationship between you as a parent and your children. (Or, perhaps if you are not a parent, between a mom and a daughter or a friend). To discipline means to give counsel and wisdom. It is teaching your children a new way of responding, making choices and how to get along with others. Of course, we'd all agree disciplining needs to start when your child is young and moldable. Trying to bend a hard dry stick is much harder than molding a soft reed! If I choose not to discipline my children, I will ruin their lives because they have no boundaries, no walls or fences around their behavior or choices. I have found being a teacher, children feel safest when they have firm loving limits put on their behaviors.

Let's Glorify: Lord, thank you it is never too late to set boundaries with my children. As I do so, I am honoring you and giving them true life and not ruin. Please help me to be a godly, loving and positive disciplinarian. In Jesus' name, I pray these things. Amen.

Let's Go! How have you given your children hope and life as you have disciplined them with God's love and teaching? Was it fair and godly? (If you do not have children, share how your parents disciplined you).

May 19

Victorious Action: Giving Back What God First Gave You!

"O our God, we thank you and praise your glorious name! But who am I, and who are my people, that we could give anything to you? Everything we have has come from you, and we give you only what you first gave us" (1 Chron. 29:13-14 NLT).

Let's Talk: In these two verses we see King David praising God in the presence of the whole assembly. The King was thanking God for allowing his son, Solomon to build His holy Temple. Solomon was also soon to be crowned the new King. David recognized everything came from God and he was offering all he had. . .the gold, his family, the wood, jewels, treasures and ebony back to God. He gave EVERY THING back to God! David knew "we are all just visitors, even strangers in this foreign land looking towards heaven. Our lives are like a passing shadow, gone so soon without a trace" (1 Chron. 29:15 NLT).

Let's Glorify: Lord God, I just want to thank you. Everything I am, everything I have today, yesterday or in the future is from your gracious and loving hands! Lord, I offer it back to you. Help me to remember my life is "a passing shadow." Let me live differently today knowing this truth. In Jesus' name, I pray. Amen.

Let's Go! Have you released everything back into God's loving hands? Do you realize everything you are and will become is due to His loving grace?

May 20

Victorious Action: My Place of Safety!

"I love you, Lord; you are my strength. The Lord is my rock, my fortress, and my savior; my God is my rock, in whom I find protection. He is my shield, the power that saves me, and my place of safety" (Ps. 18:1-2 NLT).

Let's Talk: The Lord is your rock, fortress strength and Savior! As you call out to Him you will find security for your mind and body. You will find peace and comfort from your emotional distresses. God is your place of safety. Your cries will reach His sanctuary. He will hear you with His own ears (Ps. 18:6 NLT).

Let's Glorify: Lord, thank you for inspiring King David's words. You saved him over and over again from his enemies. I know you will continue to do this for me, too. Thank you for being my mighty fortress where I can run to safety every time! How I love you! In Jesus' name, I pray. Amen.

Let's Go! In what situations has God proven to you He is indeed your rock, your fortress and your mighty Savior? Have a discussion about how God has been your rock and fortress lately.

May 21

Victorious Action: Quench Your Thirst!

"O God, you are my God; I will seek you eagerly. My heart thirsts for you, my body longs for you in a land parched and exhausted, where no water can be found" (Ps. 63:2 CJB).

Let's Talk: Have you ever been really thirsty? I mean like, your mouth is so dry you are going to die without some water, right away? I sure have! There are times when I have been sick and woken up in the middle of the night with my mouth absolutely parched. Sometimes when I run, I feel this way too. At other times, my life has felt dry as I have waited on the Lord to move and create something new in my life. How about you? Are you waiting in the dry heat of summer, yearning for some refreshment for your soul? Are you crying out to Him, seeking Him eagerly? He is our true source of soul and spirit refreshment! Just as my vegetable and flower gardens need watering every day or they will wilt and produce less fruit, your soul needs watering, too.

Let's Glorify: Jesus, I need your holy and living waters through the Holy Spirit to quench my thirst! When I do not spend time with you, I try to quench my thirst with the stuff and ideas of this world. Worldly things are a temporary fix and cannot satisfy my thirsty heart need for you, my living God! Lord, I am coming to you now for refreshment. Please renew me within Holy Spirit, as dew waters the morning grass. In Jesus' precious name, I pray. Amen.

Let's Go! Are you choosing to spend time with Jesus today so your soul and spirit can be quenched with His living water? Go to Him and ask Him to soothe and refresh your weary heart and soul today!

May 22

Victorious Action: Knowing God Keeps His Promises!

"O Lord, God of Israel, there is no God like you in all of heaven and earth. You keep your covenant and show unfailing love to all who walk before you in wholehearted devotion" (2 Chron. 6:14-15 NLT).

Let's Talk: As you walk before Him with wholehearted devotion and love, God promises to keep all of His covenants with you. A covenant is a promise from God that He most certainly keeps with His believers today and always. God also promises to show you **unfailing love!** This is not just any kind of love, but a love that is unending and unconditional. It cannot be revoked! It is not an earned love; it just is because when God sees you, He sees you through the lens of looking at His beloved Son, Jesus!

Let's Glorify: Lord, thank you for loving me and showering me with your unfailing love even on the worst of my days! Thank you I can trust you in all of my messy circumstances. How I praise you and thank you for loving me even when I am broken. How I thank you for your covenantal promises throughout the Bible! In Jesus' name, I pray. Amen.

Let's Go! Because of God's unfailing love, how will you risk sharing His love by witnessing to someone today? Share with each other some ideas about how to witness.

May 23

Victorious Action: Knowing His Great Comfort!

"I will come to you" (Jn. 14:18).

Let's Talk: In this scripture, Jesus was reassuring His disciples after His death and crucifixion. He wouldn't leave them as orphans but would be coming back again to them. Another version of this Bible verse says, **"I will not leave you comfortless"** (KJV). Through the Holy Spirit living inside of you, Jesus comes to you in your distress and in your pain. He will bring you peace in your pain. He will not leave you alone nor will He abandon you. **He will come to you!**

Let's Glorify: Jesus, thank you for living inside me through the miracle of the Holy Spirit. Thank you for always being with me. I do not have to feel abandoned or alone because you are with me. Thank you for such great comfort, peace and love. In your name, I pray. Amen.

Let's Go! How do you know Jesus is with you today? Share with each other how He has come to you and given great peace, comfort and love.

May 24

Victorious Action: Giving All That You Are to ALL That He Is!

"Have I not commanded you? Be strong and courageous. Do not be afraid; do not be discouraged, for the Lord your God will be with you wherever you go" (Josh. 1:9).

Let's Talk: After the death of Moses the servant of God, God spoke to Joshua, Moses' assistant: "Moses my servant is dead. Get going. Cross this Jordan River, you and all the people. Cross to the country I'm giving to the People of Israel" (Josh. 1:1 MSG). "In the same way I was with Moses, **I'll be with you. I won't give up on you; I won't leave you.** You are going to lead this people to inherit the land that I promised to give their ancestors. **Give it everything you have, heart and soul**" (Jos. 1: 5-6 MSG, emphasis mine). God calls us to be strong and have courageous faith in Him, not ourselves. He commands you (it's not optional!) to be brave and not get discouraged because He promises to be with you wherever you go with whatever dreams He has divinely given to you! Commit yourself and your dreams to Him and watch to see how He can multiply them!

Let's Glorify: Lord God, thank you as I cross the mighty Rivers of Jordan in my life, you promise to be with me wherever I may go! I do not have to look at the fierce rushing waters of my circumstances; I can look to you instead for help. You give me faith filled courage as I go after the dreams you have dreamed for me! Lord, please increase my faith and belief in you today! In Jesus' awesome name, I ask these things. Amen.

Let's Go! Where do you need to rely on Him today, asking for strength and courage? **Are you willing to give God everything you have, heart and soul to ALL that He is? Will you participate in the dreams He has dreamed for you?**

May 25

Victorious Action: Believing Nothing is Too Hard for God!

"Is anything too hard for the Lord? I will return to you at the appointed time next year, and Sarah will have a son" (Gen. 18:14).

Talk about great joy! Sarah laughed to herself when she overheard the news from the angel of the Lord to her husband. She said under her breath, "A baby at my old age?" When confronted, she was afraid and so she lied and said she did not laugh. How many times have you and I laughed to ourselves when God has asked us to do something? Certainly I have. I have found in the really big works He has called me to do, I have questioned myself by questioning Him. Then God responds by whispering to my heart, **"Is anything too hard for the Lord"** (vs. 14, emphasis mine).

Let's Glorify: God, nothing is too hard for you! Lord, I want to have this truth ready on the tip of my tongue by having it embedded deeply into my heart first! Lord, let me believe you and not question what I have the privilege to do for you by serving others. In Jesus' name, I pray. Amen.

Let's Go! Have you ever laughed because of what God is telling you to do? Do you truly believe nothing is too hard for the Lord? Talk about this with your mom, daughter or special friend.

May 26

Victorious Action: Live in Peace!

"Do not repay anyone evil for evil. Be careful to do what is right in the eyes of everyone. If it is possible, as far as it depends on you, live at peace with everyone" (Rom. 12:17-18).

Let's Talk: When I was a lot younger, it took a few knocks off my throne to learn how to get along with my co-workers and working with the public! I was a new believer and just happened to read (the above) scripture. These words really helped me to speak up as necessary and if it was not really needed, to keep my opinions to myself! Romans 12:21 also really taught me how to deal with rudeness: **"Do not be overcome by evil, but overcome evil with good"** (emphasis mine). I learned to give great service with a positive attitude and a smile. Then, I started to enjoy living at peace with *most* people.

Let's Glorify: Jesus, I know there are appropriate times to speak up for what is right and true. Lord, there are times to be quiet, too. Help me to know the difference. Help me love others unto you, with your supernatural love and kindness. This is how I am to overcome evil with good. Let me always remember the way I serve others is a reflection of how much (or how little) I love you. In your name, I pray. Amen.

Let's Go! Have you ever repaid evil for evil? What did you learn from this? How can you overcome evil with good today?

May 27

Victorious Action: Even from Birth, You Are My God!

"I was thrust into your arms at my birth. You have been my God from the moment I was born" (Ps. 22:10 NLT).

Let's Talk: You are wanted! YOU have always been wanted by the King and God of the universe! This makes you a royal princess! He has been your God from the moment of your birth and He will never stop adoring you. Confess and give up any shame, guilt or remorse you may have today. God is seeking you and He wants to heal and transform the messy, broken, even shattered pieces of your life. He will weave a beautiful tapestry out of the shards of your experiences. You will see His amazing handiwork woven through you.

Let's Glorify: Jesus, sometimes I do not want you to see the messes I've created from poor choices, neglect or just plain laziness. Today, I am asking you to forgive me of my wrong choices. I am asking you to cleanse me and renew my heart all to your glory. Lord, I want to be healed from my past. I receive your forgiveness right now. Thank you for your redeeming power. In your healing name, I pray. Amen.

Let's Go! Do you realize you are a royal princess, a daughter of the Most High God and King? Where do you need to ask and receive His forgiveness today?

May 28

Victorious Action: Walk with Integrity!

"The godly walk with integrity; blessed are their children who follow them" (Prov. 20:7 NLT).

Let's Talk: Integrity starts with having an honest intention. Integrity calls you and me to proceed with honesty. Maintaining your commitments even when it is not fun anymore or convenient shows the true character of a person. People (and parents) who live right, God will bless their children who follow their example.

Let's Glorify: Lord, please help me live a life of integrity. I realize this is such an important character to have and model to our children and to the world around us. Jesus, help me to remember that I am a reflection of your integrity and love to my children. In Jesus' name, I pray. Amen.

Let's Go! When is it truly hard to live a life of integrity? Does it help to realize God blesses you (and your children) as you walk in His integrity?

May 29

Victorious Action: Knowing God's Greatness!

"Oh, how great are God's riches and wisdom and knowledge! How impossible it is for us to understand His decisions and His ways" (Rom. 11:33 NLT).

Let's Talk: Can you really fathom how great God is? I sure cannot! His thoughts, His infinite wisdom are so above my head! You can be grateful He has everything under His thoughtful and wise care. In fact, all that He does is with considerable thought and foresight because He knows all your ways even better than you do! You can rest in His sovereign care and love even if you do not understand His ways and resolutions.

Let's Glorify: God, I know you are great! Please expand my vision to see and know your greatness so I can praise and worship you more! Help me to trust you and your decisions even if I do not understand them right this moment. You are a good God! I am trusting in you. "You cause everything to work together for the good of those who love God and are called according to His purpose for them" (Rom. 8:28 NLT). Thank you, Jesus for this promise! It's in you I place my trust. Amen.

Let's Go! How have you seen God's wisdom and greatness? How has He worked a really hard situation into something good?

May 30

Victorious Action: Give Yourself to Jesus!

"Let me hear of your unfailing love each morning, for **I am trusting you**. Show me where to walk, **for I give myself to you**" (Ps. 143:8 NLT, emphasis mine).

Let's Talk: Do you need some guidance and leadership today? Are you feeling badly? Or, is one of your children sick today? God will give you His unfailing, loving kindness this morning as you **put your trust and faith in Him**. He desires to lead you, guide you and show you the way as you give yourself and your loved ones whole-heartedly without reservation.

Let's Glorify: Jesus, I need to know your precious and unfailing love today, even right in this moment. Lord, help me trust you a little bit more today. I give myself to you, unashamedly and whole-heartedly. Let my thoughts and actions reflect how much I love and adore you. In your name, I pray. Amen.

Let's Go! Are you willing to give yourself to Jesus whole-heartedly? Why or why not?

May 31

Victorious Action: Jesus is in Your Midst!

"When two of you get together on anything at all on earth and make a prayer of it, my Father in heaven goes into action. And when two or three of you are together because of me, you can be sure that I'll be there" (Matt. 18: 20 MSG).

Let's Talk: Jesus is among us as we pray and gather together! That is so comforting to me! It is pretty astounding to realize when two of us gather to pray, God our Father goes into action to help us! We have an all-powerful Savior and God who is available to us 24/7 willing to help us in our time of need! What great privilege and blessing you and I have when we gather together in His holy Name!

Let's Glorify: Dear Jesus, thank you for hearing my prayers whether I am by myself or when I am with two or more. I am so thankful you eagerly wait to hear what I have to say and request. Lord, I do not take this lightly and know you will answer in your divine timing and perfect way. Lord, I ask my prayers to be fashioned and formed by the Holy Spirit living within. May I always pray your will be done. In your powerful name, I pray. Amen.

Let's Go! How will your prayers change knowing Jesus is in your midst? Open your hearts to each other.

June

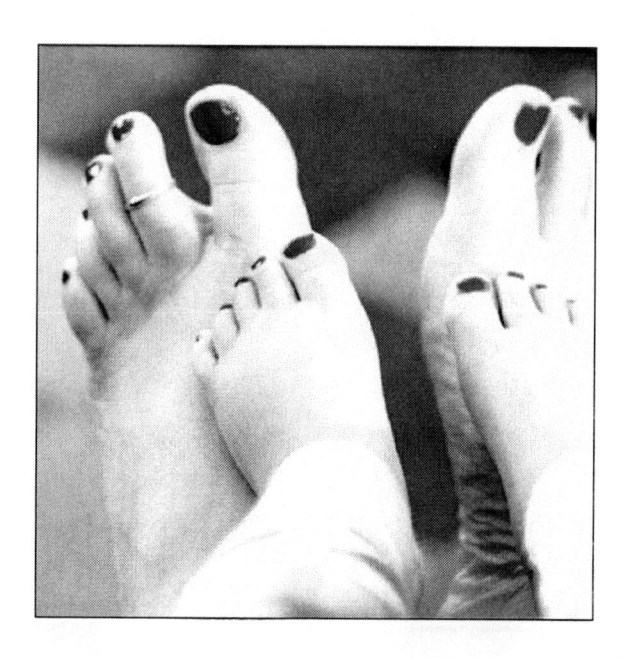

"Dear Daughter, Take my love with you now and into the time that I will never know. It is as much a part of you as breath. Or your identity."
Charlotte Gray

June 1

Victorious Action: Receiving God's Free Gift of Grace: Jesus!

"And since it is through God's kindness, then it is not by their good works. For in that case, God's grace would not be what it really is—free and undeserved" (Rom. 11:6 NLT).

Let's Talk: Grace: it is a freely given gift and quite undeserved! There is nothing you can to do earn salvation! You just need to accept and open His priceless gift called grace. Jesus is the gift that keeps on giving through His act of love poured out on that lonely day. Our Savior, has justified us through the redemption that came through His sacrifice on the Cross (Rom. 11:3, paraphrased).

Let's Glorify: Thank you, Lord I am saved from the punishment of sin because of your loving-favor. I have done nothing to earn eternal life. Thank you for showing me that Jesus is your only Son, born of a virgin. I believe the scriptures that tell me Jesus died on a cross, paying the penalty for my sins. As a result of my wholehearted belief and commitment to follow Jesus now, I will get to go to heaven and spend the rest of eternity with you, Lord. Thank you! I am so blessed! In Jesus' name, I pray. Amen.

Let's Go! Have you opened up God's free gift of grace, saying yes to Jesus as the Lord of your life?

June 2

Victorious Action: Knowing Eternal Life is Found Only in Jesus!

"For God loved the world so much that He gave His one and only Son, so that everyone who believes in Him will not perish but have eternal life" (Jn. 3:16).

Let's Talk: Your Salvation, eternal life is only found in a relationship with Jesus Christ! His sacrifice on the cross saves you. You have **a**ssurance because Jesus poured out His blood on the cross, for YOU! (Even if no one else existed, He'd die just FOR YOU!) Your Savior **l**oves you and cannot bear thought of you not being in heaven with Him. Jesus death and resurrection makes Him the **V**ictorious One! He is happily your **A**donai, which means Lord or Master. Jesus has **t**enacious love and care for you! During His ministry on earth, He showed **i**mmeasurable love by following His Father's will. He is **o**mnipresent and He is the God who sees you every moment of your life. He is your Savior. No other **n**ame can save you!

Let's Glorify: Dear God, thank you for Jesus, your only Son! He makes a way when there was no other way to have a relationship with you. Jesus is my Savior, my access to you! Thank you that your plan of salvation is simple and anyone can receive Jesus' gift. Lord, help me to remember to pray for others to believe in Jesus so they will experience the most loving relationship ever! Thank you for eternal life. In Jesus name, I pray and thank. Amen.

Let's Go! Take the **bold letters** (**above in Let's Talk**) in order and write them in your book. What word did you spell?

June

_____Write a prayer of thanksgiving to Jesus, telling Him what He means to you._____

June 3

Victorious Action: Open Your Heart To Jesus!

On the Sabbath we went outside the city gate to the river, where we expected to find a place of prayer. We sat down and began to speak to the women who had gathered there. One of those listening was a woman from the city of Thyatira named Lydia, a dealer in purple cloth. She was a worshiper of God. The Lord opened her heart to respond to Paul's message. When she and the members of her household were baptized, she invited us to her home. "If you consider me a believer in the Lord," she said, "come and stay at my house." And she persuaded us" (Acts 16: 12-15).

Let's Talk: This woman, Lydia was a successful businesswoman, a dealer in purple cloth. In Biblical days, the color purple was a royal and majestic color worn by kings and the wealthy. Lydia, scriptures say "was a worshipper of God and the Lord opened her heart" (vs.14d, paraphrase). **It is God who opens a person's heart,** shining His holy light into it, **so one can desire to know and receive Jesus.** So many times, a person's heart is plagued with sin and is not open to hearing about Jesus. Maybe they have even become antagonistic against hearing the Good News. God will not let this person go. He will keep working and gently keep knocking on their heart, so they can "hear my voice and open the door, I will come in and eat with that person, and they with me" (Rev. 3:20). Lydia was persuasive because she wanted to hear more about Jesus from the disciples. She invited the disciples into her home to dine and make them comfortable. Do I do the same with you, Jesus?

Let's Glorify: Lord, open my heart so I can hear from you. I want to know you. I want to follow you with all that I am. God, help me to be

June

mindful there are people who have not yet heard the knock on their heart and accepted Jesus. Let me be kind and sensitive to where they are spiritually. I do not want to put a fire hose of religion in their heads when they were just asking for a small drink of water. In Jesus' name, I pray. Amen.

Let's Go! How earnestly are you listening to the knock on your heart when God is trying to get your attention? Take someone to lunch or dinner and share Jesus with them gently; praying God will open their hearts to Him.

June 4

Victorious Action: Gaining Christ!

"I consider everything a loss compared to the surpassing greatness of knowing Christ Jesus my Lord, for whose sake I have lost all things. I consider them rubbish that I may gain Christ" (Phil. 3:8).

Let's Talk: What Paul is expressing in this scripture is the fact that nothing compares to "the excellency of the knowledge of Christ Jesus my Lord" (Phil. 3:8 KJ21). There is nothing sweeter than drawing closer in deeper intimacy with Jesus! Recognizing and understanding Him more fully and clearly is the goal; everything else is worth losing.

Let's Glorify: Jesus, you are a pearl of great price! In fact, I cannot put a price on your life; you are beyond estimation! Thank you for sharing your life with me. I am so grateful to be a follower of yours. Lord, draw me in a deeper relationship with you, the Author and Perfector of my faith. I give you all the praise and glory! In your name, I pray. Amen.

Let's Go! Have you found knowing Jesus to be worth more than anything else in your life?

June 5

Victorious Action: Look for Your Joy in His Commands!

Ps. 119:143 says, "As pressure and stress bear down on me, I find joy in your commands."

Let's Talk: Are you passionate and thankful for all Jesus is doing in your life? If not, ask Jesus to renew your hope and joy in Him! Ask Him for a fresh touch, a fresh revelation! Do you agree with me, that there is NOTHING like the fresh fire of the Holy Spirit falling upon you? What I mean by this is, He gives you a special word, a thought, a promise in the Bible that is divinely apportioned for you, TO YOU! And you know in your heart it is JUST FOR YOU! It's like a divine HUG of joy and love! Right in that moment, you are experiencing "fullness of joy in His presence!" What a blessing!

Let's Glorify: Lord Jesus, I thank you for your special joy that resides within me because of the Holy Spirit living inside. Lord, thank you for the peace that comes when I am following and seeking you. Thank you for the Spirit as your guarantee that He will give us the inheritance He promised and that He has purchased us to be his own people. All praise and honor to you, the Trinity! In your joy and love, I pray. Amen.

Let's Go! Being joyful is a state of our soul and spirit intermingled with Christ's. Joy comes from a secret intimacy with our Savior, through the Holy Spirit living within. Are you experiencing His joy? Why or why not?

June 6

Victorious Action: Bragging On the Lord! (Not Yourself!)

"In God we make our boast all day long, and we will praise your name forever" (Ps. 44:8).

Let's Talk: Do you brag on the Lord? Or sometimes do you forget and take on some of the glory for yourself? It's easy to do! I have to constantly remind myself, all good things come from the Lord and to praise and thank Him inwardly and outwardly. When I remember to praise the Lord and I express it out loud, I am giving others the courage to say why they are thanking Him, too. **He is our only reason to boast!** You and I are never to give our praise away to little gods or to ourselves. **Remember to praise Him even when His answer to you is no.**

Let's Glorify: O God, I give glory to you all day long and constantly praise your name.(Ps. 44:8 NLT). Please forgive me Lord when I keep some of the praise for myself instead of giving it right back to you. Lord, even when I am disappointed with the answer you give me, I will trust you and boast of your greatness! Help me to remember all good things come from your hand and loving heart! In your great name, I praise. Amen.

Let's Go! Have you given your praise away to yourself or to a little god? Ask the Lord for forgiveness. He will immediately forgive! Praise Him! Discuss this openly with your mom, daughter or friend.

June 7

Victorious Action: Believing You Are Valuable!

"What is the price of five sparrows—two copper coins? Yet God does not forget a single one of them. And the very hairs on your head are all numbered. So don't be afraid; you are more valuable to God than a whole flock of sparrows" (Luke 12:6-7 NLT).

Let's Talk: In the early morning, I love to sit on my deck and have my quiet time with the Lord. I am usually greeted by several small finches and sparrows resting in our vegetable garden. Sometimes a hummingbird comes screaming by looking for its feeder. I marvel at these small creatures and the intricacy in which our Creator has made these birds and even the soft feathers covering them. God has taken great care in designing these small birds and He has taken great care in creating you! Isn't it amazing He knows the number of hairs covering your head? You are valuable, wanted and loved by the Almighty, omnipotent God!

Let's Glorify: God, thank you for creating me and all of nature. I am so grateful you do not forget about me. Instead you delight in me and see my tears, collecting them in a bottle. Help me to be reminded every time I see a bird, how valuable and loved I am by you! In Jesus' name, I pray. Amen.

Let's Go! What is your favorite kind of bird? Ask God to help you remember how valuable and loved you are when you see or think of this kind of bird.

June 8

Victorious Action: Thanking Him in Your Fiery Trial!

"Do you see what we've got? An unshakable kingdom! And do you see how thankful we must be? Not only thankful, but brimming with worship, deeply reverent before God. For God is not an indifferent bystander. He's actively cleaning house, torching all that needs to burn, and He won't quit until it's all cleansed. God Himself is Fire" (Heb. 12:28-29 MSG).

Let's Talk: God does "actively clean your house" your heart, your spirit and attitudes! He allows you to go through fiery trials to refine you, so you will come forth as gold. You will come forth with pure, undiluted, solid faith. God also burns off all the extraneous things that you place before Him. The Holy Spirit will move in your heart encouraging you to get rid of the old habits, thoughts and attitudes that are not of Him. Let Him have free reign in the cleansing process!

Let's Glorify: Lord, even though the fiery trials are uncomfortable and I feel singed going through them, I can thank you and praise you. God, you are drawing me closer to you. Thank you for teaching me about myself in your spiritual refining process. There is glory coming, just around the corner, so help me to hang on (1 Pet.4:13, MSG, paraphrased). With reverence to you, I pray. Amen.

Let's Go! Do you think you will get to the point where you reverently thank God for your fiery trials and what He is teaching you? Share with each other.

June 9

Victorious Action: Waiting on God!

"For wisdom will enter your heart, and knowledge will fill you with joy" (Prov. 2:10 NLT).

Let's Talk: Not only do you receive wisdom in your heated waiting times through the Holy Spirit's power, you also receive joy! You and I need God's wisdom and joy in our fiery times of waiting, because we really need to have a good attitude while we try to make sense of what is truly happening! If you do not, you will want to take matters into your own hands and shorten the wait, creating your own happy ending. Unfortunately what I have found is I usually create a mess of things instead and make the wait even longer!

Let's Glorify: Lord, help me to stay in the wait with you. Jesus I want to make good use of this time and draw closer to you even now. Lord please show me what I am to learn or change about myself during this waiting period. Point out any bitterness or anger I may have toward myself or anyone else. Help me to forgive_____ today. May you receive all the praise, honor and glory. In Jesus' name, I pray. Amen.

Let's Go! Are you in a waiting season right now? Are you **content to wait on God** or **are you trying to create your own happy ending?**

June 10

Victorious Action: Receiving His Hand of Blessing!

"You hem me in behind and before, and you lay your hand upon me" (Ps. 139:5).

Let's Talk: Knowing God protects you on every side, including the front and back helps in the insecurity of uncertainties. When **God lays His hand upon you, it is for a blessing** not a curse! As the Lord Almighty encircles you, **He will protect you in your waiting room.** I have found waiting on the Lord can be productive or pitiful! Being productive is definitely a better choice! I can seek Him more. I can do some research about what I believe He is calling me to do. I can get up and get some exercise. I can journal my thoughts and pray more than I have ever before! **I can get still before Him in prayer.** This is the most productive and trusting act I can do!

Let's Glorify: God, thank you for laying your hand of blessing upon me as I wait in you. Lord, help me to know when to be still and when to be productive as I wait for you to move. God, increase my faith and help me to believe you are with me. **I am choosing not to fret or worry, but wait productively in you.** In Jesus' name, I pray. Amen.

Let's Go! In your waiting room of uncertainty **are you productive or pitiful?** What can you do that is positive while you wait for God to act on your behalf?

June 11

Victorious Action: Believing He Cares for You!

"Cast all your anxiety on Him because He cares for you" (1 Pet. 5:7).

Let's Talk: This is one of the first scriptures I learned to memorize over thirty years ago! I grew up fearful and a worrier! Maybe you can relate. I was fearful of what *might* happen. I was worried about other's opinions. I was a poor example of a people pleaser. I would even pray to act appropriately! The Amplified Bible tells you to **"Throw all your concerns, once and for all on Him,** for **He cares for you affectionately and cares about you watchfully**" (1 Pet.5:7, emphasis mine). Now, realizing how much God loves me and is for me, I can let go of others approval. I am choosing to have inner peace over anxious outer appearances.

Let's Glorify: Lord God, my Abba Daddy. Thank you that you see me, love me and watch over me. You do not want me to worry, fret or be filled with anxiety. Help me to trust your loving care and watchful eye today and every day. In your loving name, I pray. Amen.

Let's Go! Knowing God cares for you affectionately and cares about you watchfully (dutifully, attentively, vigilantly) can you cast all your anxiety on Him today?

June 12

Victorious Action: Having a Great Refuge and Strength!

"God is our refuge and strength, an ever-present help in trouble" (Ps. 46:1).

Let's Talk: He is always near to you in times of great trouble. Jesus will help in your distresses; He is readily found! The God-of-Angel-Armies protects you! When you are feeling weak, cry out to Him for strength. He will provide new energy and endurance. When you are feeling unmotivated, He will give you new creativity! When you are sad and lonely, Jesus will give Himself to you. He has felt all the same emotions you have. He understands YOU. He knows you completely.

Let's Glorify: God, I cannot thank you enough for always being near to me. I can face anything because of your great strength and help. I want to remember to run to you when I need a harbor of relief. You are my sanctuary. You are my true peace and source of inner joy! How I praise you! In Jesus' name, I pray. Amen.

Let's Go! How have you experienced God as your ever present help in your trouble? Discuss with the special ladies in your life.

June 13

Victorious Action: Knowing the Hope of Jesus!

"And hope does not put us to shame, because God's love has been poured out into our hearts through the Holy Spirit, who has been given to us" (Rom. 5:5).

Let's Talk: His hope will not lead you disappointment. God, through the Holy Spirit living within you, has flooded your heart with His love! You can be full of joy here and now even in your difficulties because of the confident hope you have in Jesus! Hope in Jesus will never fail to satisfy your deepest need! Turn to Him right now and know His love!

Let's Glorify: God, I am beyond grateful for your love! Thank you for the Word that reiterates your love and hope poured into me over and over again through the power of the Holy Spirit. Thank you for always meeting me at my deepest need. In your powerful, loving name, I pray. Amen.

Let's Go! Has His great hope and love flooded your heart in a time of difficulty? Please share with each other.

June 14

Victorious Action: You Can Be Pleasing to God!

"The Holy Spirit descended on Him in bodily form like a dove. And a voice came from heaven: "You are my Son, whom I love; with you I am well pleased" (Luke 3:22).

Let's Talk: God and Jesus receive great joy in their relationship! God, Jesus and the Holy Spirit delight in each other and value their triangular relationship so much! God has supreme happiness in His Son, Jesus! Jesus gave His Father reverent submission in all God asked Him to do. You can receive great joy in your relationship with the Trinity (God, Jesus, the Holy Spirit) as you listen and obey His leadings.

Let's Glorify: Jesus, I want to have reverent submission to what you ask me to do. Lord, I love you and am grateful that you died for me. May my thoughts, prayers and relationship to you be pleasing. Thank you for sending me the Holy Spirit to guide, correct, lead and pour out your amazing love and hope inside me. It's all to your glory, I pray. Amen.

Let's Go! When have you felt Jesus' love and delight? Discuss over lunch, if possible.

June 15

Victorious Action: Anointed with the Oil of Joy!

"You have loved righteousness and hated wickedness; therefore God, your God, has set you above your companions by anointing you with the oil of joy" (Heb. 1:9).

Let's Talk: Jesus was anointed by God, the Father **with the "oil of joy!"** Jesus is a joyous Savior and He shares His joy with you through the Miracle within, the Holy Spirit! As a result, you have a claim to the consistent experience of HIS undiluted joy! He does not expect you to walk around earth just barely surviving. He wants you to bloom and thrive as you walk with Him along the path He has set before you. Will you have rocks and roots that you will stumble on? Of course. You can still offer up praises of thanksgiving because He will always be with you and that is a promise! Ask Him for a reminder of His precious love today. I bet you will see it or know it within your heart, so be on the look out!

Let's Glorify: Jesus, I thank you that you are a joyful Savior, redeemer and restorer! Thank you for sending the Holy Spirit to deliver your amazing love and joy deep within me! Lord, when I am upset, worried or angry let me recall this scripture. I want to remember I serve and worship a joyful King that sees me and loves me no matter what happens! In your joyful name, I pray. Amen.

Let's Go! Where do you need Jesus to anoint you with His oil of joy today? Will you choose to praise Him even when you do not feel like it?

June 16

Victorious Action: Having Inner Peace!

"And the peace of God, which transcends (or surpasses) all understanding, will guard your hearts and your minds in Christ Jesus" (Phil. 4: 7).

Let's Talk: Do you need His precious peace today? The word **peace** in Greek is "**shalom.**" It means peace, completeness, welfare and health. This about covers your life in full! In the Old Testament, the word peace is used 237 times! It's a state of being at ease, with harmony in your soul and mind. It is pretty evident if your inside is calm or crazy then your outside is going to reflect what is going on! Isaiah prophesied **our Prince of Peace, Jesus** in Isaiah 9:7. Isaiah said, "His government and its peace will never end. He will rule with fairness and justice from the throne of his ancestor David for all eternity. The passionate commitment of the Lord of Heaven's Armies will make this happen" (NLT).

Let's Glorify: Jesus, thank you for protecting my heart and mind. You are my Prince of Peace! Your peace is available to me at all times even when I do not understand how this can be. I am so grateful for your loving presence and passionate commitment to me. In your everlasting name, I pray. Amen.

Let's Go! Have you ever experienced the peace of God in the midst of chaos? How can you explain this to someone else?

June 17

Victorious Action: God Speaks Tenderly in the Desert!

"I will lead her into the desert and speak tenderly to her" (Hosea 2:14).

Let's Talk: Have you ever noticed when you are in a time of great concern (worry equals sin!) over something, God will place you in the desert so you can have a wilderness experience alone with Him? God has something for YOU, some jewels He wants to teach you and give you in this seemingly dry time, where He strips away the non-essentials. You see God needs to get you quiet and alone so He can bring you into utter dependence upon Him. If you are in SIN, He is asking you to give it up to Him. "And then I'll give her back her vineyards; I'll turn the valley of Achor, that "Valley of Trouble," **into a gateway of hope"** (Hos. 2:15 VOICE, emphasis mine). Once you trust, and confess your sin to Him, your peace is restored.

Let's Glorify: Lord, you are a holy God. You want me to be in a good place with you, where I have no sin to hinder our relationship. Thank you, God you care enough to take me to a desert experience, so I can be restored back to you! Holy Father forgive me of my sins, expressly _____. I know once I confess and turn from my wretched ways, you will turn my Valley of Trouble into a gateway of hope. Thank you, Jesus' for shedding your blood so I can be cleansed as white as snow. In your holy name, I pray. Amen.

Let's Go! Are you in a desert time in your life? Discuss this time or another desert experience with each other. What did you learn about God during this dry time?

June 18

Victorious Action: Allow Jesus to Change You!

So he ran ahead and climbed a sycamore-fig tree beside the road, for Jesus was going to pass that way. When Jesus came by, He looked up at Zacchaeus and called him by name. "Zacchaeus!" He said. "Quick, come down! I must be a guest in your home today" (Luke 19:4-5 NLT).

Let's Talk: What was it about Jesus that made Zacchaeus respond right away? I think it was Jesus noticed Zacchaeus and He knew his name! **Do you realize God notices you, loves you, even adores and delights in you?** He calls you by your name! Scriptures says, "Zacchaeus quickly climbed down and took Jesus to his house in great excitement and joy." (vs. 6) Do you invite Jesus into your house (which is your heart) with great excitement and joy, desiring to spend quiet time with Him, first thing in the morning or evening? Are you delighting in Him, eager to feast on His Word? When Jesus calls your name and gets your attention, **are you allowing Him to change you?**

Let's Glorify: Lord Jesus, thank you for knowing my name. I want you to be in my house, (my bodily temple) and my heart gladly each day. I receive you into my life joyfully and want you to have full reign in my life and my decisions. Help me live "all in" today for you. I love you. In your name, I pray. Amen.

Let's Go! Do you love the Lord Your God, with all of your heart, mind and spirit? Have you fully devoted yourself to Him? Why or why not?

June 19

Victorious Action: Resting on El-Shaddai!

"When Abram was ninety-nine years old, the Lord appeared to him and said, "I am El-Shaddai—'God Almighty.' Serve me faithfully and live a blameless life. I will make a covenant with you, by which I will guarantee to give you countless descendants" (Gen. 17:1-2 NLT).

Let's Talk: God appeared to Abram (before he was renamed Abraham) after the birth of Ishmael. God reminded him of their covenant. Even though Abram encountered hurdles and bumps on his path to the Promised Land and could get discouraged, he had to have the COURAGE and conviction to remember that God would accomplish what He said He would do! You can lay on His breast and rest easily knowing the Name El-Shaddai emphasizes God's capacity to handle any challenge that comes before His people! Shaddai means breast. God's name and identity completely satisfies and nourishes you just as a mother would to her child.

Let's Glorify: God, thank you for being my El-Shaddai, my All Sufficient One. You supply all that I need. You are my great Sustainer. Help me to rely on you just as Abraham did. Let me rest against you when I am weary. Nourish me Lord with your sweet presence. How I praise you! In your strong name, I pray. Amen.

Let's Go! Are you getting discouraged on your journey to the Promised Land? Try resting on El-Shaddai only for strength and courage today.

June 20

Victorious Action: Loving God and Keeping His Commandments!

"Know therefore that the Lord your God is God; He is the faithful God, keeping His covenant of love to a thousand generations of those who love Him and keep His commandments" (Dt. 7:9).

Let's Talk: God is Love. His name is Jehovah- Ahavah. It is God's very nature to love you, because He is love (1Jn. 4:16). Out of His love, He reveals Himself to you and seeks fellowship with you every day. He IS God! He is faithful to you. (Yes, you!) He keeps His covenants with you as you enjoy His love for you. There is one thing He asks you to do: keep His commandments, His instructions in the Bible. Not in a begrudging way, but kept because of your gratefulness to Jesus who has freely poured out His life for you. He freely gives to you so you can have eternal life. Jesus wants you to have a relationship with Him that is satisfying, loving, and deeply caring.

Let's Glorify: Jehovah-Ahavah, thank you for keeping your covenant of love to my family's generations and even way past this! Lord, I desire to keep your commandments every day. God, I am going to fail you but because your identity is love and your grace abounds, I am forgiven and free. How I love you and praise you that I am not bound up in rules and regulations. Instead, you have me in your loving heart. In Jesus' name, I pray. Amen.

Let's Go! How have you shown your love to Jehovah-Ahavah lately? How has He blessed you with His love? Ask Him to share His loving presence with you, your mom, daughter or friend.

June 21

Victorious Action: Knowing the Healer, Jehovah Rapha!

"But He was pierced for our transgressions, He was crushed for our iniquities; the punishment that brought us peace was on Him, and by His wounds we are healed" (Isa. 53:5).

Let's Talk: Jehovah-Rapha is the name which means The Lord Who Heals. His holy and sinless body took the punishment for my sins. He was broken by whips; I am made whole by His stripes. His punishment brings me peace in this life and in my eternal life! He heals my past and gives me a new day of hope, peace and blessed joy.

Let's Glorify: Thank you Jesus for being my Jehovah Rapha, my great healer! Not only do you heal me physically, but you are healing me spiritually and emotionally. I am so grateful to you. Lord, help me to share the help and comfort I have received with another today. In your healing name, I pray. Amen.

Let's Go! Where do you need healing today in your life? Ask Jesus for His healing, believing He can do anything when you ask in faith! Pray together.

June 22

Victorious Action: Living as a Beautiful Accomplishment!

"For we are God's handiwork, created in Christ Jesus to do good works, which God prepared in advance for us to do" (Eph. 2:10).

Let's Talk: Another word for handiwork is *masterpiece. You are God's divine and beautiful accomplishment!* You were born to be in relationship with the Master Creator and born anew in Christ Jesus to do good things. God planned for you to do good things and to live as He has always wanted you to live. That's why He sent Christ to make you who you are. God does not make mistakes... ever. So, live as the beauty you are!

Let's Glorify: God, thank you for making me beautiful inside and out! I am grateful for your Son Jesus coming to me so I could be made new; restoring me to the original person you have called me to be from the beginning of creation. I am blessed to be a part of your good works! In Jesus' name, I pray. Amen.

Let's Go! Think about all the things you'd like to do. Do you find it amazing God has prepared these good works for you to do *in advance?* Talk about this with you mom, daughter or girlfriend.

June 23

Victorious Action: Having His Glory Filled Strength!

"We also pray that you will be strengthened with all His glorious power so you will have all the endurance and patience you need. May you be filled with joy" (Col. 1:11 NLT).

Let's Talk: God gives you the strength to stick it out over the long haul of this life. He gives the kind of endurance that lasts and lasts. But, you must ask for it, too! **"It is strength that endures the unendurable and spills over into joy, thanking the Father who makes us strong enough to take part in everything bright and beautiful that He has for you."** (Col. 1:11 MSG, emphasis mine) "I pray that God's great power will make you strong, and that you will have joy as you wait and do not give up" (Col. 1:11 NLV).

Let's Glorify: God, thank you that you give me everything I need to hold on and endure patiently even joyfully through the long, dry, dusty days of my life! Help me to realize I can be triumphant in you, no matter what happens. Thank you for hearing my prayers. I am grateful that I can be totally honest with you. You love me just the same even when I lament and carry on. I will praise you and thank you even now. May you be glorified as I do the work you call me to do. In your sovereignty, I pray. Amen.

Let's Go! Have you experienced the kind of supernatural strength and endurance that only the Holy Spirit living inside you gives? Do you remember to thank God for this strength and energy?

June 24

Victorious Action: Spending Time with God Daily!

"My heart has heard you say, "Come and talk with me." And my heart responds, "Lord, I am coming" (Ps. 27:8 NLT).

Let's Talk: Have you heard the nudge of the Holy Spirit, wooing you to come talk to Him? Are you responding right away? Or, are you saying, "Just a minute?" Then the 'just a minute' turns into hours, days or even weeks? Jesus calls us to seek Him daily. He calls us to take up our cross and follow hard after Him. Are you seeking His face, His presence? The relationship you have with the Trinity is the most important relationship you will ever experience. Your witness and walk is important to God. Come and fill up completely in Him today!

Let's Glorify: Lord God, thank you that you want to be in relationship with me. I am so satisfied when I am in your loving presence. Please help my heart to be sensitive to your calling. Lord, I want to know the importance of being in your presence every day. By doing so, I can have a positive influence on my loved ones and the people I will encounter today. In Jesus' love, I pray. Amen.

Let's Go! Are you good about responding to God's whisper to "come and talk with Him?" Why or why not? Talk about it with your special friend, mom or daughter.

June 25

Victorious Action: Staying Brave and Courageous While You Wait!

"Wait patiently for the Lord. Be brave and courageous. Yes, wait patiently for the Lord" (Ps. 27:14 NLT).

Let's Talk: Do you have a decision to make? Pray and expect the Lord to answer you as you wait for Him to give you direction. Stay with God! Take heart and don't quit during the waiting time! You can be fearless in Him as you wait for His plan to unfold. I believe God brings me to a waiting time to get me still before Him and to draw me into a deeper abiding relationship with Him. He is working on you and creating a richer faith within you. Yes, you and I can wait patiently. A great boost while waiting is to sing praise and worship songs to Him in the beginning of your day. Tell Him all that you are grateful for. Thank Him for Jesus and sending you the Holy Spirit.

Let's Glorify: God, your ways are perfect and your thoughts are so much higher than mine. I willingly give up control of my life over to you. You can be trusted completely. Help me, Lord to be brave, courageous and even patient while I rest in you. At the perfect time, I will know what you have decided and willed to happen. Thank you for being my Emmanuel: my God who is always with me. In Jesus name, I pray. Amen.

Let's Go! On a scale from 1-10, (1 is easy, 10 is excruciating) how hard is it for you to stay brave, courageous and patient when you are in a waiting time? Discuss and laugh together!

June 26

Victorious Action: Trust the Lord with All of Your Heart!

"The Lord is my strength and shield. I trust Him with all my heart. He helps me, and my heart is filled with joy. I burst out in songs of thanksgiving" (Ps. 28: 7 NLT).

Let's Talk: The Lord is your armor, your breastplate, and your ever present help in time of trouble! He protects me and defends me. He hears your tiniest of prayers whispered out of the quietness of your heart. He helps you with your finances, your relationships, your cares and worries. As a result, are you jumping for joy, and shouting and singing your thanks to Him? How many times have you forgotten to go back and thank your precious Lord for all that He done for you?

Let's Glorify: God, thank you I can rely on you to be my shield and strength always. I want to remember to thank you right away for delivering me out of my troubles, rescuing me from harm and setting me free from my sins! **My heart is filled with an outburst of joy!** How I praise you! In Jesus' name, I pray. Amen.

Let's Go! Do you **trust the Lord with all of your heart?** Can you think of certain situations where God has rescued or liberated you? Share with each other.

June 27

Victorious Action: Joy in His Presence!

"You have made known to me the paths of life; you will fill me with joy in your presence" (Acts 2:28).

Let's Talk: There is joy in His presence! What better reason to motivate you to come to the Lord! Just sitting quietly with the Lord can bring you great peace, comfort and even contentment. As you do so, God teaches you the ways of life; how to live and walk with Him peacefully. I find happiness from the inside out all because I took the time to get still before Him.

Let's Glorify: Lord, thank you for rewarding me with joy just by getting still in your lovely presence! As I do so, you show me which path to take. As I listen and obey, I am flooded with your comforting peace, the cousin to joy! Thank you for your contagious joy. I love you. In Jesus' name, I pray. Amen.

Let's Go! Have you experienced joy when you have gotten quiet before the Lord? Talk about it with your mom, daughter or girlfriend.

June 28

Victorious Action: Proclaim His Saving Power!

"I will tell everyone about your righteousness. All day long I will proclaim your saving power, for I am overwhelmed by how much you have done for me" (Ps. 71:15 NLT).

Let's Talk: Contemplate all the wonderful ways God has delivered and restored you. Your worries begin to lift and your cares are much smaller! You can know you are going to make it another moment, another hour, another day because of God's great care and unending love! You have a beautiful history of redemption on your side! And, in the process you see how God has never left your side and loved you through some really horrendous situations! When you have daily GRATITUDE your peace returns because your focus is right! It's all on God and what He's done for you.

Let's Glorify: God, I do want to proclaim your saving power to myself and those around me. You are righteous, holy and totally more than enough to handle all my hopes, fears and shortcomings. Lord, thank you for pouring out your overwhelming love and grace onto me. Let me share your message of love and redemption to our dying world. In your righteous name, I pray. Amen.

Let's Go! Who in your world needs to hear the great news of Jesus Christ? Share today how great He is with someone else.

June 29

Victorious Action: Knowing His Perfect Peace!

"You will keep in perfect peace those whose minds are steadfast, because they trust in you" (Isa. 26:3).

Let's Talk: Do you want a solid, steadfast mind? **Stay committed** to trust Him whole-heartedly, not going back and forth on your decisions. "Though the mountains be shaken and the hills be removed, yet **my unfailing love for you will not be shaken** nor my **covenant of peace** be removed says the Lord, **who has compassion on you.**" (Isa. 54:10, emphasis mine) Sense His blessed peace washing over you as you pray and lean into Jesus.

Let's Glorify: God, thank you for your peace that is pouring over me right now, like a cool river as I read these scriptures. Lord, you are everything to me! How great is your love and compassion! Please help me to remember I can be kept in your perfect peace every day as I seek your face. In Jesus' name, I pray. Amen.

Let's Go! Commit to memory Isa. 26:3 or Isa. 54:10. Recite one of these verses to each other, knowing His covenant of peace will not be removed from you!

June 30

Victorious Action: Seek His Kingdom First!

"So do not worry, saying, 'What shall we eat?' or 'What shall we drink?' or 'What shall we wear?' For the pagans run after all these things, and your heavenly Father knows that you need them. But seek first His kingdom and His righteousness, and all these things will be given to you as well" (Matt. 6:33).

Let's Talk: Do you have a worry tugging at your heart and tearing at your peace of mind? God knows your heart. Release your worries to His loving care. Put God's work first and do what He wants knowing you can turn all your distress over to Him. Set your heart on His kingdom and His wonderful goodness toward you. Pray asking His kingdom come, and His will be done on earth as it is in heaven!

Let's Glorify: Lord, I desire to do what you want me to do today. I am seeking your will and I surrender mine. God you can do anything with a surrendered heart! God, I want to be your girl. . .the one your eyes see when they range to and fro throughout the earth, looking for a heart that is whole-heartedly devoted to you (2 Chron. 16:9a, paraphrased). I desire not to look at my worries but look to you, my wonderful Father! May it be all to your glory! In Jesus' name, I pray. Amen.

Let's Go! Are you worrying about what you will eat or what you will wear to that special event? God has you covered! Seek Him first and foremost and He will honor your heart that is purely devoted to pleasing Him. **Fun Fact!** Our church has a Sister's Closet two times a year. Women from our church and community come to shop. They may take as many articles of clothing as they like even without donating anything! It is such a blessing! There is such joy in the room as 350 plus ladies "shop for free!" Left over clothing is taken to Thrift stores or women's shelters.

July

"With a daughter, life can never, never, never be monotonous."
Pam Brown, b. 1928

July 1

Victorious Action: Reaching Out to Jesus!

"A woman in the crowd had suffered for twelve years with constant bleeding, and she could find no cure. Coming up behind Jesus, she touched the fringe of His robe. Immediately, the bleeding stopped. "Who touched me?" Jesus asked. Everyone denied it, and Peter said, "Master, this whole crowd is pressing up against you." But Jesus said, "Someone deliberately touched me, for I felt healing power go out from me." When the woman realized that she could not stay hidden, she began to tremble and fell to her knees in front of Him. The whole crowd heard her explain why she had touched Him and that she had been immediately healed. "Daughter," He said to her, "your faith has made you well. Go in peace" (Luke 8:43-48 NLT).

Let's Talk: This woman had suffered for twelve long years, probably draining her savings account and her emotional account as well looking for a cure. She had heard of Jesus' miraculous healings. She thought *if I could just touch the corner of the Master's robe, I will be healed*. So, she dared herself and reached out. It was hard because there were so many people crowding Jesus. **"Who touched me?"** Jesus asked (vs. 45, emphasis mine). The woman held her breath and looked down. She began shaking in fear and sheer exhaustion of her illness. She fell to her knees in front of her Savior, healed! **What a witness of faith she was on this day!** The whole throng of people heard her confess her faith and hope in her healer! Jesus looked into her questioning eyes. "Daughter," He said to her, "your faith has made you well. "Go in peace" (vs. 48).

Let's Glorify: God, thank you for this woman's faith. She dared to reach out to Jesus for healing and hope. She believed that her only real hope was Jesus. Today, this still stands true! He is my Savior, my healer and deliverer. Thank you for sending your only Son to save me from eternal death so I can live freely today in Him. In the powerful name of Jesus, I pray. Amen.

Let's Go! Do you have any physical or emotional concerns that need Jesus' healing touch? Are you pressing into Jesus as this woman had? Pray and ask Him for healing and guidance. Believe in faith He will indeed help you!

July 2

Victorious Action: Knowing Overwhelming Victory is Yours in Jesus!

"No, despite all these things, overwhelming victory is ours through Christ, who loved us" (Rom. 8: 37 NLT).

Let's Talk: Maybe today, God is whispering to your heart, go the extra mile in me, in my strength! Don't give up! Try a little harder, asking me for help! You see when difficulties come along with frustrations, (and you know God has called you to do something) it is not time to back down! If the Holy of Holies has asked you to do something out of your natural comfort zone, such as lead, equip or form a group, be encouraged! He will help you bring it to completion as you ask Him for guidance. **God has something to teach you about staying in Him.** Believe He has a great work for you to be a part of. He is building your faith in Him and teaching you how to build your endurance muscles in His grace and love!

Let's Glorify: Lord, thank you for giving me the victory ahead of the finish! This helps me to push against the limitations I feel I have in myself. Jesus, help me to only listen to your sweet voice and in your name I cast out the enemy's voice. All praise, honor and glory are yours, Lord. In Jesus' name, I pray. Amen.

Let's Go! Have you ever turned yourself **inside out** to go the distance with God's glorious help and strength? If so, discuss with each other what this experience meant to building your faith.

July 3

Victorious Action: Listening to the Holy Spirit!

"And you also were included in Christ when you heard the message of truth, the gospel of your salvation. When you believed, you were marked in Him with a seal, the promised Holy Spirit" (Eph. 1:13).

Let's Talk: The Son and the Holy Spirit are equal to God the Father in eternity, nature and position. Within the Trinity the Father is head, first among equals; the Son and the Holy Spirit do the Father's will, glorifying Him and making Him known; and the Holy Spirit glorifies and makes known the Son. The Trinity is equal and separate and yet one! The Holy Spirit is addressed as equal to God the Father and Jesus the Son. "Therefore go and make disciples of all nations, baptizing them in the name of the Father and of the Son and of the Holy Spirit" (Matt. 28:19). The Holy Spirit brings joy to you as a believer, giving you an inner contentment and happiness.

Let's Glorify: Jesus, thank you for sending me the comforter, the Holy Spirit! Where would I be without His guidance, love and care coming from deep within me? He is my friend, my God and trustworthy counselor. Thank you, Holy Spirit for warning me, interceding in prayer for me and speaking to my heart. I praise you and thank you for sticking closer to me than a brother! May I always remember you are not an "it" but a real person with your own personality. Be my most welcomed guest every day as we spend time fellowshipping together. In your name, I pray. Amen.

Let's Go! What thoughts do you have about the Holy Spirit? Did you learn anything new about the Holy Spirit today? Are you listening when the Holy Spirit speaks to you?

July 4

Victorious Action: Hearing the Shepherd's Voice!

"My sheep hear my voice, and I know them, and they follow me: And I give unto them eternal life; and they shall never perish, neither shall any man pluck them out of my hand" (Jn. 10:27-28 KJV).

Let's Talk: "The Lord is my Shepherd," King David said in Ps. 23. He was one of the first to write on this attribute of God. Jehovah Raah is God's special name for Shepherd. Ps.79:13 says, "We are your people, the sheep of your flock. We will thank you always; forever and ever we will praise you." As our Shepherd, He holds us closely to His heart and carries us tenderly! You can call on the name of Jehovah Raah at any time. Listen intently because as a believer you can surely hear His voice. The Holy Spirit whispers His thoughts and guidance to your heart. Following in obedience is required if you desire to hear Him more! Praise God for such a privilege!

Let's Glorify: Thank you for being my Shepherd, My Jehovah Raah. Lord, I dearly want to hear your voice every day. Help me to be a better listener! How I praise you for my eternal life which cannot be taken away. In the really stressful days, let me remember you are holding me close and are preserving me unto the glorious day you come back for your followers. How I love you. In Jesus' name, I pray. Amen.

Let's Go! Are you hearing His voice? Why or why not? Humbly get quiet before Him. Pray and ask Jesus to speak clearly to you today. Journal what He tells you. Discuss it together.

July 5

Victorious Action: Clothed in Joy!

"You have turned my mourning into joyful dancing. You have taken away my clothes of mourning and clothed me with joy, that I might sing praises to you and not be silent. O' Lord my God, I will give you thanks forever" (Ps. 30:11-12 NLT).

Let's Talk: This particular Psalm is a song of Thanksgiving. The Israelites cries have been heard by God. The terrible plights of slavery, persecution and accusation are now history. They resurface here only to remind you of God's faithful deliverance. **Have you mourned? It too will be history. Yahweh will turn your weeping and grief into joyful dancing.** He does take away the sad sackcloth look from your face, your body and your spirit! He will clothe you in radiant joy! You will be saying, "Come and let me tell you what my great God has done for me!"

Let's Glorify: Yahweh, thank you for turning my deep grief into joy and thanksgiving. I want to share with others how faithful and loving you are. Thank you for being with me when I have been in the pit of despair. How awesome I serve a God who turns my mourning into joyful dancing! I praise you! In Jesus' name, I pray. Amen.

Let's Go! Have you ever been in a mourning time? How has Yahweh turned your heartache into joyful dancing? **Share with each other.**

July 6

Victorious Action: God's Gracious Hand is Upon You!

"And praise Him for demonstrating such unfailing love to me by honoring me before the king, His council, and all His mighty nobles! I felt encouraged because the gracious hand of the Lord my God was on me" (Ezra 7:28 NLT).

Let's Talk: Ezra was a scribe and priest during the reign of King Artaxerxes. Ezra was commissioned to teach the Law of Moses to the Israelites and rebuild the Temple of the Lord. He also took the Israelite remnant out of Babylon slavery. **"The gracious hand of God was upon me"** was stated five different times in the eight chapters of Ezra. This action of God throughout the Bible is often understood to convey healing, blessing or the gift of the Holy Spirit. It also indicates the conferring of authority upon individuals for the purpose of ministry.

Let's Glorify: God, thank you for your gracious hand of support and blessing upon me today. Lord, I do not want to go or be anywhere without your loving hand and Holy Spirit upon me. Please guide me and direct me. Help me to listen intently to your leadings. Lord, help me to be careful to know when I am starting to be a slave to any of the world's ideas. Thank you for your favor. In Jesus' name, I pray. Amen.

Let's Go! Where is God's gracious hand upon you? **Have you ever been a slave to the world's teachings or ideas?**

July 7

Victorious Action: Doing Work that Has Value!

"But on the judgment day, fire will reveal what kind of work each builder has done. The fire will show if a person's work has any value" (1 Cor. 3:13 NLT).

Let's Talk: What kind of work do you do? Isn't this a common question you ask when you meet someone for the first time? I know this is true of me. I guess I am trying to get a feel for a person's personality quickly. Only God knows your heart and your real motives (Jer. 17:10). It is true, the quality of each person's work will be revealed in time as it is tested by fire at the judgment seat of God. Believers are reconciled to God and cannot lose their salvation. Your work however will be tested by fire. Only the lasting, eternal work will be rewarded and the others will be burned up.

Let's Glorify: Jesus, I want to do your lasting work. Please point me in the right direction! I do not want to waste time and energy going down the wrong path. Let me be and do all that you have made me for! I ask that I would enjoy the work you have given me. May it be all to your glory. In your holy name, I pray. Amen.

Let's Go! How do you feel about the work you do? Do you volunteer anywhere? **Ask God to show you the work He'd like you to do or confirm the choice you have made.**

July 8

Victorious Action: Be Someone Else's Joy and Give Hope!

"After all, what gives us hope and joy, and what will be our proud reward and crown as we stand before our Lord Jesus when He returns? It is you" (1 Thess. 2:19 NLT).

Let's Talk: Timothy is giving the Thessalonians a great report. He is telling them they can stand before Jesus steadfast and secure because of their walk in Him! Not only will you be with Jesus, but heaven is your reward and inheritance. It is a place of great and priceless value, awaiting you, the redeemed! In heaven, your faithful service will be rewarded and the redeemed will be given resurrection bodies for service in the heavenly realm. You will receive a crown of never-ending glory and honor. How exciting! So, be encouraged and stay after being a good, loyal and faithful servant, for great is your reward!

Let's Glorify: God, I want to be that good, loyal and faithful servant here on earth. I know I can have satisfaction in the work you have given me. My identity is not to be tied up in my work. No, my identity is rooted in your love for me instead! Lord, help me to be a Christ centered witness as I go about my daily work. May I glorify you mightily. In Jesus' name, I pray. Amen.

Let's Go! Who is a source of joy and hope to you? Are you a source of joy and do you give hope to someone else? Discuss with each other.

July 9

Victorious Action: Rewarded According to the Fruit of Your Own Doings!

"I, the Lord, search the heart, I test the mind, Even to give every man according to his ways, According to the fruit of his doings" (Jer.17:10 NKJV).

Let's Talk: God knows everything that is in your heart! He knows your inner motives even before you do! He tests the mind to see if you will stop and examine your thoughts and actions. If you are not careful to examine yourself, checking in with your emotions and real motives, **pride can take root.** Examine yourself and ask yourself what you believe about Jesus, God's only Son. "I will reward each person for what he has done. I will reward him for the results of his actions" (Jer. 17:10 NOG). The results of your actions produce good fruit or sickly fruit. You have a decision to make!

Let's Glorify: Yahweh, you know all my thoughts. You know when I lay down and when I get up. Before I say a prayer you know what I will be asking. You see all of my deeds. Lord, let me do what is pleasing to you. I pray to develop luscious great fruit. Help me to examine my heart daily. May you receive all the praise, honor and glory. In Jesus' name, I pray. Amen.

Let's Go! What do you like about the God of the Angel's Armies to be able to search your heart? What do you not like about this and why?

July 10

Victorious Action: Hope in the Lord Alone!

"So be strong and courageous, all you who put your hope in the Lord" (Ps. 31:24 NLT).

Let's Talk: How do you deal with fear? The courageous woman responds to pain by not running away or being impulsive. She prays in God's spirit, strength, and firmness. Courage may, accordingly, be defined as strength of purpose of will in the presence of life's sufferings. It is absolutely important your courage is always made to rest upon the promises and presence of **Emmanuel** which means **He is with you.** More important than physical courage, although it may involve this, is moral courage. The courage of endurance, the cousin to patience, is the will to accept the pains and frustrations of life and **still live with integrity.** For the Christian, courage is possible in the measure that she knows herself to be in God's almighty hands and under the protection of her heavenly Abba Daddy!

Let's Glorify: Abba Daddy, help me to remember I have nothing to be afraid of. You promise to be with me at all times. I can call on your many names for deliverance, peace, patience and blessed assurance. Help me to courageously endure the really hard stuff in my life with patience. In Jesus' name, I pray. Amen.

Let's Go! Do you need to have courage faith today in the midst of your suffering? **Call on the name of Emmanuel. He will not fail you!**

July 11

Victorious Action: Surrendering Good for His Best!

"Whoever finds their life will lose it, and whoever loses their life for my sake will find it" (Matt.10:39).

Let's Talk: This is such a paradoxical Scripture! Jesus taught His disciples this lesson. You must die in order to truly live! Die to yourself and your ways. Surrender what is good for His best. Do what is right in His eyes, not what the world says it is okay to do. Seeking Him first above all else, not consulting your friends first. When something puzzles you, ask for His direction. Ask for help. True life is found in Jesus. You and I get caught up in our wants, our dreams and desires. He knows you the best. He knows you completely. Certainly He can give you a fulfilling career and life that will matter for eternity.

Let's Glorify: Jesus, I want to wholeheartedly give myself to you. I lose my life, my dreams and desires to your best plans. You know what will fulfill me and I trust your plans for me. Truly, you have the best plans and a future for me. Help me to stay surrendered to you. Please give me the endurance to fulfill your will in my life. In your faithful name, I pray. Amen.

Let's Go! Have you truly surrendered your good for God's best plan for your life? It takes a lot of trust and faith in the Eternal One! He is absolutely trustworthy and faithful!

July 12

Victorious Action: Ask in Faith!

"But when you ask, you must believe and not doubt, because the one who doubts is like a wave of the sea, blown and tossed by the wind" (James 1:6).

Let's Talk: Asking in faith begins with knowing God loves you and is for you. If I ask half heartedly I am not asking in belief. My attitude shows I believe there is a 50-50 chance of my prayer being heard or answered. My doubts do not hinder God's ability to answer my prayer. It is my lack of faith that hinders me and my vision to see the answered prayer! I have got to decide once and for all, today to believe in His omnipotence because "Nothing is impossible with God" (Luke 1:37).

Let's Glorify: God, increase my belief in you! When I look at how you rescued the Israelites time and time again, I can have faith that you are my God and you can do ANYTHING! May I pray according to your will, never doubting and being tossed around by my uncertainties. Thank you for hearing me. You are my Rock eternal (Isa. 26:4). In Jesus' name, I pray. Amen.

Let's Go! Do you have any doubts today? **Read Hebrews Chapter 11.**

July 13

Victorious Action: Living Under Abba Daddy's Wings of Love!

"But those who hope in the Lord will renew their strength. They will soar on wings like eagles; they will run and not grow weary, they will walk and not be faint" (Isa. 40:31).

Let's Talk: Jesus called God, His Father, "Abba." Abba is the personal name for Daddy. Do you need your Abba Daddy's strength today? It is yours as you pray and ask for it. So many times I have prayed and asked for His physical or emotional strength. He has always given it to me through the energizing power of the Holy Spirit. Being under His wings means you are comforted, being near and dear to His heart. You are covered by His love and the blood of Jesus. You are sheltered and taken care of. God loves to do this for His beloved. But, you must ask! As a result, you will have renewal of strength, trust, peace and joy! Remember to thank Him for such favor and loving care!

Let's Glorify: Abba Daddy, you are a wonderful and caring Heavenly Father! Thank you for always helping me when I call on your name! You are so kind and gracious. You want your believers to soar, fully energized and engaged, listening to the Holy Spirit. I am so grateful for your help every day! In Jesus' name, I pray. Amen.

Let's Go! Do you feel faint and worn out today? Pray and ask for the Holy Spirit to energize you, so you can soar on wings like eagles! Pray together asking for His strength to empower you.

July 14

Victorious Action: The Lord is My Stronghold, My Safety!

"The Lord is my light and my salvation whom shall I fear? The Lord is the stronghold of my life of whom shall I be afraid" (Ps. 27:1).

Let's Talk: As a follower of Jesus, you have ability to face the future with confidence. This is possible because of your relationship with God. The Holy Spirit is pouring His love and life into your heart and mind. You can have confidence in what God can do, what He will do in the future because of His Holy nature. You can remain optimistic in uncertain times, because God's character never changes. Waiting in faith and standing on the Word of God's promises is your light. He is your stronghold and strong tower! You do not have to be afraid today or tomorrow.

Let's Glorify: God, thank you for your Word and your loving promises. I can go to them at any time and I will find you, comforting, loving and encouraging! Nothing can come against me, so I do not have to be afraid. You have me securely in the palm of your hand. You hold my salvation safely. I am excited to be with you one day in heaven. How I love you! In Jesus' name, I pray. Amen.

Let's Go! Are you afraid today? Write Ps. 27:1 on an index card and carry it with you today. Read it several times throughout your day. Claim this promise for your life, asking God to be your stronghold.

July 15

Victorious Action: Rebuilding the Ruins of Your Life!

"I replied, "The God of heaven will help us succeed. We, His servants, will start rebuilding this wall. But you have no share, legal right, or historic claim in Jerusalem" (Neh. 2:20 NLT).

Let's Talk: Have there been areas of your life that have crumbled? **Arise and build!** Do what the Lord is asking you to do. Do not worry about what others say to you *or about you!* The God of heaven **will help you succeed** as He gives His **favor** to you! Maybe you need to rebuild a relationship gone sour. Maybe you are having financial ruins. Or just maybe you've had an addiction and you are tired of it. You just want to break free. Come clean before the Lord, ask for forgiveness. He is loving and forgives immediately. He will help you make it through your devastation.

Let's Glorify: Thank you, Jesus for being a loving God. You know my devastation in my life. I want to confess to you my part in all of this. Thank you Lord I do not have to fix myself. As I walk in you, you gently point out new ways for me to respond that are honoring to you. You teach me new ways to help rebuild the ruins in my life. You increase my confidence as I grow strong in you. I am so grateful for your transformation in my life! In your precious name, I pray. Amen.

Let's Go! Where do you need help rebuilding the ruins in your life? Ask Jesus for help and then accept His loving and gentle help. Discuss with your mom, daughter or girlfriend.

July 16

Victorious Action: Living in Harmony with Others!

"I appeal to you, dear brothers and sisters, by the authority of our Lord Jesus Christ, to live in harmony with each other. Let there be no divisions in the church. Rather, be of one mind, united in thought and purpose" (1 Cor. 1:10 NLT).

Let's Talk: Paul reminds you to be in harmony with your fellow believers not quarreling as the Corinthian believers were. They were dividing up into rival groups. The Amplified Bible calls you "to be perfectly united in your common understanding and in your opinions and judgments" (1 Cor. 1:10). Jesus asks you and me to not get involved in petty arguments, or take offense. He calls us to **love more, pray more and judge less**! When we do not heed these words, the enemy gets a foot hold in our marriages, our churches and relationships.

Let's Glorify: Lord Jesus, **help me to love more, pray more and judge less!** I want to be a harmony maker not an offense breaker! I pray to unite people with a peaceable attitude, kind words and loving actions pointing to my relationship in you. When someone offends me, help me to quickly forgive knowing this is what you expect of me. May my actions and attitudes bring you glory! You are the Prince of Peace! In your name, I pray. Amen.

Let's Go! Do you have someone in your life that you need to love more, pray more for and judge less? Will you pray for them today?

July 17

Victorious Action: Putting My Faith into Action!

"Faith is the confidence that what we hope for will actually happen; it gives us assurance about things we cannot see" (Heb. 11:1 NLT).

Let's Talk: What are you hoping for today? Is it safety for your children? Is it financial provision, spiritual or emotional provision? Jehovah Jireh will provide! What evidence is God showing you so you are encouraged to move forward in an activity, career, child rearing or in your marriage? **Your faith is pleasing to Him!** You are commended as you live your life in faith, approaching the God of all mercy, love and hope. You can persevere by putting your faith into action, seeing Jesus with the eyes of your heart.

Let's Glorify: God, thank you for showing me hard evidence of who you are throughout the Scriptures. I know my faith in you, is strengthened every time I stop to praise and worship you and your awesome character. My confidence increases in you as I go through my daily life and I find you faithful and loving to me. As a result, I have more confidence that "I can do ALL things through Christ who strengthens me" (Phil. 4:13) Thank you, Jesus. In your name, I pray. Amen.

Let's Go! How will you persevere and put your faith into action today? Share with each other.

July 18

Victorious Action: Trusting God's Timing is Majestically Perfect!

"The Lord is not slow in keeping His promise, as some understand slowness. Instead He is patient with you, not wanting anyone to perish, but everyone to come to repentance" (2 Pet. 3:9).

Let's Talk: God's seemingly slowness in returning for His followers is truly His patience with mankind. Jesus does not want anyone to die and live eternally without His light, His love and goodness. Think about living without God's goodness, His sunlight casting upon His beautiful creation. It's a horrible and devastating thought. Maybe some of your loved ones and friends are in this category. I know mine are. I need to remember this Scripture on my really long and hard days when I am asking the Lord, "How much longer, God do I have to wait for you to come back?" I need to stop and pray for those who have not asked Jesus to be their Lord and Savior.

Let's Glorify: Dear Lord, I come humbly before you with repentance. Lord forgive me, please. I want to be at home with you. But, I know the importance of praying for others, so I am praying for our broken world and many friends and family members. Your timing is majestically perfect! Help me to be patient, too. Your will be perfectly done here on earth. In Jesus' name I pray, love and adore. Amen.

Let's Go! What friends and family do you know that do not have a personal relationship with Jesus Christ? Will you write a reminder card of their names and commit to pray for them until they do? Will you lovingly share the gospel with them and tell them what it has meant to you to follow after Jesus?

July 19

Victorious Action: Go the Extra Mile!

"But to you who are listening I say: Love your enemies, do good to those who hate you, bless those who curse you, pray for those who mistreat you" (Luke 6:27-28).

Let's Talk: How many times have you had to deal with a difficult person? Probably a lot and way more than you have wanted to! "Jesus loves them, too" my husband always says! God has given each of us so much grace. I try to find some common ground and maybe something about their past. If that cannot happen, I can summarize they are having a bad day or their childhood must have been really hard on them. I have decided I can pray, be cordial, even joyful knowing my Jesus has gone through similar experiences. "No one has ever seen God; but if we love one another, God lives in us and His love is made complete in us. If anyone forces you to go one mile, then go with them two miles. Give to the one who asks you, and do not turn away from the one who wants to borrow from you" (Matt. 5:42).

Let's Glorify: Dear God, please give me the endurance and patience to go the extra mile with someone who I really want to just get away from today! Help me to love _____. Lord, I want to see them through your eyes of love and compassion. Forgive me and my poor attitude. **Give me grace** for this person and help me to realize I have been given abundant grace by you, My Grace Maker! **Please bless them today.** I want to have your attitude, Lord. If there is something I need to know about their situation, would you reveal that to me. If not, I leave

July

_____ in your capable hands. In Jesus' forgiving name, I pray. Amen.

Let's Go! Who do you need to pray a blessing of grace over today? Is there someone you need to forgive? With your current attitude do you need to ask for forgiveness?

July 20

Victorious Action: Be His Disciple!

"In the same way, if you want to be My disciple, it will cost you everything. Don't underestimate that cost" (Luke 14:33 VOICE).

Let's Talk: I guess the real question comes down to this: Do I believe whatever I have, whatever I have gained is a loss in comparison to knowing and living as Jesus desires of Me? Am I willing to submit to what He asks me to do? Will He *really* **ask me to give up everything?** Yes or at least your attachment to whatever you place value in. For me, it is a willingness to submit to the authority of Jesus my Savior and to actually do what He has asked or told me to do. Over and over again we are shown in the Bible, believers are to obey God. You have a choice though, because God allows free will. He is completely trustworthy and if it is hard for you to obey and you do it anyway, this is honoring to Him. You have counted the cost of being His disciple and chose it anyway. This obedience is especially clear in the life and death of Jesus Christ. Apostle Paul said, **"But whatever were gains to me I now consider loss for the sake of Christ"** (Phil. 3:7, emphasis mine).

Let's Glorify: Lord Jesus, I am your disciple. I know this is a costly endeavor. I give ALL that I am with all that I have, knowing you GAVE your ALL to your followers through your ministry and crucifixion. I take up my cross today, laying down my plans and desires because I love you and want to serve you. Thank you for your life, your teachings and all you have made possible for me. I embrace what you are doing in my life. In your holy name, I pray. Amen.

Let's Go! Have you laid down your life for all that Jesus is and has given to you? Or, are you still counting what it will cost you?

July 21

Victorious Action: Praise Him with Lips Filled with the Fruit of Praise!

The Lord says: "These people come near to me with their mouth and honor me with their lips, but their hearts are far from me. Their worship of me is based on merely human rules they have been taught" (Isa. 29:13).

Let's Talk: When your heart is far away from the Lord, honor and reverence for Him is gone. You find that worship made of man's rules is flat and unsatisfying. If you have given praise to an idol, this will make your life empty and lonely, too. But, the Lord will draw you back again, creating wonder upon wonder! God will caress your empty heart and show you what is truly worth praising! Now your spirit begins to soar as you think of how great He is! You can sing His praises right now!

Let's Glorify: God, I come to you with lips filled with the fruit of praise. I am motivated and moved by your great loving-kindness. Let my heart be in synch with yours with thankfulness. How I praise you and thank you for all that you do for me and my family! I am rejoicing before you and your greatness. In your almighty name, I pray. Amen.

Let's Go! Is your praise and worship based on human rules or is it based on the genuine praise you have in your heart for all that God has done for you? Ponder these thoughts and share with each other.

July 22

Victorious Action: Set Free from Sin and You Know It!

"We know that our old sinful selves were crucified with Christ so that sin might lose its power in our lives. We are no longer slaves to sin. For when we died with Christ we were set free from the power of sin" (Rom.6: 6-7 NLT).

Let's Talk: Your old self is gone! It's been crucified along with Jesus' crucifixion. Your sins have been buried with Christ. Sin, all the rotten things you do or have done has lost its power over you! You are no longer a slave to what you do not want to do! You have true freedom in Jesus! Praise Him! Thank Him! Share with others His life giving message of hope and everlasting life! He is our true Liberator and Freedom Fighting Warrior!

Let's Glorify: Lord Jesus, thank you for your true freedom! Let me rely on this fact: my old nature is gone because you have paid the complete and full price. I am free indeed! Thank you my priceless, Savior! In your redeeming name, I pray. Amen.

Let's Go! Are living like you know you have been set free from your sins? Or is shame, guilt or defeat over your sins dragging you down? Pray together.

July 23

Victorious Action: Saying Yes to the King's Invitation!

Jesus replied with this story: "A man prepared a great feast and sent out many invitations. When the banquet was ready, He sent his servant to tell the guests, 'Come, the banquet is ready.' But they all began making excuses. One said, 'I have just bought a field and must inspect it. Please excuse me.' Another said, 'I have just bought five pairs of oxen, and I want to try them out. Please excuse me.' Another said, 'I now have a wife, so I can't come'" (Luke 14:16-20 NLT).

Let's Talk: Invitations were sent out. The King's special signet ring embossed each invite on fine papyrus paper. Finally the big day arrived! It was time to come to the great banquet. The King waited with great anticipation, knowing His guests would be exceedingly thrilled at what He had prepared. Suddenly, the guest list dwindled leaving room for many new guests. Excuses flowed like a river. It was tragically sad. **God calls and few answer the knocking on their heart!** Other **priorities** and people seemed more important to these partygoers than listening to Jesus and obeying Him.

Let's Glorify: Jesus, I do not want to miss the opportunity of hearing your voice and receiving your invitation "To come." I have said yes to your invitation and believe **Jesus is the only Son of God. I believe He was crucified on a cross for my sins, died and rose again three days later.** I believe Jesus is alive, sitting at the right hand of God, the Father in heaven even now. As a result of my belief, I have received the counselor, the Holy Spirit to guide, comfort, care for me and be my companion. Help me to listen closely to your other invitations to love and obey you. In Jesus' precious name, I pray. Amen.

Let's Go! Have you said Yes to King Jesus' invitation? **Why or why not? Ask questions if you have any confusion about what it means to be a follower of Jesus Christ.**

July 24

Victorious Action: Boasting in Him Alone!

"My grace is all you need. My power works best in weakness." So now I am glad to boast about my weaknesses, so that the power of Christ can work through me" (2 Cor. 12:9 NLT).

Let's Talk: Do you need Christ's grace and power to rest on you and in you? I know I do! Just like Paul, you can share your past and its messy parts because God has redeemed, rescued and delivered you from that time. He will use your past experiences to help someone else. It does feel like **a blessing and a risk** at times when you step out of your comfort zone and share what He has done in your life. When you rely on the love He has for you instead of other's approval rating, Christ's supernatural power is manifested through your weaknesses.

Let's Glorify: Jesus, thank you for delivering me from past sins and today's wrong doings. I am your girl and I desire to seek your approval not anyone else's. Help me to speak love and truth into others' lives, sharing my testimony of faith as appropriate. May I boast in you alone. I pray this all to your glory. Amen.

Let's Go! Where have you seen Jesus' power worked best in your weakness? Share with you mom, daughter or special friend.

July 25

Victorious Action: Being One with Jesus!

"I am praying not only for these disciples but also for all who will ever believe in me through their message. I pray that they will all be one, just as you and I are one—as you are in me, Father, and I am in you. And may they be in us so that the world will believe you sent me" (John 17:20-21 NLT).

Let's Talk: Jesus calls you to be one with the Father and Himself As a result, as believers we can have complete unity because of their relationship. We are commissioned to love one another and forgive freely, **letting no bitter root spring up!** The enemy desires to see believers divided because it causes arguments and tears in the church body. This renders us ineffective in bringing Jesus' saving message of love and hope to our dying world.

Let's Glorify: Lord Jesus, thank you for your glory freely given to your Father and Holy Spirit so I may be one with you! Draw me closer to you today. Give me a love for all believers, making allowances for their faults. I have been graciously forgiven and I want to do the same for others. In your saving love, I pray. Amen.

Let's Go! Have you ever experienced disunity in your family? What was the outcome? God can work through any challenge as you pray and forgive others.

July 26

Victorious Action: Producing Good Fruit!

Jesus replied, "Now the time has come for the Son of Man to enter into His glory. I tell you the truth, unless a kernel of wheat is planted in the soil and dies, it remains alone. But its death will produce many new kernels—a plentiful harvest of new lives" (John 12:23-24).

Let's Talk: It is the paradox of life and death! You and I can get so caught up in holding other people, things and ideas as our identity. All of these seem so important and feel so utterly important! In fact, at times they feel so important you can feel as if you will die without them! Instead, you need to let your life, **your seed of this life, yourself, your gifts, and talents** fall to the ground willingly, lovingly into the hands and heart of Jesus. This is what Jesus did so many would be saved! He did all of this to His Father's glory!

Let's Glorify: Lord Jesus, I willingly let my seed, **all that I am**, all my dreams and heart's desires fall to the ground. Plant me fully in you. I know you will catch me bringing my life to full fruition as you deem necessary. May my life **produce good fruit and be a beautiful witness**. In your holy name, I pray. Amen.

Let's Go! What "seeds" of your life have fallen to the ground into Jesus' loving heart and hands?

July 27

Victorious Action: Lingering in Jesus' Presence!

"Remain in me, and I will remain in you. For a branch cannot produce fruit if it is severed from the vine, and you cannot be fruitful unless you remain in me. Yes, I am the vine; you are the branches. Those who remain in me, and I in them, will produce much fruit. **For apart from me you can do nothing**" (Jn. 15:4-5, emphasis mine).

Let's Talk: Linger, persist and abide are all words that mean **"remain."** Jesus Christ described Himself as the true vine, the source of life and growth for all believers. The vine is also an image of peace and security for Christ's followers. You as a branch, grow out of Jesus the vine. The vine nourishes and feeds the branches. Your very spiritual sustenance depends on how closely you remain or abide in Him and to Him. Producing luscious fruit in your life is a direct result of clinging to the vine. You will receive a blessing as you linger in His presence!

Let's Glorify: Jesus, thank you for being my vine that I can cling to. As I hold onto you, you are holding onto me. Thank you for the peace, comfort and security I experience when I am remaining in your loving presence. I pray to grow luscious, beautiful fruit as I grow in you and your ways. When I am apart from you, I do not grow. Prune me as necessary, knowing it is for my spiritual growth and maturity. Help to abide even closer to you during these times. In your name, I pray. Amen.

Let's Go! What is your favorite kind of fruit? Are you growing this kind of fruit in your life as you remain in Jesus? Discuss as you take a walk together through your garden.

July 28

Victorious Action: Be Humble and Seek His Face in Prayer!

"If my people, who are called by my name, will humble themselves and pray and seek my face and turn from their wicked ways, then I will hear from heaven, and I will forgive their sin and will heal their land" (2 Chron. 7:14).

Let's Talk: Humble yourself, pray, seek His face, asking His will be done in the matters of your life. When the Holy Spirit whispers **what you need to change** in your thoughts, attitudes and actions, listen whole-heartedly! Do what He asks of you. God will hear your prayer. He promises to right the wrongs in these scriptures.

Let's Glorify: Lord God, I choose to humble myself before you. Please forgive me of my pride of wanting to_____ so I could feel "good about myself instead of letting you fill up my "neediness vacuum!" I humbly ask for forgiveness of my sins. In your blessed name, I pray. Amen.

Let's Go! Will you seek His face humbly and ask for forgiveness of your sins? He is just and faithful to forgive you right away when you come to Him with a repentive heart. I am so glad for this fact! Pray together asking for forgiveness in any area of your life.

July 29

Victorious Action: Knowing Love is the Greatest Virtue!

"If I gave everything I have to the poor and even sacrificed my body, I could boast about it; but if I didn't love others, I would have gained nothing" (1 Cor. 13:3 NLT).

Let's Talk: Only what you do with a heart of love will last. If there is no love, no matter how hard you have worked, there is no gain! You can do a lot and work in your God given gifts and talents, but without love your work and life are worthless and meaningless! "These three virtues that should characterize a believer's life will last forever—**faith, hope, and love**—and the greatest of these is love" (1 Cor. 13: 13 NLT, paraphrased).

Let's Glorify: Jesus, you are love! Yours is a pure and undefiled love which is never proud or envious. Please help me to fill up with you and your loving-kindness so there is no room in my heart for judgment, sarcasm, envy or pride! Let me do all things with your love, Lord. In your holy name, I pray. Amen.

Let's Go! Have you ever done a job, volunteered or showed up to help someone without exhibiting love? How was your patience level that day? Pray and ask Jesus to fill you up with His love for the people you are serving today.

July 30

Victorious Action: Committed Travel Plans!

"And how blessed all those in whom you live, whose lives become roads you travel; They wind through lonesome valleys, come upon brooks, discover cool springs and pools brimming with rain! God-traveled, these roads curve up the mountain, and at the last turn—Zion! God in full view" (Ps. 84:5-7 MSG).

Let's Talk: A pilgrimage is a journey made to a holy or revered place as an act of devotion or duty. You are blessed as you seek God and His strength along the pilgrimage of this life. As believers, we are longing for a better country—a heavenly country. Dear one, set your heart on committed travel plans and the better country called heaven. Glimpse at earth and yet hold your gaze on heaven and seeing God in full sight!

Let's Glorify: Lord, you are a cool pool of refreshment in my spirit! Please travel through my life as you will, directing my paths. Help me God to see you and know you through the lonesome times. Someday, I will have a full view of you! I will be known as I am fully known by you. Help me to know myself better as I experience your love, joy and companionship today. I cannot wait to see you face-to-face! In Jesus' love, I pray. Amen.

Let's Go! What are some of your favorite roads to travel on? Describe them to each other. Go on a road trip together!

July 31

Victorious Action: Knowing You Are on a Grand Adventure!

"God, who got you started in this spiritual adventure, shares with us the life of His Son and our Master Jesus. He will never give up on you. Never forget that" (1 Cor. 1:9 MSG).

Let's Talk: Every time you think of your mom or daughter, what adventurous memories come to mind? God has you on a great adventure, too! He has your life story already figured out! You have the opportunity to partner with Him, the Majestic One as He shares Jesus' life and love with you! "Just think—you don't need a thing, you've got it all! All God's gifts are right in front of you as you wait expectantly for our Master Jesus to arrive on the scene for the Finale. And not only that, but **God himself is right alongside to keep you steady and on track until things are all wrapped up by Jesus**" (1 Cor. 1:7-9 MSG, emphasis mine). He will never give up on you, no matter what!

Let's Glorify: God, I thank you for my mom, daughter and friends. I thank you for all the adventures we have been on together. I cannot wait for the next one! Lord, I thank you for her love and the light of Jesus I see emanating out of her. Enrich her in every way with all kinds of knowledge of you. Let her life testify to your great love to those around her. Thank you for keeping us steady and on track until Jesus comes back. May our lives be lived all to your glory and praise. Amen.

Let's Go! Send your mom, daughter or friend a card or bouquet of flowers just because you love her! Remind her of an adventure you have shared together!

August

"There is one thing I'd like my daughters to remember. Always start with God's love for you! Permanent change begins with experiencing God's love, forgiveness and grace first within you. Then you can become a dispenser of His love and grace, forgiving freely!"
~Holly LaChappell

August 1

Victorious Action: Believing Jesus is God's Son!

In John 20:29, Jesus told Thomas, one of His disciples, "Because you have seen me, you have believed; blessed are those who have not seen and yet have believed."

Let's Talk: Do you believe Jesus is truly the Son of God? (See John 3:16) Why or why not? You are called to believe in Jesus in whom you cannot see with your eyes. I find in my doubting moments, I am like doubting Thomas! Jesus whispers to my heart, "I want you to believe what I believe about you." How many times have I put myself down, ridiculed myself and got stuck in shame? I need to remember Jesus' pure, unconditional love. I need to remember His sacrifice on the cross. I am forever grateful! I am reminded right in this moment how much I am loved and cherished!

Let's Glorify: Dear Jesus, thank you for loving me, no matter what! Thank you for your compassion and unfailing love, even when I do not love myself. I believe you are the Son of God and I thank you for your lavish love poured out on my behalf at the cross. In your precious name, I pray, Amen.

Let's Go! Take a walk or a run through God's beautiful nature. Creation shouts its praises to our Great Creator God blessing His Holy Name for all He has done! "Worship the Lord in the splendor of His holiness" (Ps. 96:9b).

August 2

Victorious Action: Lighten Your Load!

"When I said, "My foot is slipping!" Your unfailing love, O Eternal One, held me up. When anxiety overtakes me and worries are many, Your comfort lightens my soul" (Ps. 94:18-19 VOICE)

Let's Talk: Are you worried about many things today? Anxiety and worry are blinking warning lights to draw near to the Lord. **Let God's assuring words sooth your soul** (Ps. 94:19 GW). When anxiety starts to build, take a deep breath. Inhale Jesus and His life. Exhale your stress to Him. Quietly meditate (consider, ponder) on scriptures that bring you calmness. His support will bring you relief. You can experience joy in the midst of your stress as you start to release your pent up anxiety. Joy and gratitude can be your response to all that God has done for you!

Let's Glorify: Jesus, thank you I can turn to you at any moment of the day and release my worry and anxiety to you. Lord, I want to breathe you in and let go of my control and concerns. At the end of the day, help me to realize everything will be okay because you are with me always and eventually I will have great joy seeing you face-to-face! Savior, lighten my load as I rest in you. Thank you for taking on my cares. How I love and appreciate you. In your name, I pray. Amen.

Let's Go! Do you need to lighten your load today? **Give it up to Jesus knowing He CAN handle anything you are dealing with.** How can you lighten someone else's load today?

August 3

Victorious Action: Remaining Faithful to God Your Whole Life!

Then Miriam the prophet, Aaron's sister, took a tambourine and led all the women as they played their tambourines and danced. And Miriam sang this song "Sing to the Lord, for He has triumphed gloriously; He has hurled both horse and rider into the sea" (Ex.15:20-21 NLT).

Let's Talk: We first read about Miriam when she was about 10-12 years old. She was watching after her baby brother Moses after her mother placed him in the Nile River so he would not be killed by Pharaoh's men. She was bold and asked the Pharaoh's daughter who found Moses, "Should I go and find one of the Hebrew women to nurse the baby for you" (Ex. 2:7 NLT). Miriam grew up to be a mighty woman of God, a prophetess leading the Israelites in song and dance. She criticized Moses the leader (and her brother) of the Israelites for marrying a Cushite woman as they journeyed for forty years through the desert. Miriam and Aaron said, "Has the Lord spoken only through Moses? Hasn't he spoken through us, too?" But the Lord heard them. Now Moses was very humble—more humble than any other person on earth" (Num.12:2-3 NLT). Miriam was struck with leprosy scriptures say, because she criticized her brother Moses. It appears she was jealous against him and his leadership.

Let's Glorify: God, thank you for the story of Miriam. You endowed her with leadership skills, the gift of singing, making music and writing poetry. Lord, I see Miriam with all of her gifts and yet pride rose up in her heart creating criticism of her brother Moses and his leadership. She became jealous and wanted more. Lord, forgive me when I have a jealous heart. It is wrong! Let me overcome envy with your love, grace and kindness. Let me remember she was struck with leprosy for her jealousy so I will be detoured from any bitter thoughts. In your holy and righteous name, I pray. Amen.

Let's Go! Do you have any jealousy today? Where does it come from? Is it insecurity or pride? Or, wanting more of something? Pray and confess your pride and jealousy to the Lord, asking Him to remove it.

August 4

Victorious Action: Your Tears Are Gone!

"For the Lamb at the center of the throne will be their shepherd; 'He will lead them to springs of living water. 'And God will wipe away every tear from their eyes" (Rev. 7:17).

Let's Talk: Jesus is the Lamb of God (the living sacrifice) and yet He is also your holy Shepherd. He leads you gently to His springs of cool, refreshing living waters today and in heaven. He will be at the center of heaven. You won't miss seeing Him in all His glory! God Himself will wipe away every tear from your beautiful eyes. He will welcome you home, His good and faithful daughter. How He loves you, the Bride of Christ!

Let's Glorify: Jesus, thank you for being my living sacrifice so I can live with you in heaven for all of eternity! Thank you for paying the price, the ultimate sacrifice *for me*. Today, lead me to your springs of living water in the center of your loving heart. I want to know you more. God, I tear up knowing you will wipe away not only my tears, but the tears of my dear friends and family who have struggled in this life, too. I am so grateful. I praise your holy name! Amen.

Let's Go! Ask Jesus to lead you today by His cool, refreshing springs of living water. Let Him wipe away your tears of sorrow, regret and pain. Together pray and thank Him for His loving sacrifice.

August 5

Victorious Action: Stockpile Treasure in Heaven!

"Don't hoard treasure down here where it gets eaten by moths and corroded by rust or—worse!—stolen by burglars. Stockpile treasure in heaven, where it's safe from moth and rust and burglars. It's obvious, isn't it? The place where your treasure is, is the place you will most want to be, and end up being" (Matt. 6:19-20 MSG).

Let's Talk: You know you cannot take your material treasures, your possessions to heaven! What can you take with you to your new and glorious home? Well, for starters your good works in volunteering and your generous time and money given to the weak and the poor. How about your attitude of your love and gratitude for Jesus for all He has done for you? Jesus is not against wealth and possessions because He believes them to be evil. What makes your possessions a problem is when you obsess over having more and more and desiring only the best of the best. If we value what our Lord values rather than what our society values, then we'll meet our basic needs while giving to the poor who do not have adequate means.

Let's Glorify: Jesus, thank you for your example of caring for the poor, the broken, the weak and the hungry. Give me your eyes to see people who are in need. Help me to desire to help others and not turn a blind eye. Remind me Holy Spirit when I am starting to stockpile possessions to look deeper within myself as to why I think I need more stuff. What I need is more of you, Lord! Thank you for your generous nature. Let me be like you, Lord. In your name, I pray. Amen.

Let's Go! What motivates you to help others? **Have you ever bought something to fill a void in your heart?** (Yes, I sure have, too!)

August 6

Victorious Action: Shoulder Each Other's Burdens!

"My spiritual sisters, if one of our faithful has fallen into a trap and is snared by sin, don't stand idle and watch her demise. **Gently restore her**, being careful not to step into your own snare. **Shoulder each other's burdens**, and then you will live as the law of the Anointed teaches us. Don't take this opportunity to think you are better than those who slip because you aren't; then you become the fool and deceive even yourself." (Gal. 6:1-3 VOICE, emphasis mine).

Let's Talk: It is easy isn't it, to think "I'd never do that. . .or, what was she thinking?" Then, before you know it, you have gotten yourself into a similar sticky situation! We are to help and bear each other burdens as sisters in Christ. As Moms and daughters, it can be difficult at times to speak the truth because we do not like confrontation. It's uncomfortable and we do not want to create a break in our relationship. The scriptures however, tell you and me to **gently restore your loved one.** Quietly with love tell them your concerns. Be tender and initiate the conversation. Remaining tender is a powerful way to build intimacy.

Let's Glorify: Lord, you call me to forgive and reconcile myself and others to you. Help me not to lecture but listen emphatically. Let be speak your truth in love and encouragement. Help me to wait for the Holy Spirit to move in me and stir in her to help solve the problem. I do not have to fix her or solve her problems. I leave that up to you, Lord. May your will be done in a non-judgmental atmosphere. God, I love _____ and I want the best for her! In your grace, I pray. Amen.

Let's Go! Do you need to restore someone back to the loving truth of Jesus? Make sure you pray beforehand and ask the Holy Spirit to guide you with gentleness and empathy.

August 7

Victorious Action: Let No Bitter Root Strangle Your Heart!

"See to it that no one falls short of the grace of God and that no bitter root grows up to cause trouble and defile many" (Heb. 12:15).

Let's Talk: Do not miss or forfeit the grace of God! Notice how wonderful, kind and generous He has been to you! When you get discontented or start comparing yourself to some else, **a bitter root can twine around your heart, strangling out the grace of God.** Holding onto hurts and grievances makes bitterness grow. Bitterness can grow into hate. Holding onto hate can lead to death of a relationship, missed opportunities to witness Christ's light and holds you back from God's calling on your life! Plus, bitterness can wreck your health!

Let's Glorify: Jesus, I do not want to be a bitter filled person! Help me not to be offended so easily but give grace and kindness the way you give to me! Lord, I want to be a forgiving person to others, not letting the bitter vine of unforgiveness to strangle and squeeze my heart. Thank you for forgiving me and my sins. In Jesus' holy name, I pray. Amen.

Let's Go! Mom or daughter, do you need to apologize to each other? **Forgive freely and love each other, just as Jesus does.**

August 8

Victorious Action: Knowing God Comforts Me!

"As a mother comforts her child, so will I comfort you; and you will be comforted over Jerusalem" (Isa. 66:13).

Let's Talk: Your Abba Daddy could not ever forget you. The picture here in this verse is a loving mother comforting her child while nursing her. A mother cannot forget her baby when she nurses. God has made a woman's body to bring life to the baby forming within and then she gives life as she nurses. This scripture also depicts a mother hugging her child close and taking delight in her offspring, bouncing her on her knee. Certainly, just as a mom cannot forget the special bond she has with her child; neither will your Holy Father in heaven forget about you. It is impossible!

Let's Glorify: Abba Daddy, how I thank you for this picture of love! Lord, if there is a woman out there reading this devotional and her relationship was not want she desired when she was growing up, would you help her to forgive today, if necessary? Lord, put special friendships in her life that helps promote healing, love and understanding. You are a great Dad to your people. How we love you, Lord! In Jesus' name, I pray. Amen.

Let's Go! Thank your Mom or daughter for the special God given bond you have between each other. **Tell each other what you have always admired about each other.**

August 9

Victorious Action: Do Not Limit the Holy One!

"Again and again they tested God's patience and provoked the Holy One of Israel" (Ps. 78:41 NLT).

Let's Talk: The GNV Bible (Geneva) version of this scripture says, "They returned and tempted God, and limited the Holy one of Israel." This is such a sad scripture! The Israelite's tested God's patience over and over again! They did not believe Him and His promises. They forgot all the miraculous things He showed them in their journey to the Promised Land. They failed to obey Him and they questioned Him over and over again, even though God had proven how faithful He was. Unfortunately, you and I can act the same way! Remember, that He will provide for you as you move in faith!

Let's Glorify: God, I want to believe you and trust you with my entire being. Lord, I can do this when I remember the history I have in you. My faith increases when I do not lean on my own understanding, (Prov. 3:5-6) but look to you and ask, "What do you want me to do? What direction should I move in?" Then, I move in faith and you supply for me out of your glorious riches (Phil. 4:19). God, you are AWESOME! I thank you for helping me always. Please let me always remember this and not doubt you. In your almighty name, I pray. Amen.

Let's Go! Are you limiting the Holy One of Israel by your lack of faith or obedience? **Discuss a time when you had great faith or only a little faith.**

August 10

Victorious Action: His Words are Faithful and True!

Then he said to me, "These words are faithful and true." And the Lord God of the holy prophets *sent His angel* to show His servants the things which must shortly take place (Rev. 22:6 NKJV, emphasis mine).

Let's Talk: Angels are God's spiritual messengers with the special role of making known God's work of salvation. Angels announced the foretelling of the birth of Jesus and John the Baptist. Two angels dressed in white announced Jesus' resurrection to Mary Magdalene at the tomb, that first Easter morning (John 20:10). Two angels appeared to some of the disciples after Jesus was taken up before their very eyes. As they strained to see Him rising into heaven, two white-robed men suddenly stood among them. They said, "Jesus has been taken from you into heaven, but someday He will return from heaven in the same way you saw Him go" (Acts 1:10-11). Suddenly and soon, Jesus will come back to earth for His followers! So, be ready!

Let's Glorify: Lord Jesus, I am excited for you to come back for your believers. I pray for those who do not have a personal relationship with you yet. May I be a positive light shining into their lives. Thank you for your messengers, your angels who come to share what must shortly take place. May I be found doing exactly what you have called me to do in the meantime. All praise, honor and glory are yours. Amen.

Let's Go! Are you ready for your Savior to come back for you, His beloved bride of Christ? Who are you praying for to receive His precious love, joy and relationship?

August 11

Victorious Action: Be Happy in Your Hope!

"Be happy in your hope, stand your ground when you're in trouble, and devote yourselves to prayer" (Rom. 12:12 CEB).

Let's Talk: How do you keep your faith alive and burning brightly for the Lord? Do you memorize Scriptures so you get the Word into you? As you do this, the Holy Spirit will bring these Scriptures to mind so you can draw strength from them! Pray them back to the Lord. Be a watchful servant of Jesus Christ, remembering He is coming again for you! As you are waiting for His glorious return, remain cheerful in your hope and keep your outlook looking up!

Let's Glorify: Jesus, I want to remain happy in the hope I have in you. I am praying expectantly in my trials and errors, looking to you the Author and Perfector of my faith. Help me to remember to pray first and worry. . . never! All praise, honor and glory to you, my Savior! Amen.

Let's Go! What do you do best when you find yourself in tough, discouraging times? Are you happy in your hope? Do you stand your ground and never waver? Or, do you devote yourself to prayer? Discuss with each other over coffee, if possible!

August 12

Victorious Action: Executing Small Tasks Masterfully!

"His master replied, 'Well done, good and faithful servant! You have been faithful with a few things; I will put you in charge of many things. Come and share your master's happiness" (Matt. 25:21).

Let's Talk: All of your abilities and skills originate from God and are to be dedicated to His glory and the good of others. Think about the gifts and talents God has given to you. The small tasks you have executed well with a giving and grateful heart just might get you a promotion! In God's economy honorable service is rewarded with larger jobs to do! The message is to do your best every time, no matter the size or value placed on the assignment! The Lord sees all your efforts. **He gives you the sense of joy and blessedness when you are finished!**

Let's Glorify: Jesus, I want to serve you well and love you well as I serve others. Help me to not measure the size of the job in relationship to my worthiness. Let me count it all joy to have the opportunity to be used by you for your Kingdom purposes. Help me to be compelled by your gracious love as I do your work. In your name I pray, love and adore you. Amen.

Let's Go! Discuss with each other some of the gifts and talents God has blessed you with. How do you serve others while utilizing these gifts? Choose an event where you can serve together.

August 13

Victorious Action: Knowing His Everlasting Love and Kindness!

"I have loved you with an everlasting love; Therefore I have drawn you with loving kindness" (Jer. 31:3 NASB).

Let's Talk: Sometimes I really need this verse because I am feeling low about myself. Or, maybe I have just faced some great disappointment. God whispers to my heart, "I love you with an endless love. Believe what I believe about you: you are worthy and I could never forget about you! He is kind hearted, thoughtful and gentle towards you. He knows exactly what to say to your hurting heart. Trust His love and goodwill toward you, drawing near to His tender heart and compassion!

Let's Glorify: God, I am so blessed you love me as much as you do! Thank you for loving me with unfailing love and giving me your sweet loving kindness. You are everything that is good! I love you. In Jesus' name, I pray. Amen.

Let's Go! When do you typically need to read and internalize Jer. 31:3? Share with you mom, daughter, aunt or sister in law how much God loves them!

August 14

Victorious Action: Knowing the Creator God!

"For in Him all things were created: things in heaven and on earth, visible and invisible, whether thrones or powers or rulers or authorities; all things have been created through Him and for Him" (Col. 1:16).

Let's Talk: All things were created by God's own Son and everything was made for Him. Every detail was crafted through His design, by His own hands (Col. 1:16 VOICE). His visible creations are the evidence of people, beautiful nature, the stars and the moon in the night time sky. Heaven, angels, His unseen hand moving through you as the Holy Spirit are examples of the invisible creation. As a believer, living keenly aware of Jesus' mighty power in the visible and invisible all the time takes conscious practice. God however, through creation makes what is hidden, concrete and knowable, so that you may know and enter into sweet fellowship with Him, the living God!

Let's Glorify: Lord, thank you that you make real to me, your living presence. I see your hand in the beauty of nature. I see your creative touch in each fragrant flower in my garden. Thank you for making me and living inside of me. I want to be aware of your loving presence today. I draw near to you now. In Jesus' name, I pray. Amen.

Let's Go! Where do you mostly experience God's living creation? Is it through your children's laugh or, in the beauty of a sunrise? Perhaps in some of your dearest relationships? Talk about it with each other.

August 15

Victorious Action: Humbly Get Along with Others!

"I want you to get out there and walk—better yet, run!—on the road God called you to travel. I don't want any of you sitting around on your hands. I don't want anyone strolling off, down some path that goes nowhere. And mark that you do this with **humility and discipline**—not in fits and starts, but steadily, **pouring yourselves out for each other in acts of love**, alert at noticing differences and **quick at mending fences**" (Eph. 4:1 MSG, emphasis mine).

Let's Talk: Paul implores the Ephesian believers and you today, to life a life worthy of your calling because God is the one doing the calling! He calls us as believers in humility and unity to get along together. We serve the same God with the same purpose of sharing His love with our world. **It is good we are different as believers.** All of us bring unique gifts and talents given by God to be used for His purposes. Let your sweet personality shine, all to His glory and building up the body of Christ and others.

Let's Glorify: Thank you, Lord that you give each of us a different personality and unique gifts and talents. Jesus, help me to use my gifts all to your glory; not mine. I want to live out my calling in a way that I bring maximum glory to your name. Help me to get along with others all the while I am pleasing to you, my Savior. In your holy name, I pray. Amen.

Let's Go! What are your unique God given gifts and talents? Have you discovered them yet? Talk about what gifts you see in each other. Are you using them to serve God and the body of Christ?

August 16

Victorious Action: Getting Still Before the Lord!

"He says, "Be still, and know that I am God; I will be exalted among the nations, I will be exalted in the earth" (Ps. 46:10).

Let's Talk: God asks you to be still before Him, trusting that He is in control. Whatever is going on in your world, "The Lord of Hosts is with you; the God of Jacob is your stronghold" (Ps. 46:11). He promises to go before you. He promises to uphold you with His righteous right hand. There is a blessed peace when you get still before Him, seeking His face. But, you must get *still and quiet*. It is in the stillness that you hear the Holy Spirit's whisper to your longing heart. It is in the silence of the moment you are drawn to Jesus' loving heart, yearning for only Him. *Rest and enjoy being still before Him.*

Let's Glorify: Jesus, thank you for desiring a relationship with me. I want to slow down and give you first place in my life every day. I need to consciously slow down and meet you in the quietness of the morning or the still of the night. I am so thrilled to be on this **journey of love** with you. I trust you and know that you have my world and the world at large under your sovereign control. Someday, all nations upon this earth will exalt you. Come Lord Jesus, come. In your saving name, I pray. Amen.

Let's Go! Do you enjoy meeting with Jesus in the early morning or later in the evening? Is there anything stopping you from meeting with your Savior? Discuss with your best friend.

August 17

Victorious Action: Having Holy Spirit Hope, Peace and Joy!

"I pray that God, the source of hope, will fill you completely with joy and peace because you trust in Him. Then you will overflow with confident hope through the power of the Holy Spirit" (Rom. 15:13 NLT).

Let's Talk: Apostle Paul is saying in this Scripture that he prays, "As you experience your faith, may you bubble over with hope by the power of the Holy Spirit!" Don't you want that kind of hope? The kind that overflows and oozes out of you because you are so infused with the Holy Spirit? I sure do! God gives you an abundance of joy and peace in the heart of your faith as you fully trust in Him. Then, your confident hope increases because of the Holy Spirit's power living and breathing inside of you!

Let's Glorify: Jesus, I am so grateful you have given me the great comforter and encourager, the Holy Spirit. May I always be aware of His quiet and yet powerful presence, spurring me on in faith. I am grateful for the hope that is stirred within me because of His joy and love. I am so grateful He never leaves me. Holy Spirit, may I have your fullness of grace and joy within me always and pass it onto others. In Jesus' name, I pray. Amen.

Let's Go! What has it meant to you knowing you have the Holy Spirit's joy, peace and hope inside of you? Has He been quiet and gentle within you lately? Or, has He been loud and boisterous? Share with each other.

August 18

Victorious Action: Come Near to God!

"Come near to God and He will come near to you. Wash your hands, you sinners, and purify your hearts, you double-minded" (James 4:8).

Let's Talk: Sometimes you and I can have a divided heart when it comes to being loyal to God. We can have selfish pursuits that only focus on our goals and our wants. Drawing near to God demands you and I come to Him, asking for forgiveness of our double mindedness. Are you looking to the world for satisfaction and wholeness instead of looking to Him? You can love what is good and bad all at the same time! Your mind is double minded because you do not quite trust Him for your contentedness and your self-esteem. You are still trying to fill up the void in your heart with more of the world.

Let's Glorify: Lord, I am here to say I am sorry because I can so easily look to the world and pursue earthly means over resting in you to fill up my soul. God, I want to delight in you. My self-esteem and confidence are in you alone. I am here to please you and not other people. May my life characterize the trust and love I have for you. In Jesus' name, I pray. Amen.

Let's Go! Are you acting with a double-mindedness? Pray together and ask God to fill you up better than the world.

August 19

Victorious Action: Knowing God Gives Rest!

"Unless the Lord builds a house, the work of the builders is wasted. Unless the Lord protects a city, guarding it with sentries will do no good. It is useless for you to work so hard from early morning until late at night, anxiously working for food to eat; for God gives rest to His loved ones" (Ps. 127:1-2 NLT).

Let's Talk: This Psalm was written by King Solomon. He knew a lot about building as he oversaw the construction of the Lord's Temple. He asked for the Lord's almighty power and empowering blessing to be upon him and the workers. It is the same for you and me. We need the Lord's hand upon every area of our lives. At the end of the day, you need blessed rest. This comes directly from the Father's loving heart to His beloved. He enjoys giving you sweet, blessed relief as you slumber. God is the great dream maker!

Let's Glorify: Father God, thank you for that great night of rest. You knew how exhausted I was! Lord, I do not want to build my life without you. You are my rock and my strong foundation. I need your wisdom and guidance every day. Help me to work in moderation and live my life in moderation. Let me excel though in seeking you out, in prayer and meditation. Let be a great worshipper for who YOU ARE in my life. Thank you for all the wonderful ways you bless me. You are awesome! I am so grateful to be your daughter. In your almighty name, I pray. Amen.

Let's Go! Are you intentionally building your life on God's ways as your firm foundation? Are you helping your children, grandchildren, nieces and nephews do the same?

August 20

Victorious Action: Being Grateful for Your Parents!

"Children are a gift from the Lord; they are a reward from Him. Children born to a young man are like arrows in a warrior's hands. How joyful is the man whose quiver is full of them! He will not be put to shame when he confronts his accusers at the city gates" (Ps. 127: 3-5 NLT).

Let's Talk: Children are God's best gift (vs. 3, MSG). As a daughter, you are such a gift to your mother! God knew this when He placed you in your particular family. Your family may have not been perfect (mine either!) but God's plans are perfect. He knew exactly who your parents would be and what your family dynamics would be like. Your home life, good or not so great has shaped you into the lovely woman you are today. Be grateful for your parents because they helped make you into the wonderful woman you are today!

Let's Glorify: Lord God, thank you for my parents. They were not perfect but neither am I. I have not been the perfect parent, but I choose to rely on you and your love for me and my family. I choose to forgive my past and live richly and fully today in your great love. I pray my mom and daughters will live an abundant life, relying solely on you. Be glorified today in our lives. In Jesus' name, I pray. Amen.

Let's Go! If possible, plan a fun outing today with your mom or daughters. Recall some silly memories of your childhood over lunch or dinner and record each other's voices telling the stories.

August 21

Victorious Action: Skipping Through Open Doors of Opportunity!

"These are the words of Him who is holy and true, who holds the key of David. What He opens no one can shut, and what He shuts no one can open. I know your deeds. See, I have placed before you an open door that no one can shut" (Rev. 3:7-8).

Let's Talk: In this scripture the Lord is speaking directly to the church of Philadelphia. God said to them, "I see what you've done. Now see what I've done" (vs. 8) God opens and closes doors for you. **Figuratively, doors relate to opportunity. Doors open and shut** in an answer to your prayers. God is the door master and He knows what is best for you. If He gives you an opportunity by opening a door no one will be able to take that blessing away. You will need to act and apply the blessing to your life by walking or maybe even skipping through that divine door!

Let's Glorify: Lord, I do not want to miss the opportunity when you open a door of blessing for me. Let me be prayer ready, attentive and watching for your gracious hand working on my behalf! Let me move in faith and courage when I sense your guiding hand upon my life. God, lock the doors of a non-opportunity I am not to go through. Thank you Jesus for being my door into salvation and the bridge access to God, the Father. In your glorious name, I pray. Amen.

Let's Go! Is the Lord opening up any **divine doors of opportunity** for you? Are you hesitating counting the cost before you walk through it? Pray about this with your trusted friend, mom or daughter.

August 22

Victorious Action: Knowing You were Made for Such a Time as This!

"Maybe you were made queen for just such a time as this" (Est. 4:14 MSG).

Let's Talk: Esther, in the Old Testament was a Jew. She was brought into the King's palace to one of his concubines. King Xerxes was very pleased with Esther and made her his queen. Haman the King's right hand man hated the Jewish people. He persuaded the King to annihilate the entire Jewish race. Queen Esther knowing the fate that faced her people approached the King even though he had not called upon her. She knew approaching the King unbidden could cause her to be killed. King Xerxes extended his golden scepter to her. Esther was able to tell the King what was really going on and thereby saved the Jewish people from annihilation. There's an opportune time to do things, a right time for everything on the earth. There is a huge need to discern when that opportune time is. Looking at your history with Jesus is vitally important to see where He is leading you and what He has brought you to.

Let's Glorify: Lord, you extend your golden scepter to me; it's called grace! Thank you for your loving mercy and grace. Jesus, **help me to discern when it is time to make a decision** and then act upon what you are moving me towards. Help me to know when I am to wait as well. In Jesus' name, I pray. Amen.

Let's Go! Have you ever been in a situation where you just knew God made you for such a time as this? Describe what happened to each other.

August 23

Victorious Action: Knowing God is Always Thinking about You!

"How precious to me are your thoughts, God! How vast is the sum of them" (Ps. 139:17).

Let's Talk: "How precious it is, Lord, to realize that you are thinking about me constantly! I can't even count how many times a day your thoughts turn toward me. And when I waken in the morning, you are still thinking of me" (Ps. 139:17-18 TLB). His thoughts are rare and beautiful! And yet, God is relentlessly thinking about you. He sees what makes you cry. He knows your heart and sees the love you have for your family and friends. He even hears the frustrations you murmur under your breath! God, the creator of heaven and earth cherishes YOU beyond measure!

Let's Glorify: Jehovah Ahavah (God is love), thank you for your priceless thoughts about me. I am so pleased you think about me constantly. I am so grateful **you love me relentlessly.** I can stand tall and confident in your love. Thank you for your constant care and watchful eye over me and my family. In your Son's name, I pray. Amen.

Let's Go! When do you really need to know that Jehovah Ahavah is constantly thinking about you? Discuss with each other.

August 24

Victorious Action: Check Your Pride at the Door!

"But knowledge puffs up while love builds up" (1 Cor. 8:3).

Let's Talk: Pride goes before a fall! Knowledge makes you and me proud, while love is the other centered, helping verb! It is love that helps someone grow and develop mentally and spiritually. Love edifies. When you love God and seek His way, you open your life up to the Holy Spirit for true wisdom and guidance. The Message bible shares: ". . .but sometimes our humble hearts can help us more than our proud minds. We never really know enough until we recognize that God alone knows it all" (1 Cor. 8:3 MSG). Eve in the Garden of Eden wanted to be like God because she knew He was all knowing. She placed her desire of wanting knowledge (pride) over her love relationship with God. Eve was deceived into thinking knowledge was the better thing over having love and caring about what God wanted. Consequently, her lack of obedience shattered what she and Adam enjoyed. They were cast out of the Garden of Eden.

Let's Glorify: Jesus, thank you that you alone know it all. You know me better than I know myself. Please forgive me when I get proud in my own abilities or act stubbornly because I feel my way is right and the only way. I want to be other centered and build other's up in your love. Today I choose to have humble obedience before you because I know you have something great to teach me. I do not want to miss out on your divine jewels of love! In your holy name, I pray. Amen.

Let's Go! Do you have any areas in your life where you are feeling "puffed up?" What should you do about these feelings? Share with each other honestly and confess these thoughts to God.

August 25

Victorious Action: Knowing I am Held Up by God!

"So do not fear, for I am with you; do not be dismayed, for I am your God. I will strengthen you and help you; I will uphold you with my righteous right hand" (Isa. 41:10).

Let's Talk: Jesus is such a comforter when you are grieving, filled with anxiety or great discouragement. Jesus personally knew great sadness and grief. When His friend Lazarus died and his sister Mary was weeping, Jesus saw her sorrow. "He was deeply moved in spirit and troubled" (John 11:33). Even in the hardest of your heartaches, God and Jesus will strengthen you and help you with their loving presence. Your help may come from a friend who comforts you with the same comfort they have received in their time of trouble. The Lord may show you special scriptures to cling to. He promises to uphold you with His righteous right hand. God keeps His promises so you can fully count on Him!

Let's Glorify: Jesus, thank you for helping me in the dark moments of my life. Grief feels like a long dark tunnel. I am grateful because when I am in the darkness, you are there. You bring me your healing light of love and compassion through the promises in your Word. Thank you for my family and friends who listen to my feelings of sadness and even anger during this time. I am so grateful you understand me and my feelings. I love you. In your name, I pray. Amen.

Let's Go! In your grieving time, great anxiety or discouragement, how has God upheld you with His righteous right hand? Share your feelings with each other.

August 26

Victorious Action: The Bright Morning Star's Light Lives in You!

"I, Jesus, have sent my angel to give you this testimony for the churches. I am the Root and the Offspring of David, and **the bright Morning Star**" (Rev. 22:16, emphasis mine).

Let's Talk: Jesus is the radiant and brilliant Morning Star! As a descendent of David the King, and His Father the Most High God, Jesus has royal blood. You as His descendent have royal and priestly blood in you as well! His light is often used in Scripture as a symbol of the presence of God in the world. Light is especially associated with salvation, purity and the Word all because of Jesus. Share with believers the light filled Good News of Jesus. **Share with not yet believers, too!**

Let's Glorify: Jesus, you are the illuminator of my thoughts and motives. You are the great light that shines through believers. Someday, in heaven you will illuminate the land. "There will be no more night. They will not need the light of a lamp or the light of the sun, for the Lord God will give them light. And they will reign for ever and ever" (Rev. 22:5). How wonderful this is going to be! How I praise you and thank you for your great light illuminating the darkness in our world. In your light filled name, I pray. Amen.

Let's Go! In what area of your life do you need Jesus to illuminate and help you get a clearer view of what is truly going on? Pray together asking Jesus to illuminate your situations.

August 27

Victorious Action: Praising Your Mighty God!

"Then I heard what sounded like a great multitude, like the roar of rushing waters and like loud peals of thunder, shouting: "Hallelujah! For our Lord God Almighty reigns" (Rev. 19:6).

Let's Talk: Praise is the natural response of believers to God for all that He does. We are to praise Him with all that we are at all times and in all places. You can give Him adoration in music, thought, and song and in all areas of your life! God helps believers to praise Him through the Holy Spirit. Hallelujah translates as "praise the Lord!" You can praise the Lord in church, hiking outside in nature, driving to work or in your office. **At all times** you can declare the wonders and righteous deed of the Lord! **He reigns today and for evermore!** This is the best reason to offer up your lips and heart full of praise!

Let's Glorify: Almighty God, you are wonderful to me! When I pause to reflect on what you have done for me by sending your Son, Jesus to die on my behalf, I just have to **praise you with all that I am!** Thank you for your grace, mercy and unconditional love every day. Thank you for the beauty of nature. I thank you for my dear family and where we live. May I praise you every day and forevermore! All praise, honor and glory are yours. In your Son's name, I pray. Amen.

Let's Go! Where is your favorite place to praise and worship God? **Praise Him now together.**

August 28

Victorious Action: Count it All Joy!

"Consider it pure joy, my brothers and sisters, whenever you face trials of many kinds, because you know that the testing of your faith produces perseverance. Let perseverance finish its work so that you may be mature and complete, not lacking anything" (James 1:2-4).

Let's Talk: Testing 1, 2, 3! Your faith will be tested today. There is no doubt about it! There are a lot of great reasons to persevere under your fiery trials. Patience is developed within as you persevere. The patience of Jesus is evidenced in His relationships with His disciples and the people He encountered. He patiently taught them and mentored them. He showed immense perseverance through His sufferings unto the cross. As a follower of Christ you are called to reveal patience in all of your relationships and activities.

Let's Glorify: Jesus, thank you for your example of great patience and perseverance. I have thought of your sacrificial journey to the cross over and over again when I am trying to finish running a race, riding my bike for far too many miles or teach a class at the gym. Lord, you are more than enough! I can walk, run and move in you throughout my life physically, spiritually and mentally. You are building my perseverance muscles making me mature and complete. Thank you for helping me! In your great name, I pray. Amen.

Let's Go! Is the testing of your faith creating patience and perseverance in your life? Why or why not? Remember the **F.A.I.T.H.** acronym! You have **Favored Assurance in the Holy Of Holies** as **you persevere in Jesus!**

August 29

Victorious Action: Receiving God's Blessedness from His Actions!

"Blessed (enjoying enviable happiness, spiritually prosperous—with life-joy and satisfaction in God's favor and salvation, regardless of their outward conditions) are the **makers and maintainers of peace**, for they shall be called the sons (and daughters) of God" (Matt. 5:9 AMP, emphasis mine).

Let's Talk: In this Beatitude, we are called to turn from evil and do good; seek peace and pursue it" (Ps. 34:14). As you witness to your family, in your patience and love you are being a lovely peacemaker! In your diplomatic efforts, you have the opportunity to reconcile quarreling family members. The word "shalom" or peace in the Old Testament is defined as comprehensive wholeness and well-being. When you pursue this kind of peace you are promoting the welfare of others. God desires wholeness and peace of mind for you and your family.

Let's Glorify: God, I want my family to be at peace. This scripture says when I am a maker and maintainer of peace then I will be blessed and called your child. Lord, please give me the desire to be a pursuer of your peace and goodness today. In Jesus' name, I pray. Amen.

Let's Go! Who is the peacemaker in your family? Discuss with your mom, daughter or special friend.

August 30

Victorious Action: Being Pure in Heart!

"Blessed are the pure in heart, for they will see God" (Matt. 5:8).

Let's Talk: The pure in heart have a wholehearted devotion, loyalty and focus on Jesus and surrendering their dreams and desires for His perfect will. As a person that is pure in heart, you will know what's on God's heart because you have a singular focus and devotion to do His will! Having a sold out heart for God is not easy, but it is doable! It does begin with a wholehearted devotion and wanting please Him above pleasing the world. As you do, you will witness and shine Jesus' light by your attitude and demeanor.

Let's Glorify: Lord, I want to be that gal your eyes see "when your eyes range throughout the earth to strengthen those whose hearts are fully committed to you" (2 Chron. 16:9). I want to do what you re calling me to do and embrace the privilege it is to do your work. I pray to serve with a great attitude out of my love for you and people. May it be so, all to your glory! In Jesus' name, I pray. Amen.

Let's Go! What does it mean to you to be **pure in heart before the Lord?** Look up some scriptures that define pure in heart and wholehearted devotion.

August 31

Victorious Action: Receiving His Crown of Beauty and Joy!

... ."and provide for those who grieve in Zion—to bestow on them a crown of beauty instead of ashes, the oil of joy instead of mourning and a garment of praise instead of a spirit of despair" (Isaiah 61:3).

Let's Talk: Joy is a quality or attitude of delight and happiness, which is truly found in the work of God as Father, Son and Holy Spirit. Joy is found in being in the presence of Jesus, totally loved and accepted. As you praise and worship Him with all that you are for all that He has done for you, joy wells up inside. Gratitude flows freely. Think about going to a wedding. Being in Jesus' sweet presence is like the joy and celebration you experience there. Revelations 17:9 likens the day to Jesus coming back for His faithful ones at a wedding. . . ."and give Him glory! For the wedding of the Lamb has come, and His bride has made herself ready." Linger in His presence. As you do so, **He turns your ashes into beauty and anoints you with His oil of joy!**

Let's Glorify: Jesus, thank you for crowning me with beauty and grace instead of depression and discouragement. Thank you for my new clothes of praise instead of wearing an attitude of despair! I am excited for you to come back for your followers, your Bride! And yet, Lord I am praying for the pre-Christians who do not have a personal relationship with you, *yet*. Let me be a light that shines brightly your love and joy so others will be drawn to you. In your precious love and joy, I pray. Amen.

Let's Go! Describe the last wedding you went to. Was it a happy and joyful celebration? What made the wedding joyful? (I am assuming it was joyful!)

September

"I am not a perfect mother and I will never be. You are not a perfect daughter and you will never be. But put us together and we will be the best mother and daughter we would ever be."
~ Zoraida Pesante

September 1

Victorious Action: Be a Salty Witness!

"You are the salt of the earth. But what good is salt if it has lost its flavor? Can you make it salty again? It will be thrown out and trampled underfoot as worthless" (Matt. 5:13 NLT).

Let's Talk: There are baking salts, cooking salts and finishing salts. There are sea salts and rock salts, and salts that have been seasoned or smoked. And, of course, there is the much respected Kosher salt. Salt is a preservative. It helps to flavor foods otherwise it is bland and boring. Salt enhances the other flavors in food. Salt is still an important ingredient today and in Biblical times. Jesus' teaching here reflects the importance of salt as a preservative and seasoning. God wants your witness to last, or be preserved every day until He comes back for His beloved. "Salt is good for seasoning. **But if it loses its flavor, how do you make it salty again**? You must **have the qualities** of salt among yourselves and **live in peace** with each other" (Mark 9:50 NLT). What are the qualities of salt? Long lasting, flavor enhancer and persistent taste. You can be all of these things to those you are around as you maintain your salty witness!

Let's Glorify: Jesus, thank you that you will help me to maintain my saltiness as I spend quiet time with you. Lord, I want to be found witnessing to others with a salt filled and peaceable attitude. May I think before I talk and season my words with grace and love, all to your glory. In your wonderful name, I pray. Amen.

Let's Go! Do you have a favorite kind of salt you prefer to cook with? **Share with each other some of your favorite savory recipes. Have a night of cooking together.**

September 2

Victorious Action: Giving Clemency!

"Blessed are the merciful, for they will be shown mercy" (Matt. 5:7).

Let's Talk: When you give mercy in service to others, forgiving their sins, looking past their grievances and giving compassion and understanding, you are giving *clemency.* You are blessed, Jesus is saying here because you are giving forgiveness. God gave me some thoughts about mercy and forgiveness one morning when I was in my garden. The clematis growing on the back fence was absolutely beautiful and full of white fragrant blossoms. What I did not notice at first, the clematis had grown so much it was wrapping its vines around a rose bush growing below it. If I didn't trim the plant, it would strangle the rose bush and cause it to die. It is the same with our hearts! When you do not forgive and give *clemency,* unforgiveness vines wrap around your heart, creating a foothold for the enemy to do damage to your heart, your soul, health and relationships! **Forgiveness is totally worth the effort you put into it.**

Let's Glorify: Jesus, thank you for your teachings. You understand my heart and my tendencies. Lord, I want to be a great forgiver and freely give *clemency.* I understand as I forgive others, I am also forgiven. Savior, thank you for being my example of what true forgiveness looks and acts like. Thank you for forgiving all of my sins. I am eternally blessed. In your precious name, I pray. Amen.

Let's Go! Do you have any clematis vines of unforgiveness **encircling your heart? Will you choose to forgive today?**

September 3

Victorious Action: Knowing He Will Never Depart from You!

"The one who sent me is with me; He has not left me alone, for I always do what pleases Him" (John 8:29).

Let's Talk: Jesus while He lived on earth was a picture of His faithful Father. He lived as faithfully as God His Father is faithful. "I can do nothing on my own. I judge as God tells me. Therefore, my judgment is just, because I carry out the will of the one who sent me, not my own will" (John 5:30). "Righteousness will be his belt and faithfulness the sash around his waist" (Isa. 11:5). God never left Jesus to figure out His life and He will not leave you, either! What are you doing today that pleases the Lord?

Let's Glorify: God, thank you for your faithful love to me. You have promised to never leave me nor forsake me. You are righteous, just and fair. Your unfailing love and faithfulness came through Jesus Christ to me and I am the happy recipient! I know I can persevere and get through the long, hard days as I rely on your love for me. I am so appreciative of this fact! In your amazing love, I pray. Amen.

Let's Go! How has Jesus been faithful to you? Write a prayer of thanksgiving for all the ways He has proven Himself faithful to you!

September 4

Victorious Action: Shining Jesus, the Light of the World!

"You are the light of the world—like a city on a hilltop that cannot be hidden. No one lights a lamp and then puts it under a basket. Instead, a lamp is placed on a stand, where it gives light to everyone in the house. In the same way, let your good deeds shine out for all to see, so that everyone will praise your heavenly Father" (Matt. 5:14-16 NLT).

Let's Talk: You are either **a bright light or a dim bulb** of a witness to your family! They see you the most and hear you speak the most! What are the words, or the sayings your husband, children, your siblings remember you saying over and over again? What does your home life say about your relationship with Jesus, the Light of the world? What actions do you believe you will be remembered for? Your light filled witness will not be hidden in your home because the Holy Spirit lives within.

Let's Glorify: Heavenly Father, I want to shine brightly always so all the praise will come back to you. God, I am not perfect and I want to be able to say I am sorry or I was wrong to my dear family. I do not want to get so stuck in my ways of doing things, that I cannot learn something new from you or my family. Help me to take constructive criticism in stride, knowing you discipline those you love. May all glory, praise and honor shine on you today. In your holy name, I pray. Amen.

Let's Go! What are some of your daughter's or mother's favorite sayings? Talk about it and make a list!

September 5

Victorious Action: Worship in Spirit and in Truth!

"But the time is coming—indeed it's here now—when true worshipers will worship the Father in spirit and in truth. The Father is looking for those who will worship Him that way" (John 4:23 NLT).

Let's Talk: You and I are to worship God the Father in spirit and truth. This means we worship Him through the leading of the Holy Spirit's help, God who is spirit and truth. We worship the truth about Him that we find in the Word. Jesus, the only and unique Son of God, who is identical with God, has made God known, telling us all about Him. This endless knowing and understanding of God came through Jesus, the Messiah. He is a one-of-a-kind God-Expression, who exists at the very heart of the Father" (John 4:24 MSG, paraphrased). When we do not worship in spirit and truth, we are simply practicing religion and not a relationship. Matt. 5:18 says, **"These people honor me with their lips, but their hearts are far from me."** "No one has ever seen God. But the unique One, who is Himself God, is near to the Father's heart. He has revealed God to us" (John 1:8 NLT).

Let's Glorify: God, understanding the uniqueness of the Trinity can be confusing at times! Open the eyes of my heart so I may understand and know the Trinity, which are God, Jesus and the Holy Spirit. You are three separate persons and yet you are one. I want my worship and prayers to be pleasing to you with a heart that is in synch with your heart of truth. In your holy Son's name, I pray. Amen.

Let's Go! Write this scripture in your own words. "These people honor me with their lips, but their hearts are far from me" (Matt. John 1:8 NLT). What does this scripture have to do with **worshipping the Father in spirit and in truth?**

September 6

Victorious Action: Basing Your Self-Respect on God's Opinion!

"She is clothed with strength and dignity, and she laughs without fear of the future" (Prov. 31:25 NLT).

Let's Talk: Are you confident about the future? This Proverbs 31 woman is! She is a strong person, and people respect her. She has laughter and rejoices in the Lord and the work He has given her to do. She is positive and wears a smile as her best apparel! She deals with others fairly. Her self-respect is based on her relationship with God and in God. When I felt secure, I said, "I will never be shaken" (Ps. 30: 6). She rests securely in the Lord. This woman does not compare herself to someone else. She knows she is uniquely designed by God for His purposes. She rests in their love relationship and His opinion of her.

Let's Glorify: Lord, I want to be a strong woman, confident in your love for me. I want to embrace and rejoice in the work and life you have given to me. Let me the kind of Proverbs 31 woman who deals with people fairly and with kindness. God, help me not to compare my life with another's. You have given each of us a unique calling. Let me hold onto you and **I will never be shaken.** In your powerful name, I pray. Amen.

Let's Go! Are you feeling shaky about your future? Will you rest securely in the Lord, knowing He has you in the palm of His hand? Pray together asking Jesus to calm your nerves and give you His blessed reassurance today.

September 7

Victorious Action: Speaking Kindness and Wise Words!

"When she speaks, her words are wise, and she gives instructions with kindness" (Prov. 31:26 NLT).

Let's Talk: Have you ever heard this expression? "No matter what your message is, you are wrong if you did not say it with kindness." It is true! If your words are spoken in arrogance or with great anger, your loved one cannot hear what you are saying, because all they can hear is your tone and emotion. The Proverbs 31 Woman verse 26 is a great example to emulate. **Not only does she speak with wisdom, but she also speaks kindly.** Maybe taking a deep breath and pause are in order *before you speak what is exactly on your mind!* Maybe *a quick prayer asking the Holy Spirit* to give you pleasing and wise words to speak is a good idea. Listening more than you speak with a lot of kind eye contact shares with your family member how valuable they are to you. Sensible, thoughtful advice is the law of grace on your tongue.

Let's Glorify: Jesus, I want to give wise words of love and encouragement. I know loving kindness comes from you. I receive this when I am in your holy presence, so I pray to make time for these precious moments with you daily. Let be build up my family and not be a woman who is known to tear them down. Let the law of grace be on my tongue and in my thoughts. May I live my life as a Proverbs 31 Woman all to your praise! In your name, I pray. Amen.

Let's Go! When is it hard for you to speak a kind word to your family member? Next time in the heat of a battle, **prepare yourself beforehand**. Know if you will need to take a **deep breath and pause** before speaking and **say a quick prayer asking the Holy Spirit** to give you pleasing and wise words to speak.

September 8

Victorious Action: Being Faithful, Loyal and Committed to Your Family!

"Her children stand and bless her. Her husband praises her: "There are many virtuous and capable women in the world, but you surpass them all" (Prov. 31:28-29 NLT).

Let's Talk: Faithfulness, loyalty and commitment with our family relationships are important to God. These virtues are witnessed in your marriage and family providing dutiful provision and care. These virtues are evidenced in your loving attitudes and trustworthy speech and conduct. When we get off track and are overwhelmed with life's demands and never ending schedules, we can seek out God and His help and loving care. "**Act with love and justice**, and always depend on Him" (Hosea 12:6 NLT, emphasis mine). The word translated "love" is the Hebrew word **"hesed"** which expresses the loyalty and faithfulness that should characterize the life of God's people. As you give your family "hesed" kind of love, you are blessed by your family!

Let's Glorify: Lord, please help me today to be the kind of wife and mother or daughter that serves generously, faithfully and gives "hesed" love. Jesus, when my schedule gets too busy, I need to pause and be restored to you. "Lead me beside quiet waters and refresh my soul" (Ps. 23:3). Let me take a deep breath in you, filling me up with your love and patience. May I love and serve all to your glory and honor. In Jesus' name, I pray. Amen.

Let's Go! Are you having any commitment issues in serving your family faithfully? Where do you need to ask for help? Pray for each other.

September 9

Victorious Action: Having Reverence for the Lord!

"Charm is deceptive, and beauty does not last; but a woman who fears the Lord will be greatly praised" (Prov. 31:30 NLT).

Let's Talk: It is true, beauty can fade away with time and can be only skin deep! But, have you noticed a beautiful woman who just glows because she has lived a life spent with Jesus? She radiates His holiness! "The woman to be admired and praised is the woman who lives in the Fear-of-God" (Prov. 31:30 MSG). It is **reverence for who God is** and **what He has done** in your life that creates a holy awareness about what you will or will not do in your life. The Word says about Jesus, "There was nothing beautiful or majestic about His appearance, nothing to attract us to Him" (Isa. 53:2 NLT). Looks can be misleading and as people we can boast in our looks or think we are better than we truly are. God sees your inner reality and looks into your heart, your thoughts and emotions. This really creates a reverenced awe of the One who created you!

Let's Glorify: Lord, even Jesus the scriptures share, didn't have anything about His appearance that would draw us to Him. I believe your Spirit living inside of Him drew people to His side and penetrated their thoughts. God, I can't be in Jesus' presence and not be changed! Help me to remember looks are not as important as having a relationship with Jesus. This is the utmost importance! I want to live and believe it is living a godly life now versus having worldly opinions about my external appearance is what truly matters. In Jesus' holy name, I pray. Amen.

Let's Go! Have you ever tried living up to the world's standards of appearance and clothes? Share a funny story about this with each other!

September 10

Victorious Action: Set Apart as Holy to the Lord!

"You have been set apart as holy to the Lord your God, and He has chosen you from all the nations of the earth to be His own special treasure" (Deut. 14:2 NLT).

Let's Talk: When you encounter the Living God, you will be changed, set apart and made holy. In the eyes of the world, you are *just different*. You find yourself no longer watching *those* movies, or gossiping. God Himself has chosen you to be His special jewel! He has put His Spirit into you to guide, correct and make you righteous. You are called to obey Him and keep His covenant. You are His special possession and He loves you more than you will ever know this side of heaven!

Let's Glorify: Lord, I am no more defined by the world, than Jesus is defined by the world (John 17:16 MSG, paraphrased). Lord, I desire to be different from the world's views and ways. God, I want to obey you and hear your voice speaking to my heart. Change me as you see fit for I am trusting you and your holy ways. Thank you that I am your special treasure! Jesus, help me to obey you out of a heart that absolutely is in love with you! In your precious name, I pray. Amen.

Let's Go! How are you different from the world and its ways? **Discuss with your mom, daughter or friend.**

September 11

Victorious Action: Bring Joy to His Heart!

. . ."so that you may live a life worthy of the Lord and please Him in every way: bearing fruit in every good work, growing in the knowledge of God" (Col. 1:10 NIV).

Let's Talk: How do you live a life worthy and pleasing to the Lord? By walking in Him daily, talking to Him and then praising Him for answered prayer. Leading other's to His heart of love, to His way of doing life. Living in Him proves you belong to Him alone. You produce fruit, because you are listening intently to Him as you go about your daily life. Paul and Timothy were praying for the holy and faithful people in Colosse. "We are asking God that you may see things, as it were, **from His point of view** by being **given spiritual insight and understanding**. We also pray that your outward lives may bring credit to your master's name, and that you may **bring joy to His heart** by bearing genuine Christian fruit, and that your knowledge of God may grow yet deeper" (Col. 1:8-10 PHILLIPS, emphasis mine).

Let's Glorify: Lord God, you are holy and majestic. I thank you for the good fruit you produce in my life as I live, move and breathe in you. Thank you for the good works you have given me to do. I want to bring joy to your heart. Jesus, teach me more about you so my love may grow deeper in you. May it be all to your glory. Amen.

Let's Go! How do you bring joy to God, the Father's heart in your daily walk? **Discuss over coffee or tea.**

September 12

Victorious Action: Believe in Jesus and Be Saved!

"For God so loved the world that He gave His one and only Son, that whoever believes in Him shall not perish but have eternal life" (John 3:16).

Let's Talk: Jesus came to save you and all the lost in our world, not pass sentence on it. Any person **who believes in Him is not judged at all.** It is the one who will not believe who is **already condemned**, because she **will not believe Jesus is God's only Son** and that He exists. "This is the judgment—that light has entered the world and men have preferred darkness to light because their deeds are evil. Anybody who does wrong hates the light and keeps away from it, for fear her deeds may be exposed. But anybody who is living by the truth will come to the light to make it plain that all she has done has been done through God" (John 3:16-19 PHILLIPS). Anyone can have a whole and lasting eternal life in God's One of a kind, Son Jesus!

Let's Glorify: Lord Jesus, I pray whoever reads this devotional today has a relationship with you. If they do not, I pray they would read **John 3:16** with fresh eyes and an open heart. **Their eternity (where their soul will live after they die) is at stake.** Jesus, a relationship with you is too important just to glide over. In your holy name, I pray. Amen.

Dear reader, if **you have not received Jesus** as your **personal Savior** you can right now. If someone you know hasn't either, you can lead them through this simple **ABC prayer.** Dear Jesus, **A- I accept that you are God's only Son. B- I believe you died on the cross for my sins. C-I confess that I have lived my life totally for myself and my ways. I ask you to forgive me right now. I choose to follow you the rest of my days as best as I can. Thank you, Lord Jesus! In your name, I pray. Amen.**

If you prayed this prayer let someone know. I suggest you start going to a church that believes in teaching from the bible and learn more about following Jesus. Buy a bible and write your name with your new birthday in it! Congratulations! I look forward to meeting you in heaven some day!

Let's Go! When did you receive Jesus as your Savior? How has your life changed? Pray for the people you know to accept Jesus as their Savior.

September 13

Victorious Action: Share Each Other's Burdens!

"Share each other's burdens, and in this way obey the law of Christ" (Gal. 6:2 NLT).

Let's Talk: We are called to help and share each other's troubles. Keep your critical comments to yourself when someone's life isn't going so well. For who knows? You may need forgiveness and help one day, too! How can you help carry the load of someone else's burden? The answer is prayer and more prayer! Also, ask how you can help them practically. What are their needs? Is it cleaning their house, running errands or watching their children? The law of Christ teaches to love our neighbors as you love yourself (Matt. 22:39).

Let's Glorify: God, in today's fast paced world, I do not stop to notice the needs around me. Lord, I want to do better and give caring compassionate help. Let me see with the eyes of your heart the people you place into my path today, sharing their troubles with Christ's love. Thank you for letting me be your hands, feet, arms and toes to someone today. In Jesus' caring name, I pray. Amen.

Let's Go! Do you need to slow down so you can notice the needs of other's? Who is it God has placed in your life right now, that you can help carry their burdens?

September 14

Victorious Action: Take Delight in the Lord!

"Take delight in the Lord, and He will give you your heart's desires. Commit everything you do to the Lord. Trust Him, and He will help you" (Ps. 37:4-5, NLT).

Let's Talk: Taking delight in the Lord is seeking what He wants. Notice everything He does for you. "He has dressed me with the clothing of salvation and draped me in a royal robe of righteousness" (Isa. 61:10 NLT, paraphrased) Delight and give joyful thought of how wonderful He is to you. Matt. 6:33 has a similar message as Ps. 37:4-5. "But seek first His kingdom and His righteousness, and all these things will be given to you as well." It reminds you to set your priorities correctly, aligning with God's purposes. His purpose is that you and I would **have love as our highest goal** in all areas of our lives. God always gives us His best and your heart desires as He sees fit! He gives more than you could ask or imagine. So, commit your family, your work, your ministries and friendships all to Him! Trust Him and He will help you today!

Let's Glorify: God, I love you! You are my great Lord, loving, kind and near to my heart. You long to give me the desires of my heart but you ask me to delight in you first. Lord, I surrender my plans and commit all that I am to all that you are. In your majestic name, I praise and delight in. Amen.

Let's Go! How will you delight and give praise to God today? Will you choose to trust Him with your heart's desires?

September 15

Victorious Action: Love!

"Let love be your highest goal" (1 Cor. 14:1 NLT).

Let's Talk: Love is having true affection for God and man, growing out of God's love for and in us (1 Cor. 13:13 AMP). So, let love be your motivation to please God and help people. "If I had the gift of prophecy, and if I understood all of God's secret plans and possessed all knowledge, and if I had such faith that I could move mountains, but didn't love others, I would be nothing" (1 Cor. 13:2 NLT). Think about all the women's events you have attended or even worked on. If the event is fancy and decorated to a T, but the women serving do not have love or give grace, it would be meaningless! Let love compel your motives, set your sails and attitudes! If your love of Christ is not your guiding force, you have gained nothing!

Let's Glorify: Lord Jesus, I want to love with your love, serve with love and lead with love. Help me Savior to let love be my highest goal. You are my excellent example of sacrificial love, putting other's needs above my own. I pray to let the overflow of my heart and words to be a life filled with you first. May it be all to your glory. Amen.

Let's Go! Where is Jesus calling you to express His love today? Pray together and ask for some unexpected places and people to share His love to!

September 16

Victorious Action: Turn Your Anger Over to Jesus!

"Stop being angry! Turn from your rage! Do not lose your temper—it only leads to harm" (Ps. 37:8 NLT).

Let's Talk: Stop being mad, furious, irritated and ticked off! I am not saying you can never be angry and neither is God. What the scriptures are saying is *do not let your anger be your first and foremost emotion.* You see, when anger and rage are your default emotion, you are always reacting from a position of defense. Losing your temper overshadows your love for Christ and others. What is behind your wall of anger? Could it be fear? Anger is usually a secondary emotion. Fear could be hiding behind your angst and rage. Do not let your bad temper be your downfall and harm. Look at your past issues and ask God and others for help. Repent and confess asking God to show you your triggers.

Let's Glorify: Lord Jesus, I confess my angry tendencies to you right now. Lord, I do not want anger to drive me and my reactions. God, I do not want my anger or temper tantrums to tarnish my witness for you. **Soften me up with your oil of love and forgiveness.** Your blood poured out forgives all my sins, my grievances and heals my hurts. In Jesus' name, I pray. Amen.

Let's Go! What makes you really mad? Talk about it and your feelings out loud with your mom daughter or friend. Then, pray, releasing it to Jesus' and His transformational heart healing ways!

September 17

Victorious Action: Keeping a Revival in Your Heart!

"Then you will call on me and come and pray to me, and I will listen to you. You will seek me and find me when you **seek me with all your heart**" (Jer. 29:12-13, emphasis mine).

Let's Talk: Do you need renewal in your life, your home, job or ministry? Then I suggest putting into practice Jer. 29:12-13 on your knees or in a posture of total heart submission! **Call on Him. Pray fervently** and continuously. **God promises to listen** to you! **Seek Him** with all of your heart and with all of your might. Confess any sins and **pray for a new stirring within you. God answers those kinds of genuine prayers.** When you turn to Him and you are broken, knowing He is your ONLY help and solution, He's going to show up! Thank Him for what He is doing as He answers your prayers and petitions. Leave room for God to move in His sovereign ways. He can do so much more than you might even be dreaming about! "Lord, I have heard of your fame; I stand in awe of your deeds, Lord. Repeat them in our day, in our time make them known; in wrath remember mercy" (Hab. 3:2).

Let's Glorify: Lord, I have heard of your fame; I stand in awe of your deeds. God, there is no God like you! I am so grateful you are in control of my life and my family's lives. Lord, would you **create in us a revival,** a yearning after seeking your face every day so we can be effective as followers of Jesus Christ? Lord, I pray for families that desire a closer, more intimate walk with you. God through the Holy Spirit's power, remind us to confess our sins daily so we can be renewed and effective in your

Kingdom's work here on earth. May our lives be all to your glory. In Jesus' name, I pray. Amen.

Let's Go! Do you have any areas in your life that need renewal, or a fresh start? Pray and ask God to begin a revival in your heart.

September 18

Victorious Action: Believing God is Bigger than Your Giants!

"So they began to spread lies among the Israelites about the land they had explored. They said, "The land we explored is one that devours those who live there. All the people we saw there are very tall" (Num. 13:32 GW).

Let's Talk: Have you ever noticed it is when you are trying to do the Lord's will that you run into opposition? You are moving forward and whack! You run headlong into a giant! Maybe your giant is an injury or an unexpected delay in your plans. Maybe God has something for you to learn as you face your giant. He will strengthen your faith as you rely on Him. Do not let the land (your circumstances) devour and detour you when God has asked you to do His work!

Let's Glorify: Dear Lord, help me to keep my eyes upon you alone. It does not matter the lies that are told about me or to me. I know what you have spoken to my heart and I will stay the course. Help me, Jesus to rely on you no matter how huge the giants appear. Grow my faith in you. You are bigger and greater than any giant or opposition I will face. In your almighty name, I pray. Amen.

Let's Go! Do you have any giants lurking in your mind? What stops you from going all the way; completing what He has called you to do? Talk about it!

September 19

Victorious Action: Knowing You Are His!

"But we have this treasure in jars of clay to show that this all-surpassing power is from God and not from us" (2 Cor. 4:7).

Let's Talk: Clay was a common material used in making clay pots in biblical times. **You are a like a fragile clay vessel** and yet you carry around in you **the Excellency of the power of God**. You carry His precious Message in you, in the unadorned clay pots of your ordinary life! Paul was saying, while he was going through the worst, you're getting in on the best Jesus has to offer! God does cares about what He creates. "He who formed you, Israel: **"Do not fear, for I have redeemed you; I have summoned you by name; you are mine"** (Isa. 43:1, emphasis mine). Aren't you so glad you are His? He knows you need His help every day. Ask Him and give Him all the glory. The powerful life of Jesus is available to you!

Let's Glorify: Lord, thank you for creating me. You know my strengths and my weaknesses. I come to you today broken and need of your holy repair. Thank you that you never turn me away for I am yours. I do not have to have fear, for you have redeemed me and make me whole! How comforting these facts are to me! How amazing it is that your great power is displayed through the fragile clay jar that I am. May I use my body to glorify you and take the light of the Good News to others. In Jesus' name, I pray. Amen.

Let's Go! Where are have you seen your mom, daughter or great friend shine His Good News to others? Share with each other your insights.

September 20

Victorious Action: Love Mercy and Walk Humbly with Your God!

"O people, the Lord has told you what is good, and this is what He requires of you: to do what is right, to love mercy, and to walk humbly with your God" (Mic. 6:8 NLT).

Let's Talk: You and I are to deal fairly and honestly with others and do them good. We can be pleasing to God in our thoughts, our actions and daily communion with Him, conforming our will unto God's will. To love mercy (which means kindness and understanding) delights in giving it away to others. As we do so, we render our good service unto God. You are called to stay in fellowship with Him by keeping up your communion with God, studying to approve yourselves to Him in integrity. All of this must be done humbly as you walk, dance, skip and even hop scotch in Him! All of your thoughts must be conformed to the will of God because you "have the mind of Christ" (1 Cor. 2:16).

Let's Glorify: God, I want to do what is right before you and others. Help me to be a loving person who shows compassion and understanding. Help me to remember I am nothing without you and to remain humble before you. Every good thing comes from you! I want to serve and praise you alone, today. In your Son's name, I pray. Amen.

Let's Go! What does this scripture mean to you? Discuss with each other how you can implement loving mercy and walking humbly before the Lord.

September 21

Victorious Action: Knowing Your Kinsmen Redeemer!

"So Boaz took Ruth and she became his wife. When he made love to her, the Lord enabled her to conceive, and she gave birth to a son. The women said to Naomi: "Praise be to the Lord, who this day has not left you without a guardian-redeemer. May he become famous throughout Israel! He will renew your life and sustain you in your old age. For your daughter-in-law, who loves you and who is better to you than seven sons, has given him birth" (Ruth 4:13-17).

Let's Talk: What a turnaround in Ruth's and Naomi's lives! Ruth was Naomi's daughter in law. Naomi's husband and her two sons Mahlon and Killion had died leaving the two women to fend for themselves. Ruth would not leave her Mother in law, saying "Don't urge me to leave you or to turn back from you. Where you go I will go, and where you stay I will stay. Your people will be my people and your God my God" (Ruth 1:16). So, they headed to Moab where Naomi knew she had some relatives. God was behind the scenes divinely arranging their new lives. Ruth found herself working in Boaz's field (Ruth 2:3). He was her Kinsmen Redeemer and told his reapers to leave behind stalks of grain for Ruth to pick up. They soon married and both women were blessed when Ruth gave birth to a son named Obed. The grown up Obed became the grandfather to King David! It is wonderful how *a baby can renew your life and sustains you* in your golden years!

Let's Glorify: Lord Jesus, thank you for being my Kinsmen Redeemer. Thank you for divinely guiding my life, especially when it appears I am at a dead end. Thank you for helping me and reconciling me in my troubles and pain. Please help me to remain faithful to you and my family and extended family. Increase my faith as I walk closely to you in all that I do. How I love and appreciate your faithfulness to me! In your precious name, I pray. Amen.

Let's Go! Ruth was blessed by God because of her faithfulness to her mother in law and to Himself. How has God sustained you as you have remained faithful to your family and Him?

September 22

Victorious Action: Listening to His Authority!

"Never has a man spoken the way this man speaks" (Jn. 7:46 NASB).

Let's Talk: No mere man can speak the way Jesus does because He holds ALL authority and power given to Him by God His Father! He has divine insight into God's heart. Jesus is part of the Trinity: God, Son and the Holy Spirit. His words are greater than the words of any other person who has ever spoken! I think this is why the Holy Spirit's voice (when I am truly listening) is so distinct and His message is true. The Holy Spirit speaks the exact message He hears from God and delivers it to you.

Let's Glorify: Jesus, you are all knowing. Your words (the Bible) "are alive and active. Sharper than any double-edged sword, it penetrates even to dividing soul and spirit, joints and marrow; it judges the thoughts and attitudes of the heart" (Heb. 4:12). Lord, cleanse me right now as you know my thoughts and attitudes. May my meditations be pleasing to you. In Jesus' name, I pray. Amen.

Let's Go! Are Jesus' words (spoken to you through the Word or the Holy Spirit) asking you to change today? Have a conversation about what you believe He is asking you to change.

September 23

Victorious Action: Responding in Faith Even When It's Excruciating!

"Then Pharaoh gave this order to all his people: "Throw every newborn Hebrew boy into the Nile River. But you may let the girls live" (Ex. 1:22 NLT).

Let's Talk: Jochebed, Moses' mother in the Old Testament, had to move in great faith. Her story profoundly stood the test of time because she was obedient to God. He gave her guidance when she was seeking what she should do with baby Moses. She had a mother's fierce kind of love for her baby. The edict had gone out to the Hebrew homes. Pharaoh gave the grim order to kill all the Hebrew baby boys. How wrenching it must have been for Jochebed to put Moses carefully into the papyrus basket, which she had lovingly coated in tar and pitch so it would float on the Nile River. I'm sure as a mother, Jochebed agonized over her decisions. As a mom, it's not usually a question if we love our children, but **can we really surrender them into God's care and protection?** By God's loving hand and will, Moses was found by Pharaoh's daughter. He was raised in the King's palace and yet nursed by his own mother!

Let's Glorify: Lord God, you are amazing! As I trust you wholeheartedly, you work my life out better than I could have ever expected! Lord, you can be trusted with our children and our families. Sometimes, it is hard to imagine but you love them more than I do! Thank you for the sacrifice of your own Son Jesus. What a beautiful and costly reminder of how much you love each one of us! I choose to believe you and move in faith even when it is hard to do so. In your almighty name, I pray. Amen.

September

Let's Go! Who do you need to surrender over to God's perfect care and protection? **Discuss your feelings in letting someone go, into God's loving hands.**

September 24

Victorious Action: Faith Comes from Hearing the Good News!

"So faith comes from hearing, that is, hearing the Good News about Christ" (Rom. 10:17 NLT).

Let's Talk: Before you can trust, you have to be open to listening. If life is going well for you, you may never stop to question nor listen to the Good News about Jesus. But, you must stop, listen and ponder the life of our Lord and Savior, Jesus. Unless Christ's Word is preached, there's nothing to listen to. If you never stopped to listen, you would not experience asking Jesus to be the Lord of your life!

Let's Glorify: Jesus, thank you for the very best news! Your Good News, the gospel needs to be told to all people. Lord, help me to be aware of people around me that have not placed their faith in you yet. Give me the words Holy Spirit, to share the Good News in a clear and concise manner. Thank you Lord for letting me partner with you saving souls. In your saving name, I pray. Amen.

Let's Go! Who are you praying for today to hear and receive the Good News of Jesus Christ? Will you be the one who brings this great news? Pray about it with your mom, daughter or special friend.

September 25

Victorious Action: Believing He Will Provide for You!

"For God is the one who provides seed for the farmer and then bread to eat. In the same way, He will provide and increase your resources and then produce a great harvest of generosity in you" (2 Cor. 9:10 NLT).

Let's Talk: God, the provider is more than extravagant to you! He supplies your necessities so you in turn can be generous to someone else. He expands what you give, "which grows into full-formed lives, robust in God, wealthy in every way, so that you can be generous in every way, producing with us great praise to God" (2 Cor. 9:11 MSG). God is not just interested in providing your needs. He wants you to see the needs of those around you and give graciously. He knows as you do so, you will take the focus off yourself, looking for ways to help and serve. As you do so, God is honored and you are blessed! "The seed will grow well, the vine will yield its fruit, the ground will produce its crops, and the heavens will drop their dew. I will give all these things as an inheritance to the remnant of this people" (Zech. 8:12).

Let's Glorify: God, thank you for being so generous and gracious to me. You give and give! Let my heart attitude be one of gratitude, giving out of a heart that is full of your love and generosity. Jesus, help me to notice the needs of someone else today. Please put the desire in my heart to put these prayers into action. May I honor and glorify you. In your holy name, I pray. Amen.

Let's Go! Pray and ask the Lord to show you how you can meet someone else's needs today. Share with each other what you did or are planning to do.

September 26

Victorious Action: Knowing the Hope of Your Savior!

"You faithfully answer our prayers with awesome deeds, O God our savior. You are the hope of everyone on earth, even those who sail on distant seas" (Ps. 65:5 NLT).

Let's Talk: He is the hope of all believers! You do not have to turn anywhere else for help or encouragement! Seek Him first! When you have a right standing and cleansed heart before Him, He will send His loving encouragement through other believers! He faithfully answers your prayers. Are you willing to wait, while He does? So many times, we get in the way of God's plans because we just cannot stand being in the wait any longer. Is your patience drained? Ask Jesus to pour His love and grace into you while you wait. Ask Him what He'd like to teach you as you wait patiently. No matter how far you travel away from home, even on those distant seas, God is there for you!

Let's Glorify: Thank you Jesus for how faithful you are to me! You answer my prayers even better than I can ask or imagine. I give you my life. I want to be where you are. Lord, thank you for always keeping your arms and heart wide open to me. You never stop loving me or caring about me. Help me to wait patiently. I know you are up to something good and profitable for my life. How I thank you! In Jesus name, I pray. Amen.

Let's Go! Do you like surprises? Are you willing to wait? Discuss a time you had to wait for a special surprise.

September 27

Victorious Action: Knowing God Sees Me!

Thereafter, Hagar used another name to refer to the Lord, who had spoken to her. She said, "You are the God who sees me." She also said, "Have I truly seen the One who sees me?" So that well was named Beer-lahai-roi (which means "well of the Living One who sees me") (Gen. 16:13-14 NLT).

Let's Talk: God is a God of seeing everything. Nothing slips past His view of you and your world. "Beer-lahai-roi" is His divine name which is not shown elsewhere in the Bible. It expresses the deep significance to Hagar of God's gracious revelation to her. God showed Hagar how much He loved not only her but also her son, Ishmael. Even while she was lost in the wilderness, God had seen her and revealed Himself to her in a huge way.

Let's Glorify: God, thank you that you are my God who sees me! I am not just a number but a person you have divinely made. I praise you for you have given me a purpose and a plan for my life. Jesus, help me to always turn to you, knowing you are with me. I do not have to turn to the world for satisfaction or significance. You have already given me everything I need to walk in you. I do not have to be afraid. Lord, I seek your face today. In your powerful name of Adonai, I pray. Amen,

Let's Go! Are you going through a hard time? Where do you need God to see you today? Share how you have gotten through something similar and pray for each other.

September 28

Victorious Action: Believing Jesus is Alive!

"After Jesus rose from the dead early on Sunday morning, the first person who saw Him was Mary Magdalene, the woman from whom He had cast out seven demons. She went to the disciples, who were grieving and weeping, and told them what had happened. But when she told them that **Jesus was alive** and **she had seen him, they didn't believe her**" (Mark 16:9-11 NLT, emphasis mine).

Let's Talk: Mary Magdalene was a woman who had utter devotion to her Savior and healer. She is mentioned fourteen times in the gospels. Time and time again we see Mary serving and helping Jesus and the disciples. She gave of her own means: her money, food and time to support them. What is striking is in eight of the fourteen passages Mary is named in connection with other women, and her name is at the top of the list, implying that she occupied the place at the front in service given by godly females. Through the years biblically, Mary has gotten a reputation for being a prostitute. According to biblical scholars there is no evidence to confirm this. She is referred to as having "seven demons." Her condition most likely was worse than the rest. The moment Jesus laid eyes on the cringing and deranged woman, He saw in her the caring and supportive woman who would be a great blessing to His own heart and to others. It is no wonder she was the first person to see Jesus after He had resurrected!

Let's Glorify: Jesus, you take the broken parts of me and restore me completely. You have done so many miracles in my life emotionally, spiritually and physically. How can I not want to devote myself to you and your loving kindness? Lord, let me serve you as I serve others with pure motives, all to your glory! When others do not believe you are alive, let me not get discouraged. I will remember what you have healed in my life! Thank you, for being my Jehovah Rophe, my healer. In Jesus' name, I pray. Amen.

Let's Go! What has Jesus healed in your life spiritually, emotionally or physically? Share with your mom, daughter or friend. Give Him all the glory!

September 29

Victorious Action: Be Happy!

"Be happy that your names are written in heaven" (Luke 10:20 GW).

Let's Talk: In Luke 10:1, seventy two disciples had been sent out by Jesus to heal the sick and spread the Good News. They came back rejoicing because they had cast out evil spirits. Jesus responded to them: "Don't be happy that evil spirits obey you. Be happy that your names are written in heaven." Jesus was saying it's not what you do for God but what God does for you! "The one who is victorious will, like them, be dressed in white. **I will never blot out the name of that person from the book of life,** but will **acknowledge that name before my Father and His angels**" (Rev. 3:5, emphasis mine).

Let's Glorify: Jesus, thank you my name is written in the Great Book of Life, never to be erased! Lord, I am praying for my friends and family who have not received you yet. Please knock on their heart and I pray sincerely Jesus they will answer you back. Thank you it is what you do in me that matters. All praise, honor and glory to you, my King Jesus! Amen.

Let's Go! Is your name written in the Great Book of Life? On Judgment day, Jesus will acknowledge all the redeemed names before His Father and the angels!

September 30

Victorious Action: Delight in God Holding Your Hand!

"The Lord makes firm the steps of the one who delights in Him; though he may stumble, he will not fall, for the Lord upholds him with His hand" (Ps. 37:23-24).

Let's Talk: Did you know God also delights in all the details of your life? When you have to face your failures again, He is with you. It will not be the end of you! Jesus shows you the better way to proceed. When you have hesitation because you are not sure of which way to turn, stop and pray. Ask Him. Delight in Him and get excited because He will give you the answers you are seeking! When you have difficulty in your job, at home or in a ministry, pause, breathe and pray. Just like a parent, God has your hand safely clasped in His hand. You will not fall. He will be the encourager to your shaky knees!

Let's Glorify: God, thank you for being my **Yahweh; the God who will be who He is for me.** You are a strong tower and I know you are not going to drop me or let me fall. Thank you even in my failures, you are there holding my hand tightly in yours. I want to make my first response to be prayer and gratitude every time. How I delight in you and your loving and kind ways! In Jesus' name, I pray. Amen.

Let's Go! Do you have shaky knees today? What is it you are worrying about? Pause, breathe and pray.

October

"The mother memories that are closest to my heart are the small gentle ones that I have carried over from the days of my childhood. They are not profound, but they have stayed with me through life, and when I am very old, they will still be near. . . Memories of mother drying my tears, reading aloud, cutting cookies and singing as she did, listening to prayers I said as I knelt with my forehead pressed against her knee, tucking me in bed and turning down the light. They have carried me through the years and given my life such a firm foundation that it does not rock beneath flood or tempest." ~Margaret Sanger

October 1

Victorious Action: Cast a Vision of Encouragement and Salvation into Others!

"I remember your genuine faith, for you share the faith that first filled your grandmother Lois and your mother, Eunice. And I know that same faith continues strong in you" (2 Tim. 1:5 NLT).

Let's Talk: Timothy the apprentice of Paul had the benefit of growing up in a home that loved and served the Lord. "He had been taught the Holy Scriptures from childhood, and they have given you the wisdom to receive the salvation that comes by trusting in Christ Jesus" (2 Tim. 3:15 NLT). From the record of Timothy, you see evidence of the importance placed upon positive Christian guidance and training in the home by his mother and grandmother. What a blessing to have godly parents, grandparents and mentors while you are growing up! How wonderful to have relatives that pointed Timothy toward a relationship with Jesus. Their guidance, wisdom and prayers are precious and priceless!

Let's Glorify: God, thank you for the godly people in my life. Even as a child growing up, you placed godly parents, teachers and friends in my life to point me to you. Thank you for the vision they cast in my life, encouraging me to walk with you and lean on you. Lord, let me pass this spiritual heritage onto my children and their children, bringing glory to your marvelous name. Lord, help me to take the time to pray and love them into a personal relationship with Jesus. In His name, I pray. Amen.

Let's Go! Did you have someone in your life growing up or even today, who has pointed you towards Jesus and His precious love? Write them a card of thanks. (If they are not alive, could you send one of their relative's a note about how their special relative has impacted your life in a profound way?)

October 2

Victorious Action: Free!

"So if the Son sets you free, you will be free indeed" (Jn. 8:36).

Let's Talk: The Son liberates us and we are unquestionably free! Jesus came to set you and I free from the sin that so easily entangles us. He sets you free from addictions, bad habits, bad attitudes and crazy moods! He sets you free from eternal death so you can live forever with Him! He sets you free from worry so you can know His peace. He sets you free from desiring the approval of others because He unconditionally loves you. He sets you free from the law because He came to abolish the law. He is your Freedom Fighter and Liberator!

Let's Glorify: Jesus, thank you for your liberating freedom! I am free to walk, run, dance, sing and be the person you have made me to be from the beginning! Thank you for your healing and transformational power! Lord, help me to share the freedom you have brought to me with others. I want them to experience the exhilaration of what it feels like to be healed and freed in you. How I love you and praise you! In the powerful name of Jesus, I pray. Amen.

Let's Go! Have you experienced Jesus' freedom in your life? If so, describe what this means to you. If not, you might consider asking Him for help.

October 3

Victorious Action: Acknowledging God Before Others!

Jesus tells us, "Whoever acknowledges me before men, I will also acknowledge him before my Father in heaven. But whoever disowns me before men, I will disown him before my Father in heaven" (Matt. 10:32-33).

Let's Talk: How can you acknowledge God before others and not sound like you are beating your faith over their heads? Jesus said He came to seek and save the lost. We are surrounded by lost people. Ask God to raise your awareness of others and to increase your love for them, sharing His love, light and kindness. Seek Him and pray to see the needs of others. Ask Him to help you go the extra mile for others, just as He has done for you!

Let's Glorify: Lord Jesus, give me courage and a divine nudge as to when I am to speak your love and life into others. In the meantime, let my life speak to the fact you are alive, changing me from the inside out. Let those around me daily witness your love and light because Holy Spirit you are guiding and I am whole-heartedly submitting. Let me not get caught up in my own petty pet peeves that I miss giving out your kindness and compassion. In Jesus' loving name, I pray. Amen.

Let's Go! How can you acknowledge God before others and not sound like you are beating your faith over their heads? How have you taught your daughter about Jesus' love? Share with each other.

October 4

Victorious Action: Having an "All-In" Kind of Love!

"Hear, O Israel: The Lord our God, the Lord is one. Love the Lord your God with all your heart and with all your soul and with all your strength" (Dt. 6:4-5).

Let's Talk: How do you love the Lord with an ALL IN kind of love? First of all, it takes time to get silent before Him. Lean in and hear the Holy Spirit's whispering to your heart. I have found I can have nothing more important than Jesus in my life. When I make something more important and spend more energy on it, I am setting myself up for idol worshipping. My strength is gone and I have wasted my first fruits instead of giving my God all my strength, love, soul and energy.

Let's Glorify: Dear Jesus, forgive me on those days when I place life and its pleasures and even troubles in front of you. You are the Giver of life and I desire to give ALL that I am to you. Thank you for your loving grace when I blow it! Let me be passionate for you every day! In the strong name of Jesus, I pray. Amen.

Let's Go! Where is God calling you to have an "ALL-IN" kind of love? In what way can you be more passionate for Him today? Share with each other.

October 5

Victorious Action: Staying Committed to the Lord Even in Your Sorrow!

"Oh no, sir!" she replied. "I haven't been drinking wine or anything stronger. But I am very discouraged, and I was pouring out my heart to the Lord. Don't think I am a wicked woman! For I have been praying out of great anguish and sorrow" (1 Sam.1:15 NLT).

Let's Talk: Hannah was childless. She was fervently praying to God for a child. Eli the Tabernacle priest thought she was drunk on wine. She replied to Eli, "I am very discouraged and I am pouring my heart out to the Lord" (vs.15). Hannah had prayed for a son with all of her heart. God gave her the desire of her heart and she named him Samuel, for she said, "I asked the Lord for him" (1 Sam. 1:19 NLT). After Hannah had weaned Samuel she came back to Eli to dedicate her son to the Lord. She said, "He will belong to the Lord his whole life. And they worshiped the Lord there" (vs. 28). Hannah kept her word to God and dedicated her young son to Him. Notice **they worshipped the Lord together as a family**, giving Samuel a beautiful example to follow. **God blessed her commitment** and Samuel grew into a mighty prophet for Israel.

Let's Glorify: God, I thank you for Hannah's honesty in her prayer. She was in great anguish and yet she knew it was okay to share her true feelings with you. Jesus, I praise you because you are an approachable Savior. You understand my discouragements and my sorrows. Lord, I also know when I pray according to your will, you will give me the desire of my heart, especially when you put that desire there in the first place. **Lord,**

I commit my children and family to you. May we serve you the rest of our lives. Amen.

Let's Go! Have you ever prayed to God out of great anguish and sorrow? What happened? Share with each other.

October 6

Victorious Action: Positively Expecting Jesus' Glorious Return!

"But let me reveal to you a wonderful secret. We will not all die, but we will all be transformed! It will happen in a moment, in the blink of an eye, when the last trumpet is blown. For when the trumpet sounds, those who have died will be raised to live forever. And we who are living will also be transformed" (1 Cor. 15: 51-52).

Let's Talk: With eager hope, I look forward to the day when I will be made new! My physical body is aging and my face is beginning to show it! Make up has been this girl's best friend lately! "For all creation is waiting eagerly for that future day when God will reveal who his children really are" (Rom. 8:19 NLT). God eagerly waits to reveal to you, who you truly are and were meant to be from the beginning of time. You and I will be transformed in a twinkling of an eye when Jesus comes back for His believers. That is fast! What was physical will be made spiritual. In the meantime, you can be made new today, by renewing your mind, your thoughts as you spend time with Creator God and become like Him (Col. 3:10 NLT).

Let's Glorify: Creator God, I am listening for the mighty trumpet sound blasting throughout the earth! How exciting that day is going to be! Jesus, help me to be ready by seeking you in prayer, reading and studying the Word and listening to the Holy Spirit. I am excited to be transformed into a body that will never die (1 Cor. 15:53 NLT). May I live in a positive expectation of your glorious return, remembering there are people who still have not received your Son, Jesus Christ. In His name, I pray. Amen.

Let's Go! What is encouraging to you knowing Jesus will return someday soon? Who are you praying for today to receive Jesus?

October 7

Victorious Action: Having a Peaceful Heart so I Can Have a Healthy Body!

"Then, when our dying bodies have been transformed into bodies that will never die, this Scripture will be fulfilled: "Death is swallowed up in victory. O death, where is your victory? O death, where is your sting?" For sin is the sting that results in death, and the law gives sin its power. But thank God! He gives us victory over sin and death through our Lord Jesus Christ" (1 Cor. 15:54-57 NLT).

Let's Talk: Have you lost a dear one to sickness, an accident, an addiction or even self-infliction? God tells you, "Death is swallowed up in victory" (vs. 54b). There will be a time of rejoicing, because God makes all things new. He swallows up the pain and anguish of death and sin with His Son, Jesus' great and undeniable victory! He will transform our tired and weak bodies. He will make new the bodies of those Jesus filled believers that died of cancer, disease or any other means. The Lord knows **"A peaceful heart leads to a healthy body"** (Prov. 14:30 NLT). He understands your grief and has great compassion on you. He knows this time of mourning will end and He wants you to have a peaceful heart that is full of trust in Him and what He will do when Jesus comes back again for His faithful!

Let's Glorify: Jesus, thank you for your undeniable victory in life and death. You are victorious over the death of the cross once and for all. I am so thankful, because you give me victory over an eternal death of sin and life. I am praying you help me to have a peaceful heart today so I may have a healthy body, mind and heart. May I wait patiently and live each day victoriously in Jesus. May it be all to His glory. Amen.

Let's Go! How does knowing "Death is swallowed up in victory" for Christ's followers give you a peaceful heart? Discuss it with each other.

October 8

Victorious Action: Living Out Your Faith!

"Quite frankly, I don't want to be bothered anymore by these disputes. I have far more important things to do—the serious living of this faith" (Gal. 6: 17 MSG).

Let's Talk: Do you have any petty disputes going on in your relationships? Some arguments are merely over preferences and opinions, wants or desires. Here Paul was talking about being circumcised or not. Many of the Galatian believers thought 'yes,' all men should be circumcised. Paul knew they wanted to boast in themselves for following the law and **appear outwardly righteous.** What really mattered, what really counted "was being a new creation in Christ" (Gal. 6: 15). Paul wanted to be done with these disputes and get on with the important work God had given him to do: sharing the Good News of Jesus Christ!

Let's Glorify: Jesus, thank you for your life! You did not waste your time on petty disturbances or the mini dramas that were going on around you. You kept your focus on your Father's business. I want to stay focused on you and your life. Lord, help me to turn the other cheek, forgive quickly and love freely. Lord, help me to speak the truth in love when it is necessary, pointing my life back to yours. Let me be a peaceable person who loves others deeply. In Jesus' name, I pray. Amen.

Let's Go! In your life are you trying to appear outwardly righteous caring about other's opinions more than Jesus'? Or, are you dealing with any petty disputes in your relationships? Either way, pray and ask God to give you His clear direction and heart in the manner. Biblically, the person who apologizes and is done with the pettiness is more spiritually mature!

October 9

Victorious Action: Being a Part of Jesus' Family!

Then Jesus' mother and brothers came to see Him, but they couldn't get to Him because of the crowd. Someone told Jesus, "Your mother and your brothers are outside, and they want to see you." Jesus replied, **"My mother and my brothers are all those who hear God's word and obey it"** (Luke 8:19 NLT, emphasis mine).

Let's Talk: Jesus was obedient and caring to His family. His mother Mary remembered all the things Jesus did. At the cross, Jesus saw His mother standing there beside the disciple He loved. Jesus said to her, "Dear woman, here is your son." And He said to this disciple (John), "Here is your mother." And from then on this disciple took her into his home (John 19:26-27 NLT). It is probable by then, Joseph, her husband, had passed away and that Jesus had supported her. He knew His mother's cares and grief's. He knew she would need care and compassion after His death, resurrection and ascension to heaven. In Mary's case, you can see God removed her comfort of having her son Jesus. But, He gave her another comfort in John taking care of her. Jesus led by example providing care of His mother in her old age. It is a great honor to be trusted by God to fulfill His divine assignments. John knew this and understood his job. When you truly love Jesus, you will have a happy heart to have the opportunity to willingly obey and give any service for Him and His people.

Let's Glorify: Jesus, thank you for the opportunities you bring in my life to serve you and your people. Help me to recognize the care and comfort you provide me through other wonderful people of the huge family of God! Your kindness and love are so evident! At the same time,

October

the scriptures today share your family members are those who hear your Father's word and obey it. Help me Lord to obey first and foremost today. In Jesus' name, I pray. Amen.

Let's Go! Has God brought someone in your life to bring you comfort, love and peace? Has He made you like family? Share with each other.

October 10

Victorious Action: Seek His Face!

"Look to the Lord and His strength; seek His face always" (1 Chron. 16:11).

Let's Talk: To seek means to hunt for or try to find. Searching continually for His thoughts and wisdom is the answer to all of your life's needs. As you seek the Lord and His strength, you are really yearning to know what He thinks and what is on His heart! Humbly approach Him. Give Him the respect and reverence He deserves. Then, listen whole-heartedly, turning from your sin.

Let's Glorify: Lord Jesus, I want to see you with the eyes of my heart today! Please shower me with your loving encouragement! I look forward to the day when I can look at your face and your eyes. Help me to seek your presence always and to follow hard after you, the Eternal God, who was and is, and is to come! What a day that will be when I get to hug your neck! In Jesus' name, I pray. Amen.

Let's Go! When in your life have you really depended on the Lord and His face? Have you always gone to Jesus for help? Talk about it with the special women in your life.

October 11

Victorious Action: Be Filled with the Holy Spirit!

"Don't be drunk with wine, because that will ruin your life. Instead, be filled with the Holy Spirit" (Eph. 5:18 NLT).

Let's Talk: The Holy Spirit, your guidance counselor and comforter fills you as you yield to Him. He takes up residence and lives in you when you became a believer of Jesus Christ. Did you know the burden of being filled by the Holy Spirit rests upon you? He is always ready to fill you, but will not agree to do so **unless He is in present control over you.** You are filled as you are yielded to Him and God's desires for you. He loves you and approves of you. He wants God's best for you. Can you feel the passion of the Holy Spirit wanting to speak to you and move you closer to God's heart? Do you sense Him telling you to take care of a particular task or problem?

Let's Glorify: Jesus, thank you for sending the Holy Spirit. He is such a gift! He sticks closer than a sister, a friend, a mother, or a daughter because He lives inside me. He shares exactly what is on your heart and speaks love, life and encouragement into my heart. He lets me know when I need to course correct, too! Lord, help me to not grieve the Holy Spirit by not listening to Him or continuing in sin. I want the full measure of His presence every day. In your holy and righteousness name, I pray. Amen.

Let's Go! How has the Holy Spirit nudged you closer to God's heart lately? **If you are not sensing His nudges upon your heart or mind, pray and ask God for help in being sensitive to listen to the Holy Spirit.**

October 12

Victorious Action: Start a Boomerang Effect of Love and Kindness!

"Give, and it will be given to you. A good measure, pressed down, shaken together and running over, will be poured into your lap. For with the measure you use, it will be measured to you" (Luke 6:38).

Let's Talk: Do you give to others? Or are you stingy and reluctant to share what you have, fearing you may not have enough for yourself? The way you give to others is the standard God will measure to give to you. When you give generously and cheerfully, this Scripture says in God's economy, He will bless your kind efforts. In fact, He will send blessings upon you that will spill over! In also the same way, what are your thoughts and attitudes toward others? "Don't judge other people and you will not be judged yourselves. Don't condemn and you will not be condemned. Make allowances for others and people will make allowances for you" (Luke 6:37-38 PHILLIPS).

Let's Glorify: Jesus, I want to be blessed, too! I understand generosity begets generosity. Help me to freely give of my time, energy and resources knowing I am in turn blessing you, my Savior. How it must grieve your heart to see your children being stingy and cruel to each other, when you have just given so much to each of us! Lord, forgive me when I have a critical spirit. I want to make allowances for other's differences and want them to do the same for me. Let me become a better mom, daughter and friend. In your precious love and forgiveness, I pray. Amen.

Let's Go! Is it hard or easy for you to be generous with others? **When you are generous you start a boomerang effect of love and kindness! Others will want to follow your beautiful example!**

October 13

Victorious Action: Having the Fruit of Joy!

"I have told you this so that my joy may be in you and that your joy may be complete" (Jn. 15:11).

Let's Talk: What has Jesus told you? He wants you to be joyful as He is joyful. **He wants His full and complete joy in you!** His relationship with God, His Father makes Him happy. This is His command: **"Love one another the way I loved you.** This is the very best way to love. Put your life on the line for your friends. You are my friends when you do the things I command you. I'm no longer calling you servants because servants don't understand what their master is thinking and planning. No, I've named you friends because I've let you in on everything I've heard from the Father" (John15: 11-15 MSG). What joy and privilege you have as a follower of Jesus!

Let's Glorify: Jesus, what a huge blessing it is that you call me your friend! I am praying to put my friends and family's needs before my own, praying earnestly for them. This is how you love me, laying down your life. I am so grateful you are my joyful and happy Savior. You want me to have joy as you reside in me. Thank you Lord, even though I have suffering times in my life, you are with me, enlarging my capacity for joy! Thank you for the fruit of joy that wells up within me even now! Help me to obey you fully today with a rejoicing heart. In your joyful name, I pray. Amen.

Let's Go! How do you love others the way Jesus loves you? Discuss with one another. As you do so, I pray you will experience His abundant, overflowing, immense joy!

October 14

Victorious Action: Open the Eyes of My Heart!

"I pray that the eyes of your heart may be enlightened in order that you may know the hope to which He has called you, the riches of His glorious inheritance in His holy people, and His incomparably great power for us who believe. That power is the same as the mighty strength He exerted when He raised Christ from the dead and seated Him at His right hand in the heavenly realms" (Eph. 1:18-20).

Let's Talk: There is no one like God! Do you understand this great fact? Ask God to open the eyes of your heart so you can know the hope you have in Him and eternal life! He does incomparable and unrivaled acts, healings and declarations of great love! You have an amazing victory in Him! You have the same mighty strength in you that God exercised to raise Jesus from the dead! This means, in your really long days of frustration, God will be there for you. When you experience deep heartaches, He is in your midst. At the end of the day, you still have your great hope and victory in Him, because He lives in you! God gave the executive order and His Son Jesus is sitting at His right hand helping you today. Therefore, "I will proclaim the name of the Lord. Oh, praise the greatness of our God" (Deut. 32:3).

Let's Glorify: Jesus, you are my awesome God! Thank you for the never ending hope I have in you. I am so grateful, no matter what happens today, you've got me. Emmanuel, thank you for being with me, giving me strength and victory! I am amazed and grateful I have the power and strength God exercised to raise Jesus from the grave in me through the mighty power of the Holy Spirit. What a privilege it is to be your daughter!

How I praise you and thank you! In Jesus' resurrected and glorious name, I pray. Amen.

Let's Go! Pray and ask God to open the eyes of your heart that you may know His hope of eternal life, the forgiveness of your sins and the great power for us who believe! Journal what He shares with you at the end of the day.

October 15

Victorious Action: Step Out of the Boat!

"Take courage! It is I. Don't be afraid." "Lord, if it's you," Peter replied, "tell me to come to you on the water." "Come," He said. Then Peter got down out of the boat, walked on the water and came toward Jesus. But when he saw the wind, he was afraid and, beginning to sink, cried out, "Lord, save me!" Immediately Jesus reached out His hand and caught him. "You of little faith," He said, "why did you doubt?" And when they climbed into the boat, the wind died down. Then those who were in the boat worshiped Him, saying, "Truly you are the Son of God" (Matt.14:25-32).

Let's Talk: Jesus will ask you to do the seemingly impossible, because He knows the full and true outcome! He will ask you to step out of the boat of your circumstances and move in faith! He knows He can do anything because He has conquered death! He asks you to come alive in Him and His mighty resurrection power and strength! He has some fantastic goals for you to accomplish in this life. But, you will not do it, unless you move in a positive frame of mind, making a decision to wholeheartedly count on Him! **Have you realized yet, that you have the VICTORY in Him, because He loves you?** Have you truly realized **HE IS the SON of GOD**? You do not have to be afraid! You do not have to doubt. It is Jesus who is calling you to be victorious! Step out of the boat! **Once you do, victory is yours because He is victorious!**

Let's Glorify: Dear Lord Jesus, you call me to have a joy filled abundant life. You did not call me to live a small and safe life. Lord, help me to get out of the boat when you call me. Help me to trust you completely,

October

looking into your face and your heart. When the waves of doubt start crashing around me, let me remember that "Nothing is impossible with you!" Please take away my insecurities that make me feel like I am sinking. I want to live for you. May it be all to your glory, honor and praise. Amen.

Let's Go! Are you going to step out of the boat today and move in faith towards Jesus? Discuss a time when you did (or did not) get out of the boat. What happened?

October 16

Victorious Action: Believing He is the Holy One!

"From this time many of His disciples turned back and no longer followed Him. "You do not want to leave too, do you?" Jesus asked the Twelve. Simon Peter answered him, "Lord, to whom shall we go? You have the words of eternal life. We have come to believe and to know that you are the Holy One of God" (Jn. 6:66-68).

Let's Talk: Jesus already knew the disciple's true heart feelings. He asked, "You do not want to leave too, do you" (vs.66). I think this must have really jolted their thoughts. This one question made them come to a conscious decision about who Jesus really is: the Son of God and the holy One of God. Jesus knew when it got really hard to follow Him some of the converts would indeed turn away. Peter replied, answering for the group: "Lord, to whom shall we go? You have the words of eternal life" (vs. 67). Jesus asks the same of you today. Will you stay with Him, seeking Him the rest of your days? Will you stay committed to follow Him in a love relationship? Or, will you stop believing He IS the Son of God? Jesus is the Word, the Way, the Truth and your life! He holds the keys to eternity and is cheering for you to stay strong and committed to your faith walk in Him. Ask for endurance in this race called life! He is more than enough to help you!

Let's Glorify: Lord Jesus, thank you that you already know the questions in my heart and on my lips. You know already what I am needing and what I am desiring. Help me to believe and share you, the holy One of God to those you put in my path. You are the Word and Way to eternal life. I choose to follow you all the way home. In your holy name, I pray and ask these things. Amen.

Let's Go! Do you have the question, **"You do not want to leave too, do you?"** settled in your mind? If not, pray and ask your special daughter, mom, sister or friend to pray for you so you know without a shadow of doubt that you will stay committed till you go home to be with Jesus in heaven.

October 17

Victorious Action: Knowing He Sustains You!

"The Son radiates God's own glory and expresses the very character of God, and He sustains everything by the mighty power of His command. When He had cleansed us from our sins, He sat down in the place of honor at the right hand of the majestic God in heaven" (Heb. 1:3-4 NLT).

Let's Talk: The word glory also means majesty. Majesty is Jesus' sovereign power, authority or dignity. Jesus is the brilliance and evidence of God, His Father. Jesus' love shines from the delight the Father has in Him and He in His Father. God expresses His character and personality through Jesus made flesh as He walked and ministered throughout the earth. Jesus holds you and me together. He keeps the earth spinning on its axis and the stars in their place. **He holds everything together!** He is not ruffled by the seemingly chaos of the world. He has cleansed you from your sins and is sitting in perfect control next to God the Father. You can breathe a sigh of relief as you reflect on His majestic loving presence in your life!

Let's Glorify: Lord Jesus, **thank you** for your sovereign power, grace and mercy. You do express the very nature and personality of God. You are the bridge, the Way of life so I can know God. You sustain me and my life by your perfect peace and order even when my world seems out of control. Thank you for satisfying my soul and forgiving my sins. How I love and praise you in the splendor of your holiness! In Jesus' perfect name, I pray. Amen.

Let's Go! Today, how is Jesus sustaining you? Is He satisfying your soul, nourishing your spirit or filling your heart? Have a conversation around this topic.

October 18

Victorious Action: Desiring Times of His Presence and Refreshment!

"Repent, then, and turn to God, so that your sins may be wiped out, that times of refreshing may come from the Lord" (Acts 3: 19).

Let's Talk: Do you want to be set free? Repent then and turn your heart toward Jesus. Do you need a time of refreshing? **Refreshment occurs when your weary, dry soul collides with His presence.** Sin blocks you from being in God's company. Have you ever thought of this? "Son of man, say to the Israelites, 'This is what you are saying: "Our offenses and sins weigh us down, and we are wasting away because of them. How then can we live?"' Say to them, 'As surely as I live, declares the Sovereign Lord, I take no pleasure in the death of the wicked, but rather that they **turn from their ways and live"** (Ez. 33:10-11, emphasis mine).

Let's Glorify: Lord, forgive me of my sins. I repent of_____. I turn it over to you right now. Give me a new path to walk on, one that is pleasing to you. I want times of cool refreshment, soothing my thirsty soul. Thank you the moment I ask for forgiveness my slate is wiped clean! How I praise you for that! In Jesus' precious sacrifice, I pray. Amen.

Let's Go! Do you need a time of sweet and cooling refreshment? Turn to Jesus and spend some time in His sweet presence. Talk about your experiences when your weary, dry soul collided with His presence.

October 19

Victorious Action: Cultivating the Fruit of His Imperishable Love!

"Now that you have purified yourselves by obeying the truth so that you have sincere love for each other, **love one another deeply,** from the heart. For you have been born again, not of perishable seed, but of imperishable, through the living and enduring word of God" (1 Pet. 1:22-23).

Let's Talk: Love is the answer. It has always been the answer in *getting along with others and yourself!* Love does not keep score of the sins of others. Love takes pleasure in the flowering of truth! Love is long suffering and yet sets healthy boundaries. Love always sees the best in others. Love never looks back but keeps going to the end. Love defers to others wishes and yet can also make a healthy compromise. Love forgives and does not harbor resentments. Love persists and never gives up! **His love is divine and gives true life.**

Let's Glorify: Jesus, thank you for your deep and abiding love. You are such a wonderful Savior to me! Your holy love is pure and unending! Your love is unconditional. I can rest in and rely on your love. Let it envelop me, change me, forgive me. Your divine love has saved me. Let me take your love today and make a difference in someone else's life! Thank you, Jesus! With a grateful and changed heart, I pray. Amen.

Let's Go! Who do you need to love deeply from your heart today? Pray and ask God to pour His imperishable love into your heart so you can love someone else with His supernatural love!

October 20

Victorious Action: Cultivating the Fruit of Patience!

"Be patient, then, brothers and sisters, until the Lord's coming. See how the farmer waits for the land to yield its valuable crop, patiently waiting for the autumn and spring rains. You too, be patient and stand firm, because the Lord's coming is near. Don't grumble against one another, brothers and sisters or you will be judged. The Judge is standing at the door" (James 5:7-11).

Let's Talk: Patience is defined as steadfastness under dire situations or when ill-treated. Both instances seem dire to me! How can you cultivate patience in your life today? Try making a **PACT** with yourself and Jesus at the beginning of your day! This acronym helps you to focus on Jesus first and not on your circumstances or people that you feel impatience with!

P- Praise Him! Thank Him by using one of His many Names. (Prince of Peace, Emmanuel. . .)

A- Acknowledge Him and His position in your life. He is on the throne and you are not!

C- Confess your sins that you know about and also what He brings to mind. Let go of trying to **control** everything in your life!

T- Trust Jesus for the outcomes in all areas of your life. Treat Him with love, respect and reverence. Treat others with the Golden Rule. This means, treat others the way you'd like to be treated!

"A quick-tempered woman stirs up dissension, but one who is slow to anger calms a quarrel" (Prov. 15:18 NET).

Let's Glorify: Jesus, thank you for your loving patience and kindness. I am so grateful you do not fly off the handle with me when I am anxious and get impatient with others! You are always showing me the better way to deal with life! Thank you, Lord I can count on you to calm me down. All I have to do is ask, breathing in your calmness and presence. May I have serenity, peace and patience in you today. In your forgiving name, I pray. Amen.

Let's Go! Praying for patience does not mean you are automatically going to have a ton of trials today! It does mean however, the Holy Spirit might be getting you prepared spiritually ahead of time! Why do you need an extra dose of patience with some people? Discuss it with each other! Make sure to laugh and forgive!

October 21

Victorious Action: The Secret is Christ Lives in You!

"For God wanted them to know that the riches and glory of Christ are for you Gentiles, too. And this is the secret: Christ lives in you. This gives you assurance of sharing His glory" (Col. 1:27 NLT).

Let's Talk: God's will is fulfilled in Jesus Christ! As a result, you have His strength living inside of you through the Holy Spirit. **You have His love poured out into your heart.** You have victory because Jesus was victorious on the cross! *Christ lives in you!* You get to share His happiness and joy as He transforms you into His image! Christ came for all people. Today, you just need to make the choice and accept His free and gracious gift of love, if you haven't done this yet!

Let's Glorify: God, thank you for your beloved Son Jesus, the one you love and are delighted in! The riches and glory bestowed upon Him are priceless and yet, you get to share in them! Thank you Jesus for your costly and precious obedience. You have paid the ultimate price on the cross on my behalf! How grateful I am! In your loving name, I pray. Amen.

Let's Go! Do you know Christ's secret that He lives in you? Or, have you asked Him to be your Savior? Talk about it with each other.

October 22

Victorious Action: Thanking God for the Special Women in Your Life!

"Every time I think of you, I give thanks to my God" (Phil. 1:3 NLT).

Let's Talk: Mom, daughter, sister, friend, and all the special women in between! As the Holy Spirit brings you to my mind, I smile and sometimes I laugh! You have been such a treasure in my life. You have pointed me toward Jesus. You have encouraged me when I have felt really badly about myself. You have noticed my tears and applauded my successes. You have listened to me as I have felt safe enough to pour out my heart. I have so many wonderful memories spent with you. You are precious to me and even more, loved by God. Always remember your true identity is in Him and His unrelenting love for YOU! You are a Princess, a daughter of the Most High King! Thank you for being so loving and so very special to me! I give thanks for YOU!

Let's Glorify: Lord God, thank you for the special women in my life! They are such a gift to me. Thank you Lord for using them to sharpen me as iron sharpens iron. Thank you for the guidance, mentoring and loving support. Lord, you are the Creator of friends. You call me your friend and teach me how friends should love unconditionally while speaking the truth kindly. Lord Jesus, let me be a friend that loves unconditionally. May my friendships be glorifying to you. In your Son's precious name, I pray. Amen.

Let's Go! How are your friendships lately with the special women in your life? Are you making it a point to spend time together once a week or once a month? Pray for God to open up some time to see your special friend.

October 23

Victorious Action: Devoting Yourself to Prayer!

"Devote yourselves to prayer with an alert mind and a thankful heart" (Col. 4:2 NLT).

Let's Talk: Paul was discussing family life in Colossae. The family in his day extended to the immediate family, aunts, uncles, grandparents, servants and others. In today's economy many grown children have moved back home. So, prayer is always needed in all family situations especially when your empty nest is not so empty! We are to always maintain the habit of prayer throughout the many moments of the day and night. We are called to be prepared, paying attention to what is going on in our families and the world. And, we are called to be thankful as we pray in all situations and challenges.

Let's Glorify: Lord God, you created families. Thank you for my family! Help me to be the kind of mom and wife that prays all the time. Help me to be grateful for the children and husband you have divinely blessed me with. Help me to pour into their lives love, encouragement and wisdom because I am seeking you first. Please help me to remember to pray for my own siblings and parents, too. Lord, encourage me to love, never give up on my family and offer words of kindness. As I serve my family, let me be mindful I am serving and loving you all to your glory. In Jesus' name, I pray. Amen.

Let's Go! What reminds you to pray for your family all day long? **If you are having a hard time remembering, what can you use as a tool to remember? (For example: set an alarm, write a post it note, or ask the Holy Spirit to remind you)**

October 24

Victorious Action: Pray for Each Other!

"Confess your sins to each other and pray for each other so that you may be healed. The earnest prayer of a righteous person has great power and produces wonderful results" (James 5:16 NLT).

Let's Talk: Jesus promised that praying in agreement amongst believers would unleash power for answered prayer (Mt. 18:19-20). He promises to be in our midst when two or more pray! What a wonderful comfort and something to remember! We are called to <u>pray in the name of the Lord as we call upon the power of God to move in our situation. As we do so, we are submitting to Him, because we are in union with Him.</u> **When you pray, pray in faith, never having doubt that God can do anything for you. For effective praying to occur when you pray with others, pray united as repentant sinners.** As we become real with each other, letting down our guards and confessing our sins, we can lovingly and compassionately pray for each other.

Let's Glorify: Lord, thank you for your model of prayer. I am so grateful I can come to you day or night and offer up my prayers of sadness, loneliness, grief, joy, hope and discouragement. Thank you for hearing my heart and my deepest desires. Lord, help me to pray for others, confessing my sins so there is no hindrance in my prayer life. I want my prayers to be effective and produce your wonderful results. In Jesus' powerful name, I pray. Amen.

Let's Go! Have you ever thought of Jesus being in your very midst, standing next to you as you pray with someone else? Discuss it with each other and then pray for God's will be done today in each other's lives.

October 25

Victorious Action: Praying with Praise!

"Now all glory to God, who is able to keep you from falling away and will bring you with great joy into His glorious presence without a single fault" (Jude 1:24 NLT).

Let's Talk: This scripture is considered a Doxology. A Doxology means to "praise, honor and give glory." It is used both in song and prayer. All glory to God! He will bring you into His presence without any blame or any fault! Can you imagine the day Jesus comes back for you, His faithful follower? You do not have to worry or fret. Your sins are forgiven! Jesus paid the price once and for all. You and I will have unspeakable joy and great ecstatic delight living in His presence in a beautiful paradise! Jude 1:24 says, "You will keep me from slipping or falling away from you." I know this because God has you in the palm of His hand. It is His great love that holds you tight!

Let's Glorify: Lord God, just thinking about this scripture gets me excited to go home with Jesus to heaven! Lord, I know I do not deserve heaven and yet you made a way through your only Son's life poured out as a sin offering on my behalf. Even if I were the only person alive, Jesus, you would have paid that tremendous price, *for me.* What joy! What great anticipation I have thinking about living in heaven with you! You will bring me home into your glorious presence with great joy and without a single fault! What a triumphant blessing you are to me! How I love you! In Jesus' name, I pray. Amen.

Let's Go! What are your thoughts about going home to live in heaven with Jesus? What do you think you will like the most about heaven? Discuss with each other.

October 26

Victorious Action: Knowing Your Prayers Are a Fragrant Offering to the Lord!

"And when He took the scroll, the four living beings and the twenty-four elders fell down before the Lamb. Each one had a harp, and **they held gold bowls filled with incense, which are the prayers of God's people**" (Rev. 5:8 NLT, emphasis mine).

Let's Talk: Prayers of the saints, God's people are lovingly placed by an angel into gold bowls filled with pleasing, aromatic incense (Rev. 8:3). The Lord smells these prayers intermingled with the smoke of incense of fragrant spices for burning. I envision God smiling; knowing He hears, sees and smells your prayers! Your prayers are a beautiful and special perfume to Him. How many tens of thousands of fragrant prayers have you sent up to God? Isn't it nice to know He regards your prayers as a fragrant offering? He wants you to pray and ask Him for help for yourself and others.

Let's Glorify: Lord Jesus, I bow down before you just as the four living beings and the twenty-four elders do. You are the Lamb of God and I want to worship you. I give you reverence and praise. Thank you, Jesus for hearing my prayers. It is quite amazing to know my prayers are held in gold bowls filled with incense. Thank you for the care you take with each of my prayers. In your holy name, I pray. Amen.

Let's Talk: What do like (or do not like?) about the picture of your prayers mixing with the smoke of incense?

October 27

Victorious Action: Believing God Accepts My Prayers!

"Accept my prayer as incense offered to you and my upraised hands as an evening offering" (Ps. 141:2 NLT).

Let's Talk: God hears all of your prayers. They can be prayers of praise and joy, or prayers of doubt and discouragement. Your prayers are a fragrant offering going up to Him because you are sharing your trust in Him. You are choosing to trust God with your most cherished people: your family, your husband, your sister, mom, son, friends, relatives and coworkers. At the end of the day, thank Him for all that He has brought you through. Raise your hands in praise and utmost gratitude!

Let's Glorify: Almighty God, you are worthy of my praise. May my life and work every day bring you praise, honor and glory. Lord, I want my prayers to be pleasing to you and be a sweet aroma going up. Thank you I can pray about anything and you still accept me. You alone know fully what is in my heart. I sacrifice with the fruit of lips filled with praise, all to you. In Jesus' name, I pray. Amen.

Let's Go! Have you ever held back a prayer or broken feelings from God thinking it would not be okay to pray *that or feel a certain way*? It's okay! Say it with reverent respect but do tell Him. God knows how you feel already and He loves you just the same! **Share with one another any prayers you are having a hard time releasing to God.**

October 28

Victorious Action: Praying for Success!

"So today when I came to the spring, I prayed this prayer: 'O Lord, God of my master, Abraham, please give me success on this mission" (Gen. 24:42 NLT).

Let's Talk: Do you need success today on a particular project or mission? Prayer is to be the first step not an afterthought! Make it a point to make an appointment with God in the cool of the morning. Notice, your anxiety and worry are not from the Lord, but **rather a self-centered approach to dealing with the cares of your life.** When I heard a speaker say this recently, it was a sucker punch to my mid-section! My long standing anxiety is **my way of being in control** and not turning my challenges over to the One who can help me and direct my actions and thoughts.

Let's Glorify: Lord God, help me to come to you early in the morning with my requests. You know I desire success, but even more Jesus; I want to be in communion with you. You can handle all of my worries, concerns and stress over getting a project up and running and then completed. Please give me energy and endurance Holy Spirit. Help me to listen intently to how you are directing me. Let me breathe in your calmness and exhale any apprehension I have. God, I cannot multi task out my stress, but I can focus on you alone in our sweet morning appointment. Lord, I give myself and this day to you. Thank you for loving me just as I am. In Jesus' name, I pray. Amen.

Let's Go! Are you trying to multi task excessively so you do not have to think about your stress, anxiety or worry? Schedule a sweet appointment with the Lord right now, turning your day and that project over to Him. **He can do mission impossible!**

October 29

Victorious Action: Going to Your Bethel!

"We are now going to Bethel, where I will build an altar to the God who answered my prayers when I was in distress. He has been with me wherever I have gone" (Genesis 35:3 NLT).

Let's Talk: Where is your Bethel spot? Where has God spoken to you through the quiet whisper of the Holy Spirit? Do you have a special spot where you go annually to remember and thank God for all the beautiful ways He has answered your prayers? I do. It is beautiful Lake Tahoe in Northern California. Seeing the beautiful lake and the smell of pine trees is such a faithful reminder how He has spoken His promises of joy and desires into my heart. Has He answered you while you were in distress and pain? This is a great time and place to build and remember your Bethel spot. God is so absolutely faithful! He will be with you wherever you go!

Let's Glorify: Dear Holy Spirit, thank you for whispering into my heart the answer to my prayers. Thank you for sharing with me what God wants to do in my life. I am so grateful! I want to remember to always be joyful, praising Jesus' holy name when you speak to me! Lord, I pray I can go to my Bethel place very soon. In Jesus' name, I pray. Amen.

Let's Go! Do you have a Bethel spot? Pray and ask God to make such a spot for you, where He speaks love and encouragement to your heart! If so, share where your Bethel spot resides with your mom, daughter or special friend.

October 30

Victorious Action: Believing Nothing is Too Hard for God!

"On the day the Lord gave the Israelites victory over the Amorites, Joshua prayed to the Lord in front of all the people of Israel. He said, "Let the sun stand still over Gibeon, and the moon over the valley of Aijalon." So the sun stood still and the moon stayed in place until the nation of Israel had defeated its enemies. The sun stayed in the middle of the sky, and it did not set as on a normal day. There has never been a day like this one before or since, when the Lord answered such a prayer. Surely the Lord fought for Israel that day" (Josh. 10:12-14 NLT).

Let's Talk: Joshua prayed to the Lord in front of all the people of Israel. He said, "Let the sun stand still over Gibeon, and the moon over the valley of Aijalon." On the day the Lord gave the Israelites victory over the Amorites and the sun shone brightly so the Israelites could have victory. Surely, God will fight for you, too! I have prayed not to run out of gas. I have prayed for super natural strength running half marathons. I have prayed for strength and patience in teaching children. God has always been right there, helping me with His outstretched arm! He will do the same for you. But, you must ask Him!

Let's Glorify: Lord God, nothing is too hard for you! You make the sun stand still so your purposes can be fulfilled. You ask me to pray and I will receive what I need according to your glorious and divine plan. Thank you for always giving me your loving touch when I have prayed and asked for it. I am so grateful you care about me! In Jesus' name, I pray. Amen.

Let's Go! Where do you need more of His light, strength and vision so you may proceed with His plans? Talk it over and pray for each other.

October 31

Victorious Action: Knowing There is No One Like God!

"And Hezekiah prayed this prayer before the Lord: "O Lord, God of Israel, you are enthroned between the mighty cherubim! You alone are God of all the kingdoms of the earth. You alone created the heavens and the earth" (2 Kings 19:15 NLT).

Let's Talk: God is enthroned in heaven between the mighty cherubim! Cherubim are described throughout the bible. They are supernatural angels. They are also used as decoration in the holy temple and tabernacle. "In the center and around the throne were four living beings, each covered with eyes, front and back. The first of these living beings was like a lion; the second was like an ox; the third had a human face; and the fourth was like an eagle in flight. Each of these living beings had six wings, and their wings were covered all over with eyes, inside and out. Day after day and night after night they keep on saying, **"Holy, holy, holy is the Lord God, the Almighty—the one who always was, who is, and who is still to come"** (Rev. 4:6-8 NLT, emphasis mine).

Let's Glorify: Lord God, you alone are God! You created the heavens, the earth, people and cherubim. What amazement I will have when I get to heaven to see these cherubim and Jesus! Thank you for their description! I am going to be so astonished and fascinated by what you have prepared for me in heaven! How wonderful! Holy, holy, holy are you! I praise you, God! There is no one like you! In the splendor of your holiness, I praise. Amen.

Let's Go! What about heaven are you looking forward to seeing? Discuss with the special women in your life.

November

"A mother's love is something no one can explain,
and is absolutely missed when Mother has passed away."

November 1

Victorious Action: Knowing His Eyes and Ears Are Open to My Prayers!

"O my God, may your eyes be open and your ears attentive to all the prayers made to you in this place" (2 Chron. 6:40 NLT).

Let's Talk: Solomon had completed the temple and now was praying this mighty prayer of dedication and consecration to the Lord Almighty. He is beseeching the Lord to see and hear the prayers that would be spoken in the temple. He prayed for God's spirit to be in this place saying, "Come to your resting place, both you and the covenant chest of your power" (vs. 40 VOICE). Do you have a project, a career, a child, a spouse that you are praying heavily for? Expect God to answer and give you favor! Jesus hears your prayers and holds them near and dear to His heart. He will answer you in due time. Then you will rejoice in His goodness!

Let's Glorify: God Almighty, thank you that you do hear my prayers and you see all of my needs, hurts and praises. Lord, I surrender _____ to you right now. I will unclench my hands and turn this situation over to you. Please Holy Spirit give me endurance and strength as I continue to lift up this concern to you, knowing you have everything under your control. Thank you, gracious God for caring about me and my loved ones. Lord, do more than I could ask or imagine! In Jesus' powerful name, I pray. Amen.

Let's Go! What prayer concerns are you praying about today for God to see and hear? Share with a few of the special women in your life. Commit to praying for each other.

November 2

Victorious Action: Delight in Honoring God!

"O Lord, please hear my prayer! Listen to the prayers of those of us who delight in honoring you. Please grant me success today by making the king favorable to me. Put it into his heart to be kind to me." In those days I was the king's cup-bearer" (Neh. 1:11).

Let's Talk: Nehemiah needed the King's approval to leave his work as a cupbearer and go rebuild the wall of Jerusalem. He needed his understanding. He had built a rapport with the King and Queen of Persia. Did you know he received the go ahead answer he desired? The queen was none other than Queen Esther! She dramatically helped save her people the Jews from annihilation! She knew about prayer, too!

Let's Glorify: Lord, blessed be your Name! Thank you for hearing my prayers! I do delight in honoring you. Thank you that I can pray and ask for others to be kind to me, because I need their help. Thank you for your generous and gracious hand upon me, granting me success so I can bring glory to your name. In Jesus' name, I pray. Amen.

Let's Go! Is there an area in your life God has been telling you, it's time to act? Is it time to step out in faith and answer His call? Pray and ask Him to open up doors of support and favor for you.

November 3

Victorious Action: Showing Kindness and Mercy!

"There was a believer in Joppa named Tabitha (which in Greek is Dorcas). She was always doing kind things for others and helping the poor" (Acts 9:36 NLT).

Let's Talk: Dorcas lived in Joppa, a town on the Mediterranean coast. She was part of one of the earliest Christian churches. She was considered a disciple and was also a seamstress. Through Bible history she is remembered for her acts of kindness and mercy. She showed her faith by her good works. Dorcas at one point became sick and died. Acts 9:39 shares, "So Peter returned with them; and as soon as he arrived, they took him to the upstairs room. The room was filled with widows who were weeping and showing him the coats and other clothes Dorcas had made for them." Peter got down on his knees and prayed. Dorcas was healed and got up (vs. 41). Dorcas' friends would not give up. They sent for Peter, knowing he was a close disciple of Jesus. They hoped and prayed he could bring her back to life.

Let's Glorify: Dear Jesus, you call me to pray for my loved ones and friends. Nothing is too hard for you! In their sicknesses, their grief, their daily struggles, Lord I want to pray and continue on praying fervently. Lord, if you decide not to deliver them this side of heaven, I will continue to trust you, for your works are good. Thank you for Dorcas' faithful example to do good works with mercy and kindness. Help me to be like her example. In your miraculous name, I pray. Amen.

Let's Go! Who are you praying for today? Are you praying expectantly, believing God can do anything? Pray together.

November 4

Victorious Action: Thirsting After God!

"I lift my hands to you in prayer. I thirst for you as parched land thirsts for rain" (Psalm 143:6 NLT).

Let's Talk: Are you thirsting after God? Are you dry and lifeless without His presence? Are you wondering when your next break is going to happen? Then dear sister, get quiet before Him. Take a pause. Sit at His feet, praying, asking the Holy Spirit to flood your spirit. When all that you are aches and hungers for His sweet presence, Jesus is going to fill your soul with His very presence, love and joy.

Let's Glorify: Dear God, there are times when I am so exhausted, and just plain spent. I need you so much all the time! Quench my weary spirit, filling and flooding me with your precious presence Holy Spirit. Set me on your right path and let me know you are near. Please refresh me and restore me beside your cool waters and green meadows. Thank you for your everlasting care. In Jesus' name, I pray. Amen.

Let's Go! Are you feeling thirsty in a really busy season? **If yes, encourage each other to spend some quiet time with Jesus alone. Ask the Holy Spirit to fill you with His refreshing water.**

November 5

Victorious Action: Have the Attitude of Christ!

"Is there any encouragement from belonging to Christ? Any comfort from His love? Any fellowship together in the Spirit? Are your hearts tender and compassionate? Then make me truly happy by agreeing wholeheartedly with each other, loving one another, and working together with one mind and purpose" (Phil. 2:1-2 NLT).

Let's Talk: Sisters, here is one thing, Jesus is saying, "that would complete His joy—come together as one in mind and spirit and purpose, sharing in the same love" (Phil. 2:2 VOICE). He calls us lovingly to get along with each other. He calls us to move in the same direction, with the same heartbeat and goal.

Let's Glorify: Jesus, I want to make your joy complete by loving and getting along with my sisters in Christ. Lord, increase our fellowship in the Holy Spirit as we work together to bring you glory and share the Good News of your salvation. Savior, make our hearts tender and compassionate for you and each other so we can stand united in our purpose: bringing your salvation to our dying world. Lord, have your way in me today. In Jesus' name, I pray. Amen.

Let's Go! Are you willing as mothers, daughters, friends and as special women to "complete Jesus' joy" by getting along whole-heartedly and loving each other while sharing the common goal of sharing the Good News? Discuss what happens when you do make Jesus truly happy.

November 6

Victorious Action: Making the Most of Every Moment!

"Make the most of every living and breathing moment because these are evil times" (Eph. 5:16 VOICE).

Let's Talk: The Living Bible says in Eph.15-16, "So be careful how you act; these are difficult days. Don't be fools; be wise: make the most of every opportunity you have for doing good." Time is drawing short. Who knows when Jesus will come back for His believers? I believe these Scriptures though. These are indeed difficult days. As followers of Jesus Christ, you and I are called to be a shining light, a beacon on a hill. How can you do this? Show honesty and integrity in your interactions with others. Be kind and refuse to gossip. Share your time and resources with others. Above all else, share the love of Christ. Tell people about how they may receive Jesus as their Lord and Savior.

Let's Glorify: Lord Jesus, life is but a vapor. Help me to make the most of **every living and breathing moment** I have on this earth. Let me make a difference in other's lives because I am listening to what you'd like me to do, all to your glory. Lord, remind me, it's not about my pat on the back, but it is about honoring your sacrifice. Please give me opportunities to open my mouth bravely and share your Great News! All praise, honor and glory to you! In Jesus' name, I pray. Amen.

Let's Go! Do you have a regular volunteer job? Yes or no? If not, are you willing to do at least a short volunteer job to help someone else out? Talk about it. Maybe it is something you can do together.

November 7

Victorious Action: Singing Your Heart Out to the Lord!

"Sing and make music in your heart to the Lord" (Eph. 5:19).

Let's Talk: Sing from your heart into the Lord's heart and praise Him for all He has done in your life! Talk with each other a lot about the Lord, quoting psalms and hymns, singing sacred songs. Singing releases your heart to worship expressing your joy, wonder and praise for how good and faithful the Lord is! Notice as you sing and worship the Lord, your Spirit is being filled and your attitude begins to soar! A downcast heart cannot remain there long, when praises are going up in a beautiful song!

Let's Glorify: Lord God, how I praise you! I love singing about how you deliver me and rescue me from myself and my sinful nature. I am so grateful for your love and promises! Let these precious melodies and scriptures sink deeply into my heart and spirit. I always have something to sing about for you are good all the time! In Jesus' name, I pray. Amen.

Let's Go! What is your favorite praise and worship song? Do you remember your mom, grandma, sister or aunt singing to you as a child?

November 8

Victorious Action: Recognizing Jesus' Authority!

"The Spirit of the Lord is upon me, for He has anointed me to bring Good News to the poor. He has sent me to proclaim that captives will be released, that the blind will see, that the oppressed will be set free" (Luke 4:18).

Let's Talk: Jesus has divine authority because God has exalted Him, His beloved Son. His authority to speak and act on His Father's behalf is found in forgiving your sins, pronouncing judgment and giving eternal life to those who believe in Him. So Jesus said, "When you have lifted up the Son of Man, then you will know that I am He and that I do nothing on my own but speak just what the Father has taught me" (John 8:28). Jesus has authority over nature, sin, sickness, evil and over death! His authority is recognized by others. How about you? He has been anointed to share the Good News to the poor in spirit, (this is all of us!) because He IS the Good News! He releases you, the captive sinner so you can see with clear eyes and a cleansed heart. You are set free! Praise Him!

Let's Glorify: Jesus, how I adore you! I respect your authority over all and any evil forces that might try to set up roadblocks and destruction before me. You are holy and mighty to save. I do not have to fear. You are greater in me then the enemy in the world. Thank you for your life and your sacrifice on the cross. Please forgive me of my sins. I am able to bow down victoriously and righteously before you. How I praise you! In Jesus' name, I pray. Amen.

Let's Go! The Spirit of the Lord is the Holy Spirit. Share with each other how the Holy Spirit has moved or spoken into your life.

November 9

Victorious Action: Knowing Victory Comes from Jesus!

"For the Lord delights in His people; He crowns the humble with victory" (Psalm 149:4 NLT).

Let's Talk: The Lord is pleased with His people! He will beautify and revamp your life with eternal salvation. This means you have submitted your will to Him, believing Jesus is God's Son. He holds all victory in His hand and will keep your salvation sure and safe until He comes back for you! "For the Eternal is listening, and nothing pleases Him more than His people" (vs. 4 VOICE). Jesus loves you today and forevermore. He is happy with YOU! Ask Him for help. He will give you victory in this life and in the one to come!

Let's Glorify: Jesus, thank you for my salvation! I am so happy and grateful I know what will happen to me after I leave this earthly life. I am looking forward to living with you and God, my Father in heaven some day! Thank you for the victory you have for me today! I do not have to be afraid of anything or anyone; this is not of you or your plan. "I can do all things through Christ who strengthens me" (Phil. 4:13). How I praise your Name! Thank you for being my Strong tower. In Jesus' name, I pray. Amen.

Let's Go! Where do you need to have Jesus' powerful victory in your life? Share and pray together.

November 10

Victorious Action: Releasing Your Troubles to Him!

"For you will break the yoke of their slavery and lift the heavy burden from their shoulders. You will break the oppressor's rod, just as you did when you destroyed the army of Midian" (Isa. 9:4 NLT).

Let's Talk: Are you feeling enslaved to something, or someone? Jesus breaks the yoke of slavery! He lifts the ton of bricks from your back! He never intended for you to carry the weight of the world between your shoulders. Let it go, releasing that trouble over to Him right now just as Gideon, the warrior did. Jesus is more than enough to carry you and your heavy problems! Jesus will give you great freedom, but your part is to release it to Him! Let His light and love lift and encourage you right now.

Let's Glorify: Jesus, I thank you for your glorious love and light! Thank you for taking the weight and pressure of my problems off my back. Lord, I release the strain I feel in the area of _____. Thank you for breaking the oppressor's rod and giving me true freedom! Victory is mine because of your reverent submission at the cross. I praise your powerful and victorious name. Amen.

Let's Go! Are you carrying the weight of the world on your shoulders today? Let it go to Jesus! He is more than enough to handle your life. Discuss a time growing up when you worried about something.

November 11

Victorious Action: Knowing Christ and His Mighty Power!

"I want to know Christ and experience the mighty power that raised Him from the dead. I want to suffer with Him, sharing in His death" (Phil. 3:10 NLT).

Let's Talk: Jesus has the power of life and power over life which cannot be destroyed. How? It is by the virtue of having the power of an indestructible life given to Him by God the Father. God raised Him from the dead and will do the same for you (unless you are still living) when it is time to go to heaven! Will you suffer during your time here on earth? Oh, absolutely yes! Is there profit in your pain? Yes. God is forming you into the image of His Son Jesus and developing your character, perseverance, trust and hope in Him. He is creating spiritual maturity within you. You can discover that pain and suffering expands your capability for great joy, too! Because of Jesus' death on the cross, sin has lost its power over you!

Let's Glorify: God, I do not choose to suffer on my own. Lord Jesus, I do pray to grow deeper in my relationship with you. Help me to come to know the power flowing from your mighty resurrection. Help me to be transformed into the likeness of you as I go through my sufferings. Help me to realize that I share in your death as I surrender my will over to yours. In Jesus' name I pray, and ask these things. Amen.

Let's Go! What was one of the most immature things you did growing up as a kid? Share and laugh together! More recently, how is God spiritually maturing you?

November 12

Victorious Action: Cherishing Jesus!

"We know how much God loves us, and we have put our trust in His love. God is love, and all who live in love live in God, and God lives in them" (1 Jn. 4:16 NLT).

Let's Talk: God cherishes you! Do you believe the love He has for you? Trust, believe and rely on His perfect, unconditional, never ending love for you, in you and to you! Love does not contain fear. Fear in a person means love has not been perfected within. Do you realize the Holy Spirit came to live within you the moment you received Jesus as your Savior? Let Him fully develop Jesus' love within you, casting out any doubt, guilt or fear. As you learn to rely on His love, it will dispel any shred of fear!

Let's Glorify: Jesus, thank you for your perfect and unconditional love. How I cherish you! I trust your love. Please forgive me when I doubt the love of your priceless sacrifice. Lord, you have told me and shown me your unrelenting heart of love. I do not have to live in fear of feeling I am not good enough, smart or pretty enough. My worth is mirrored in your eyes and heart of love. I cherish and thank you forever. In your loving name, I pray. Amen.

Let's Go! Do you have any fear, guilt or doubt from your growing up years or even from today? Discuss it with your friend, mom or daughter. Pray together and ask Jesus to help you with any of these feelings you might have.

November 13

Victorious Action: Make My Heart Wise, Lord!

"My child, if your heart is wise, my own heart will rejoice! Everything in me will celebrate when you speak what is right" (Prov. 23:15-16 NLT).

Let's Talk: A person, when transformed and led by the Holy Spirit, will be aware of new spiritual experiences and desires starting to stir within. The Holy Spirit's work of restoring character is beginning or renewing. These miraculous occurrences provide evidence of the grace of God at work in the life of a believer. King Jehoshaphat's heart was devoted and deeply committed to the ways of the Lord. "He removed the pagan shrines and Asherah poles from Judah" (2 Chron. 17:6 NLT). This took courage and yet Jehoshaphat was more interested in pleasing God than man. Oh, to teach this to our children when they are young!

Let's Glorify: God, thank you for your renewing process within my mind and spirit. You are developing my character to reflect Jesus' character and personality. God I am asking you to make my heart wise, true and pure. Let me seek you and your Kingdom purposes over caring what others think of me and my decisions. Let my life shine all to your glory with a devoted focus on you alone. In Jesus' name, I pray. Amen.

Let's Go! What were you taught growing up about pleasing others? Have you taught your children differently than how you were raised? Discuss this together.

November 14

Victorious Action: Let Your Old Self Be Gone!

"My old self has been crucified with Christ. It is no longer I who live, but Christ lives in me. So I live in this earthly body by trusting in the Son of God, who loved me and gave Himself for me" (Gal. 2:20 NLT).

Let's Talk: The Messiah lives in you! Your old self was buried in Christ when He died on the cross. His blood cleanses your old sin life. Your prideful self is gone. Your anger and addictions can be gone as you learn to have complete reliance on Him. You are white as snow, living in obedience and dependence on Jesus to help you. You can completely trust in Him today! The Holy Spirit empowers you to do this.

Let's Glorify: Praise you, Jesus! My old self is gone. I am a new creation in you! Slowly, but surely you have transformed and healed my old hurts. You have shown me many things about myself! The areas in my heart that you bring out to your health-giving light are restored and made new! You are worthy to be praised all day, every day! Thank you for the good work you are continuing to do in me. In Jesus' healing name, I pray. Amen.

Let's Go! Have you allowed your old self to be crucified in Christ? Why or why not? Do you realize **He gave Himself up for you, so you can be set free once and for all**?

November 15

Victorious Action: Forgive Others and You Will Be Forgiven!

"When you forgive this man, I forgive him, too. And when I forgive whatever needs to be forgiven, I do so with Christ's authority for your benefit" (2 Cor. 2:10 NLT).

Let's Talk: In this verse, Paul was sharing with the Corinthians, it was time to forgive. This man in particular, had been remorseful. Paul was encouraging them to show plainly they had forgiven him. When you do not forgive someone who has hurt you, the enemy has a chance to overtake you, grabbing the victory from a messed up relationship. Do not let this happen! Luke 6:7 tells you and me, "Do not judge others, and you will not be judged. Do not condemn others, or it will all come back against you. **Forgive others, and you will be forgiven**" (emphasis mine).

Let's Glorify: Lord, I know there is a time to confront in love and there is a time to comfort. God, give me the wisdom to know when to do these actions. I want to have a forgiving heart; praying more and judging less. I want others to forgive me quickly, too so I am choosing to be kind hearted and give others the benefit of the doubt. Please help me to get along with others, all to your glory! In Jesus' name, I pray. Amen.

Let's Go! What behavior do you have a hard time stopping? Is it judging, condemning or forgiving? Try this anecdote: "Be kind to each other, tenderhearted, forgiving one another, just as God through Christ has forgiven you" (Eph. 4:32).

November 16

Victorious Action: Working with Passionate Enthusiasm, Serving the Lord!

"Work with enthusiasm, as though you were working for the Lord rather than for people. Remember that the Lord will reward each one of us for the good we do" (Eph. 6:7-8 NLT).

Let's Talk: Are you serving whole-heartedly as if the Lord Jesus were sitting at your table? It is a great picture to keep in the fore front of your mind. When you face opposition remember the suffering Jesus went through. You are staying devoted to Him as you do your work. Do not grow weary and give up! The Lord will bless you and reward you as you keep serving and praying in faith. Your witness while you work will blaze His love all around you and others!

Let's Glorify: Jesus, I want to serve you with passion out of a heart that is in love with you! How could I ever repay you for all that you have done for me and my family? I know I cannot, but I will try in my words, deeds and actions. Let me know the depth of your love. Thank you for laying down your life for me. May I bring you glory today and make you smile. In Jesus' name, I pray. Amen.

Let's Go! Are you working and serving your family or in a job with passion and enthusiasm as if Jesus Himself was sitting at your table? Discuss it. What are some of your funniest memories sitting at your kitchen table growing up?

November 17

Victorious Action: Asking to Be Sent!

Then I heard the voice of the Lord saying, "Whom shall I send? And who will go for us?" And I said, "Here am I. Send me" (Isa. 6:8).

Let's Talk: I had the opportunity to go to Uganda on a mission trip last spring. Our pastor held a special ceremony for the young men at the orphanage. He asked them, "Who is going to step up and be a godly leader to the younger boys? Who is going to live whole-heartedly for Jesus?" A beautiful young woman jumped up out of her chair and was ready to go! She heard the call on her life from the Lord! We all laughed. I patted her on the back and she laughed heartily, too. The pastor said, "Thank you, but this is just for the young men tonight. You will have a chance tomorrow night." I loved her passion and the fact that she had heard the call of the Holy Spirit to her heart and stood up without any hesitation! Isaiah the prophet responded in the same way when the Lord asked, "Whom shall I send? And who will go for us?" (Vs. 8c) He didn't stop to count the cost to himself.

Let's Glorify: Jesus, I want to respond to the Holy Spirit's call immediately when He prompts me. Let me be ready, willing and always listening for His gentle whisper. Let me chase after you, ready to say, "Here am I. Send me!" (Vs. 8d) Let me grow deeper in love with you. May I live my life ready to go, doing the very things that bring you honor, praise and glory. In Jesus' name, I pray. Amen.

Let's Go! Do you think you will respond favorably when the Holy Spirit knocks on your heart? Will you go and share the Good News of Jesus Christ to those in your world?

November 18

Victorious Action: Having Beautiful Feet that Brings the Good News!

"And how will they preach unless they are sent? As it is written: "How beautiful are the feet of those who preach the Good News of peace, who bring glad tidings of good things" (Rom. 10:15 WEB).

Let's Talk: At one point, you responded to the Good News you heard with faith, obedience, and repentance. Now it is time to share this Great News with others! How can you do this? First of all, by sharing your story. We all have a story of what our lives were like before we met Jesus. Work on your story and try to whittle it down to one to two minutes. When you share your story, make sure you listen more than you talk! Hear people's needs, their wants and do hear their pain. It is usually their pain, their disillusionment with life that has a person searching for more. The more they are searching for is Jesus Christ! You have the answer they are looking for! Tell them about Jesus and how He has died for their sins. Tell them about God's mighty power and the fact He raised Jesus from the dead! He will raise them out of the deadness of their sins, too if they will **put their trust in Jesus!**

Let's Glorify: Jesus, you tell us "When someone has been given much, much will be required in return; and when someone has been entrusted with much, even more will be required" (Luke 12:48). Lord, you have entrusted me with salvation. You have entrusted me of living in you and your holy ways. Help me Lord, to share your Good News with others. Help me not to be afraid, but be bold sharing your amazing love. Lord, let me take as many people as possible out of the clutches of hell and bring them to heaven by sharing your message of salvation! In Jesus' powerful name, I pray. Amen.

Let's Go! Have you ever written down your testimony about how you received Jesus as your Savior? I challenge you to do this today! Make it 1-2 minutes, put it in your purse and have it ready! Practice on each other. Pray God will bring people to you that you can share His saving love with today!

November 19

Victorious Action: Shine Brightly!

"The way of the righteous is like the first gleam of dawn, which shines ever brighter until the full light of day" (Prov. 4:18 NLT).

Let's Talk: It is the season of autumn where I live. The maple trees are about to burst forth in glorious red, rusts and oranges! This morning, I watched the sunrise over the Sierra Mountains. Slowly but surely, amidst clouds and gorgeous golden rays, the sun began to come up for the day. As the sun rose, there was a golden lining illuminating the edges of the clouds. You, God's righteous one, are like this golden lined cloud! With the first gleam of dawn, you start to shine His love and light on those around you. It is evidenced as you lovingly serve and love your family. It's in the little notes you put in your kid's lunch pail. It's preparing dinner in the crockpot before you rush off to work. It's that quick squeeze and I love you to your husband and children before they leave for the day. Jesus' light within cannot be hidden. His love glow radiates out of you because of the beautiful Holy Spirit living inside you. Just as the sun rises again today by God's mighty outstretched arm, He will help your love lit witness shine again.

Let's Glorify: God, thank you for making the sun rise again. It was spectacular! You are such a God of wonders! I can count on you through every moment of the day. Thank you for seeing me. I am so grateful to know your presence within as I look at the beauty of your creation. Let me be a blessing to my family, my friends and my co-workers, as I shine your love. Let my life radiate you today. In Jesus' saving name, I pray. Amen.

Let's Go! What are you grateful for today? Share how grateful you are to your family, your mom, daughter or friend today.

November 20

Victorious Action: Resting in Your Shepherd!

"The Lord is my Shepherd, I lack nothing. He makes me lie down in green pastures; He leads me beside quiet waters" (Ps. 23:1-2).

Let's Talk: Jesus is your shepherd, your comforter and healer. He will guide you to refreshing rest. He will lead you beside cool waters. There are some trails where I live that I just love to run! I always sense Jesus' presence there. At the end of my run I have the opportunity to finish along a winding canal of fresh water. Even throughout the long, hot summer the water keeps flowing at a brisk pace. The air is clean and the sound of the water rushing over the rocks is energizing. I hear the whisper of my Shepherd, wooing me unto Him. *I restore your soul. Lean into me. Learn from me. You can make it. Just a little longer.* The rest of my day is changed and my spirit is renewed.

Let's Glorify: Jesus, thank you for being my Shepherd, guide and comforter. This life can feel like a long drawn out race at times. And yet, you tell us to run in such a way to win the prize. So, I run, walk and live intentionally seeking you every day. Lord, help me to run hard after you! It is the most important thing I need to do daily next to taking care of my family. Thank you for being with me today and every moment in it. May I live life all to your glory. In Jesus' name, I pray. Amen.

Let's Go! In your day, what do you do that draws you closer to Jesus, your Shepherd?

November 21

Victorious Action: Following His True Wisdom!

"But true wisdom and power are found in God; counsel and understanding are His" (Job 12:13 NLT).

Let's Talk: "True wisdom and real power belong to God; from Him we learn how to live, and also what to live for" (vs. 13 MSG). God sets your priorities straight. He shows you what to do and when to do it. He knows everything! Why then, would you try to consult the world to try to figure out what you should do in a particular situation? Wouldn't it be simpler and cause a lot less confusion in your life, if you went straight to the true source of ALL knowledge? I believe so! Once you pray and seek His guidance, wait with courageous faith!

Let's Glorify: God, I want to glorify you in my decision making. Lord, help me to turn to you first instead of coming to you when I am at my wit's end! Help me not to look around to see what my peers are doing. I want your perfect and pleasing will. Once you give me your answers please give me courage to obey you. I can fully trust you. May it be all to your glory. In Jesus' name, I pray. Amen.

Let's Go! Are you seeking God today for true wisdom? Are you going to follow Him? Share with each other what happened when you decided to trust Him.

November 22

Victorious Action: Inhaling Jesus' Love and Exhaling Your Worries!

"Don't be afraid, for I am with you. Don't be discouraged, for I am your God. I will strengthen you and help you. I will hold you up with my victorious right hand" (Isa. 41:10 NLT).

Let's Talk: What are you dealing with today? You do not have to choose to be afraid. **Jesus is with you.** As much as you desire to be done with this situation or project, He desires even more that you would reach out to Him and ask for His help! Stop for a moment and take a deep breath. Inhale Jesus and His love. Exhale your discouragement and worries to Him. Let His strength replace your worries. **Trust Him. Thank Him for His victory on the cross!**

Let's Glorify: Jesus, I am so grateful you are holding me up right this moment with your victorious right hand! Thank you for always being with me. Help me to rely on your love, grace and mercy today. Help me to know in the deepest part of my heart and spirit as I depend on you that you will help me through this day victoriously! Praise you Lord that you have overcome death and you are breathing your resurrection power into me! How I love you! In your name, I pray. Amen.

Let's Go! Are you afraid today or discouraged? Where do you need Jesus' victorious right hand to support you? Practice inhaling His love and exhaling your worries all day long.

November 23

Victorious Action: Shining Like a Star!

"Those who are wise will shine as bright as the sky, and those who lead many to righteousness will shine like the stars forever" (Dan. 12:3 NLT).

Let's Talk: Those who impart and teach wisdom will shine as bright as the mid-day sky! "For you are all children of the light and of the day; we don't belong to darkness and night. So be on your guard, not asleep like the others. Stay alert and be clearheaded" (1 Thess. 5:5-6 NLT). Did you know stars in the sky are often treated as symbols of the kindness and generous nature of God, and His faithfulness to His promises? "He speaks to the sun and it does not shine; He seals off the light of the stars. He alone stretches out the heavens and treads on the waves of the sea. He is the Maker of the Bear and Orion, the Pleiades and the constellations of the south" (Job 9:7-9). The Bible stresses that every source of light (sun, moon and stars) are created by God, and subject to Him. God is a God of beautiful Light. He asks you and me to walk in His brilliant and true, natural light!

Let's Glorify: God, you are such a magnificent Creator! You make all forms of light and ask me to shine as bright as the sky. Lord, you know I cannot do this without you and the Word, illuminating every thought I think and say. Thank you for your guiding Word and the Holy Spirit who pours out His love into my heart. I am so grateful to you. Help me to be wise in how I spend my days. In Jesus' name, I pray. Amen.

Let's Go! What is your favorite kind of light to see? Is it light from the sun rising over the mountains, moonlight over the ocean or the diamond studded stars in the dark night time sky?

November 24

Victorious Action: Strive to Do What is Good!

"Make sure that nobody pays back wrong for wrong, but always strive to do what is good for each other and for everyone else" (1 Thess. 5:15 NLT).

Let's Talk: Make sure you do not repay evil for evil. This is something I have tried to teach my daughters as they grew up. It is better to respond with Jesus' kindness then to lash out in retaliation. I know this sounds good; but is not always easy to do! If nothing else, turn and walk away from the rudeness and meanness that can so easily prevail in our world. While you do so, pray for that person. Ask yourself, *"What is going on behind the scenes that are making them act this way?"* Realize you might be the first person they have encountered and you are getting the backlash of their fear and insecurity. Strive to do good anyway. Jesus sees you and appreciates your loving and kind heart even when others do not.

Let's Glorify: Jesus, you are my model of how to respond in the face of wrongdoing and evil. Help me not to be vindictive or retaliate. Let me turn the other cheek, realizing everyone needs the benefit of the doubt. Let me extend grace and not take offense. God, take the sting of their words and actions and turn it into something good. Help me to forgive right away. In Jesus' loving name, I pray. Amen.

Let's Go! Is there someone you have been struggling with? Surrender them over to Jesus. Pray a blessing upon them, knowing this is what you would want for yourself!

November 25

Victorious Action: Increasing and Overflowing Love!

"May the Lord make your love increase and overflow for each other and for everyone else, just as ours does for you" (1 Thess. 3:12 NLT).

Let's Talk: In the sisterhood of women, Jesus asks our love would increase and overflow with a heart that bubbles over with the Holy Spirit's love for each other! You do not have to be jealous of another's spiritual gift. God has divinely and personally given you a unique gift that He will enable you to use and impact your circle of influence for good and His glory! Your gift is not to be compared to another's. Have you discovered your special spiritual gift yet?

Let's Glorify: Lord God, you are a holy and wonderful Potter. You have divinely molded me to fit your unique will for my life. You have created me to fulfill a specific purpose within your church. How blessed I am to have the opportunity to partner with you in ministry! Lord, show me how I am to use my gift that you have so graciously given to me. Let me go in the Holy Spirit's strength and not my own as I serve you and the body of Christ. Let me honor you and not take any credit for what you are doing. In Jesus' name, I pray and serve. Amen.

Let's Go! Take a spiritual gifts test and share with each other what God has divinely appointed for you to do! **Where will you use your gift to bless others and glorify God?**

November 26

Victorious Action: Serve the Lord With All of Your Heart!

"Whatever you do, work at it with all your heart, as working for the Lord, not for human masters, since you know that you will receive an inheritance from the Lord as a reward. It is the Lord Christ you are serving" (Col. 3:23-24 NLT).

Let's Talk: Many times your vocation is part of your ministry. All of your work, whether done at a secular job or in Christian work, should be done all to the glory of God. Are you working with all of your heart? Do you realize on the really long and frustrating days it is the Lord Jesus you are serving? This should help your attitude and focus. See Him ever before you, receiving what you have to offer through your work. Smile and relax. He is not a heavy handed task master and He does not expect you to over work. Remember to work hard and yet "Seek first His Kingdom and His righteousness" (Matt. 6:33).

Let's Glorify: God, how I thank you that you are not a heavy handed task master. Your ways are loving and kind. You want me to work hard and yet have times of refreshment and rest. Lord, when I am getting unbalanced, help me to take a break and reflect on why I might be over working. Am I trying to please man? Am I feeling insecure and trying to feel better about myself? Lord, fill me up better than anything I would try to do or perform. Help me to be a good steward of my time and gifts. May I live and work with all of my heart, done all to your glory. In Jesus' name, I pray. Amen.

Let's Go! Do you find yourself working too much as a form of distraction? What is God asking you to slow down and take a look at? Discuss it with each other.

November 27

Victorious Action: Knowing the Author and Perfector of Your Faith!

"I have brought you glory on earth by finishing the work you gave me to do" (Jn. 17:4).

Let's Talk: Jesus had meaningful work to do on earth. By trade, He was a carpenter. His earthly father Joseph showed Him his craft. Can you picture Jesus carefully creating things out of wood? Or repairing objects that were damaged? His work on the cross repairs the damage in your heart and soul. He heals the brokenness in your life. He took His work seriously, knowing it was exactly what God, His Father had ordained Him to do. His work saves you from an eternity that would have been separated from His goodness, love and light. Praise Jesus for His redeeming work!

Let's Glorify: Jesus, thank you for your true and honest work. Your very breath breathes life into my soul. Thank you for redeeming me out of the pit of hell. I am so grateful and so blessed! Jesus, you are my one desire. Let me know you more and more today. Thank you for finishing the work God, the Father gave you at the cross. You are the Author and Perfector of my faith! In your name I pray and thank you. Amen.

Let's Go! Do you have any areas in your heart that are damaged and need Jesus' healing? **Pray together and turn this area over to Jesus, the Author and Perfector of your faith.**

November 28

Victorious Action: Be a Doer of the Word!

"You must be doers of the word and not only hearers who mislead themselves" (James 1:22).

Let's Talk: You are called to be a doer of the Word, not just simply listening to the Word. You are called to apply the Word to your heart first. Then act upon what the Holy Spirit is asking you to do, change or stop doing! If you do not, it's as if you checked your reflection in the mirror, walk away and within minutes simply forget who you are and what you look like!

Let's Glorify: God, help me to have the courage and the energy to apply your Word to my life and heart. I am so grateful I do not have to do this on my own! I want to be a doer of your Word and not just a listener. Thank you for the Holy Spirit within me who will remind me of your teachings and show me how and what to change. It is my joy to do your will. In the holy and truthful name of Jesus, I pray. Amen.

Let's Go! Do you let the Word go in one ear and out the other? What do you need to do so this does not happen? Discuss with each other and stay committed to lift each up in that special area of need.

November 29

Victorious Action: Receive His Mercy at the Throne of Grace!

"Let us then approach God's throne of grace with confidence, so that we may receive mercy and find grace to help us in our time of need" (Heb. 4:16).

Let's Talk: Jesus is your help when you need it the most! "Jesus is your great High Priest with ready access to God. We don't have a priest who is out of touch with our reality. He's been through weakness and testing, experienced it all—all but the sin. So let's walk right up to Him and get what He is so ready to give. **Take the mercy, accept the help**" (Heb. 4:16 MSG, emphasis mine). Reach out to Him! Let your ego and pride go. He is more than ENOUGH to help you with all of your needs. Jesus understands your heartache. He understands your loneliness and will wipe away your tears. He will respond with tender kindness. Let Him help you!

Let's Glorify: Jesus, thank you for being my High Priest. You have suffered and experienced all that I have gone through or will go through. You understand me completely. You know exactly how to help and encourage me. Lord, I accept your help right now. Remind me that I do not have to go through life's struggles and heartaches by myself. You are more than willing to offer me help and support. I am so blessed! Thank you for your loving kindnesses which are new every morning. In your precious name, I pray. Amen.

Let's Go! Jesus is in touch with your life and knows exactly what is going on. Where in your life are you confused or suffering? Will you give it up to Him entirely? Pray about it with your daughter, mom or girlfriend.

November 30

Victorious Action: Knowing the Weight of Your Sins!

"You say, 'I am rich; I have acquired wealth and do not need a thing.' But you do not realize that you are wretched, pitiful, poor, blind and naked" (Rev. 3:17 NLT).

Let's Talk: You might be wealthy and have everything but **do you know the weight of your sins?** It's grimy. I was thinking about this as I began cleaning my kitchen today. No matter how many times I clean it, someone comes along and fixes something to eat. Then there are crumbs left on the counter or spills on the stove top. No matter how much I clean, it becomes grimy again in no time! My grimy sins hurt the Holy Spirit living within. I am sensing Him telling me, "Do not take it lightly! Your sins cost Jesus His everything!" Truly, each of us is blind sighted to our own faults. We are wretched, pitiful, poor, blind and naked! I have found it best to think twice before I choose to do something that goes against what God wants for me. The solution to mine and your sin problem is to ask for forgiveness immediately, realizing the cost to Jesus. I am a sinner in need of a holy Savior.

Let's Glorify: Jesus, no matter how many times I try to clean myself up, it is not enough. I need you to be my Savior and wash me as white as snow. Lord, I want to know the weight of my sin so I will think twice about sinning willfully. Please forgive me today. Thank you for hearing me and restoring me upon your right path. In Jesus' name, I pray. Amen.

Let's Go! Have you found yourself to be wretched, pitiful, poor, blind and naked when you are in sin? Are you placing your hope in anything besides Jesus? Talk it over.

December

"We never know the love of our parents for us till we have become parents."
~ Henry Ward Beecher

December 1

Victorious Action: Live a Grace Filled Life!

"For the grace of God has appeared that offers salvation to all people" (Titus 2:11 NLT).

Let's Talk: His unmerited favor and blessing is His grace bestowed upon you. "God made for Himself a people of His own, clean and pure, **with our hearts set upon living a life that is good**" (PHILLIPS 2:14, emphasis mine). Jesus' salvation is for all people everywhere. He is looking and calling you to live a holy life, with your heart set upon living a life that is good. What does this look like? It's loving others as you love yourself. It's sharing kindness, humility and being generous. It's having gratitude in your heart daily for ALL that Jesus has done for you and continues to do for you. And, it's seeking Him and confessing your sins daily. Living a life that is good requires listening intently to the Holy Spirit and then promptly obeying. It's not withholding love, support or encouragement from those around you. Your life witnesses to the fact that God is great and Jesus died for all!

Let's Glorify: God, I desire to be pleasing to you. Let my life reflect the goodness and the loving grace you have given to me daily. Lord, let me be mindful there are people who have a hard time letting you in. Let your selfless and pure love be a part of my character, leading others to want to know more about you and your free gift of salvation. Let love be my highest goal. May it be all to your praise and glory! In Jesus' name, I pray. Amen.

Let's Go! What does *your heart set upon living a life that is good* look like? How can you witness God's loving grace to others today? Share with each other.

December 2

Victorious Action: Accepting One Another Brings Praise to God!

"Accept one another, then, just as Christ accepted you, in order to bring praise to God" (Rom. 15:7).

Let's Talk: Who are you having a hard time with? Are you feeling judgmental and angry towards them? God knows how you feel! Could it be you are judging first, so you are not judged or rejected? Has your wall of defense gone up? God wants to tear it down and transform your heart! You need to be compassionate with yourself before you can give acceptance and compassion to another. Pray and ask Him for a better way to deal with your anger and fear.

Let's Glorify: God, I do want to bring you praise in my life! Lord, please help me to recognize when I am erecting walls as a defense mechanism. God, as I judge others, my attitude appears to say, *I am better than you*. Really God, if I am honest with you and myself, I am angry or fearful about something else and I am not dealing with my past situation very well. Thank you when I repent and ask forgiveness, it is gone immediately! I can start fresh right away, today. Thank you, Jesus for your loving forgiveness and grace. Let me extend your grace and acceptance to others, bringing glory to your name. Amen.

Let's Go! Are you feeling judgmental towards someone? Is this a reoccurring process for you? If so, confess to each other and God asking for a transformed heart. Pray and ask Him to replace your judgment with acceptance and a clean heart.

December 3

Victorious Action: Praying for Forgiveness!

Jesus said, "Father, forgive them, for they do not know what they are doing" (Luke 23:34).

Let's Talk: Have you ever had an experience where you were absolutely compelled to pray Jesus' prayer? I sure have. His prayer has really helped me through some tough moments to release my anger, shock and utter discouragement. His prayer has helped me to forgive and move forward without obsessing over someone's thoughtless deeds. I know it can help you as well! So many times as you deal with people they have not thought out what they are going to do or say. It was just a spontaneous eruption!

Let's Glorify: Jesus, how many times have I had a spontaneous eruption and hurt someone else? I have had to pray, *Father forgive me because I obviously was not thinking or being considerate.* Thank you for your model of loving forgiveness. Even in your extreme agony on the cross, you did not retaliate. Lord, help me to remember your example of forgiveness even when you were hurt, spat upon, mocked and beaten. In Jesus' name, I pray. Amen.

Let's Go! Do you need to pray Jesus' forgiveness prayer today? Or, ask God the Father for forgiveness. Talk it over with your mom, daughter or special friend.

December 4

Victorious Action: Victory in Your Battles!

"You have given me your shield of victory; your help has made me great" (2 Sam. 22:36 NLT).

Let's Talk: The NIVR Bible says, "You help me win the battle. You bend down to make me great." God says that He will stoop over to give you the victory and He does! A shield in the Bible is a piece of armor used to fend off blows or arrows from the enemy. God is described as the shield of His people; protecting, giving help, strength and favor. Faith is given to the believer to act as a shield with God's power against spiritual attack. Faith helps you to press on believing God, even when those around you think you should stop and do something else! God blesses your belief in Him! How He longs to have His people, His remnant truly believe that He will do what He says He will do! **He makes you great!**

Let's Glorify: God, thank you for giving me your shield of faith and victory. How blessed I am; your help makes me great! Thank you Creator God of heaven and earth! You stoop down and demonstrate your great love to me. Thank you for helping me win the battles in my life by overcoming my past. You are the Great I AM and yet you notice your people. How I love you and praise you! In the strong name of Jesus, I pray. Amen.

Let's Go! In what battle do you absolutely need to see His victory today? Are you praying without ceasing, believing He can do the impossible no matter how long it takes? Talk about it with your mom, daughter or special friend.

December 5

Victorious Action: Living Life All to His Glory!

"Whether you eat, or drink, or whatsoever you do, do all to the glory of God" (1 Cor. 10:31).

Let's Talk: Remember Jesus in all that you do! Start your day with Him in prayer and meditation. Be mindful of His holy presence with you throughout your entire day! Stick a few verses on flashcards in your purse. Look up a bible Scripture online on your phone or device. Apply the verse to your life. Hum and sing your favorite praise and worship songs back to Him. Notice how your spirit and mood begins to lift and become joyful as you remember Jesus and His precious love! Reading scriptures, meditating on His love and promises all day help you to live well in the moment.

Let's Glorify: God, I want my life to glorify you alone today. Help me to take the time to remember Jesus and His amazing heart work done in so many lives during His ministry on earth. His Word is still creating miracles and transformation in people today. Lord, please let me be a part of His transformational heart healing work in other's lives, done unto the glory of God. In Jesus' holy name, I pray. Amen.

Let's Go! What time of the day do you tend to forget the Lord? **Brainstorm some ideas together to help you to remember to reflect on Jesus and His earthly ministry.**

December 6

Victorious Action: Overflow with His Confident Hope!

"I pray that God, the source of hope, will fill you completely with joy and peace because you trust in Him. Then you will overflow with confident hope through the power of the Holy Spirit" (Rom. 15:13 NLT).

Let's Talk: Has He become your source of all hope? His joy will bubble up inside you when you are walking closely to Jesus, the Man of joy! You will notice His presence, His blessedness when you have been obedient to Him. Did you notice at the birth of our Messiah, the angels sang with great joy? Mary His mother treasured and pondered all the news around her son. God said, "He was well pleased with His Son and that He loved Him" after Jesus was baptized by John the Baptist (Matt. 3:17, paraphrased). When you begin to realize you have Jesus living inside of you through the power of the comforter, the Holy Spirit, you can live in peace as you trust in Him! Joy can truly be yours in the midst of trial and tribulation!

Let's Glorify: God, I choose to trust you more with a childlike faith. **I know you do not want me to worry or be stressed out. Thank you for being my Abba Daddy, whom I can count on in all seasons of my life.** Thank you for giving me blessed assurance over and over again through your Word. You give me overflowing confident hope, joy and peace as I trust in you! Lord, fill me up today with the fullness of the Holy Spirit, so I may know you and your amazing joy which only you can give! How I love you and praise you! In Jesus' name, I pray. Amen.

Let's Go! Do you fully trust Jesus today? Are you asking Him to fill you with His joy and peace as you trust in Him? Why or why not? Talk it over and **pray God would increase your joy** as you trust in Him!

December 7

Victorious Action: Appreciating the Holy Spirit!

"Since we live by the Spirit, let us keep in step with the Spirit" (Gal. 5:25).

Let's Talk: The Spirit lives inside of you. He is a gift. When you receive a gift, it is wise to treat the gift with care because it was especially given to you! The Holy Spirit is this way, too. He has been divinely given, apportioned to you to help you live a successful godly life. The Holy Spirit is not an "it." He has a definite and distinct personality as part of the Trinity. Take some time to get in step with what He is doing. **Get into His rhythm. This usually means you have to slow way down!** Lean in and listen to what He is sharing through the Word. Read it intentionally asking Him what He'd like to say to you. Seek Him and His God given guidance. The Holy Spirit speaks the deep things He hears from God the Father. He will not lead you astray. He will not go against what God says in the Bible. He can be trusted. **"The Spirit intercedes for God's people in accordance with the will of God"** (Rom. 8:27, emphasis mine).

Let's Glorify: Jesus, thank you for sending the comforter, the Holy Spirit. I am so grateful to have Him in my life to guide and direct me with God's will. Holy Spirit let me remember you are not an "it." You have a distinct personality and operate in equal power with the Trinity. Help me not to grieve you by choosing to sin or not obey. I pray to have discernment to ask for forgiveness right away so I do not break fellowship with you. Thank you for pouring your love and joy into my heart! I am so blessed Jesus put you in my life so I can experience your guiding presence and hope. In Jesus' name, I pray. Amen.

Let's Go! What do you believe "Since we live by the Spirit, let us keep in step with the Spirit," means? (Gal. 5:25). If possible, discuss this Scripture over a hot peppermint mocha or hot cocoa topped with mile high whip cream!

December 8

Victorious Action: Honor God with a Passionate Heart!

And so the Lord says, "These people say they are mine. They honor me with their lips, but their hearts are far from me. And their worship of me is nothing but man-made rules learned by rote" (Isa. 29:13 NLT).

Let's Talk: This is a stinger of a verse! **Are you honoring the Lord with your lips, but have found your heart is far, far away from Him?** Ouch! Take notice of where your heart is today. Do you desire to spend time with God, really? Is He more important than any other relationship, activity or social event? Are you weighed down with the cares of this world? As you sing and worship Him, are your lips moving but your heart is not? Maybe you are just going through the motions. Maybe this is why your life feels dry and uncertain. Get out of your spiritual malaise! Seek Him as if your entire life depended on it, because it does! **Your family needs you to passionate for God; not lukewarm.** You can influence your family and friends to be passionate for Jesus generations to come because you decided today, "But as for me and my household, we will serve the Lord" (Josh. 24:15).

Let's Glorify: God, thank you for your Word. It is true and steers me straight when I am headed down the wrong road. Jesus, I want to serve you with a heart filled with wholehearted passion. I do not want to operate on man's laws of doing things by habit and rote, because then my heart is detached. Lord, I surrender myself to you today. In Jesus' holy name, I pray. Amen.

Let's Go! How would you rate yourself on the spiritual plumb line? Are you honoring the Lord with your lips and yet your heart is far away? Or, are you loving and serving Him with wholehearted passion? How do you know the difference? Honestly share your heart with each other.

December 9

Victorious Action: Have a Heart that Desires to Obey and Glorify God!

"Lord, we show our trust in you by obeying your laws; our heart's desire is to glorify your name" (Isa. 26:8 NLT).

Let's Talk: It is one thing to hear the still, quiet voice of the Holy Spirit gently whispering to your heart. It is quite another thing to obey it. It seems obedience is the harder of the two to do! But, as Isaiah the prophet said, **"Our heart's desire is to glorify your name."** If you are going to exalt and worship His Name, **you must obey out of an attitude that trusts Him.** Think about your children, grandchildren or nieces and nephews. Have you seen them obey their parents? How did you feel? You probably thought, "Good for you!" You might have even complimented them on their good behavior. Or, if they were sulky and disobedient, your thoughts were probably not as favorable! God sees you the same way! He loves you no matter what, but He really wants you to obey Him out of a grateful and trusting heart. He wants you to obey Him as a child would her parent.

Let's Glorify: Lord God, my heart's desire is to bring your name praise. I want to obey out of a heart overflowing with love; appreciation and gratitude for all that you have done for me. Help me to realize I can trust you fully for you have good plans in mind for me! Help me to be mindful that **delayed obedience is disobedience.** I need to be ready to obey in all seasons of my life, not just when I feel like it! Lord, please increase my faith so it is like a child's faith, relying on her daddy. In your gracious name, I pray. Amen.

Let's Go! Did you ever have a time growing up when your Mom asked you to do something that made no sense whatsoever? Do you trust God enough to obey Him even when you think His plans do not make sense to you? Discuss it together.

December 10

Victorious Action: Having Victory in Death!

"He will swallow up death forever! The Sovereign Lord will wipe away all tears. He will remove forever all insults and mockery against His land and people. The Lord has spoken" (Isa. 25:8 NLT).

Let's Talk: Death is swallowed up in victory. Your victory is being held securely in Jesus' hands! Your victory is living forever in heaven, face-to-face with Jesus! Rev. 21:4 says, "He will wipe every tear from their eyes, and there will be no more death or sorrow or crying or pain. All these things are gone forever." How wonderful! There will be an end to your grief, your frustrations and your troubles! Jesus will take away all the mean things said to you or about you. There will be no gossiping or slander. The Lord has spoken and what He says always stands forever!

Let's Glorify: Lord God, thank you that you have the power and authority to wipe away all of my tears. I am thrilled to have the opportunity to live in heaven with you forever. You know me better than anyone else. I look forward to being known by you as you fully know me! Jesus, I am praying for my family members, co-workers and friends who do not have a personal relationship with you. God, my heart yearns deeply for them to know you. Let my witness shine brightly. Please give me an opportunity to speak about your changing love with them. Send me and others as you knock on their hearts to receive you. In Jesus' wonderful and saving name, I pray. Amen.

Let's Go! What tears do you need the Lord to wipe away today? Share them freely with each other. Who in your circle needs Jesus' precious salvation? Will you speak to them? Pray and ask God to open a door so you will have an opportunity to share Jesus' changing and saving love with them.

December 11

Victorious Action: Seeing God's Vision Cast into Your Life!

"Where there is no vision, the people perish: but he that keepeth the law, happy is he" (Prov. 29:18 KJV).

Let's Talk: The Message Bible of this same verse says it this way: "If people can't see what God is doing, they stumble all over themselves; But when they attend to what He reveals, they are most blessed." You are most blessed when you obey God's laws, His Ten Commandments. God will reveal His plans and vision when you are trying to live for Him. Be careful though, of only trying to keep His laws and not experiencing His love. **You cannot work for His approval. You already have it!** Come to Him with a heart filled with love. Come to Jesus with gratitude and how He has saved you from death of your sins. You need His guidance and vision casted in a loving relationship and not just a bunch of rules to keep!

Let's Glorify: Jesus, I am so grateful to be in a loving relationship with you. Thank you for your approval which I do not have to try to work for or earn. Lord, I want to try to keep what you have commanded out of reverent respect and love, not out of duty or obligation. Lord, the law can kill but your love gives life and true freedom! Let me always choose being in a loving relationship with you first. Then, out of reverent submission I will want to choose to do what is right and pure before you. Thank you for casting your vision into my life! In your name, I pray. Amen.

Let's Go! Has God ever casted His vision or plans into your life? Did you listen and obey? Discuss what happened with each other.

December 12

Victorious Action: Knowing the Lord is With You!

"In the sixth month of Elizabeth's pregnancy, God sent the angel Gabriel to Nazareth, a town in Galilee, to a virgin pledged to be married to a man named Joseph, a descendant of David. The virgin's name was Mary. The angel went to her and said, "Greetings, you who are highly favored! The Lord is with you" (Luke 1: 26-28).

Let's Talk: Oh, to be approached by an angel in dazzling white clothes! The angel Gabriel came to tell Mary the most fantastic news! He told Mary she was "highly favored and the Lord is with you" (vs. 28). Did you know **God favors you**, too? He does! He knows the number of hairs on your head. He has your name tattooed on His hand! If He wore a locket around His neck, you, His precious daughter, would be the photograph in His locket! That's what a treasure you are to Him! God promises to always be with you and never leave nor forsake you. He loves you today and will love you tomorrow. He is proud to be your Abba, Daddy! Even if you never knew your earthly dad and you wonder what he was like, God knows and understands your emotions and thoughts. Tell Him how you feel. You will not scare Him away with your honest feelings and questions. He is a perfect dad and He will *never stop loving you!*

Let's Glorify: Abba Daddy, thank you for always being there for me. How you know everything about me is just amazing! Your wisdom is beyond compare. I am so happy I can depend on you every moment of each day. Thank you for being my Emmanuel. **I love and hold onto the fact that you are always with me.** Thank you for your loving favor. I pray I make you smile today. In Jesus' loving name, I pray. Amen.

Let's Go! What do you need from your Abba Daddy today? Is it His favor or the fact He is Emmanuel, your God who is with you?

December 13

Victorious Action: Finding Favor with God!

Mary was greatly troubled at his words and wondered what kind of greeting this might be. But the angel said to her, "Do not be afraid, Mary; you have found favor with God. You will conceive and give birth to a son, and you are to call Him Jesus" (Luke 1:29-31).

Let's Talk: Anxious, greatly troubled, confused and disturbed. These are words to describe how Mary was feeling about the angel Gabriel's words. How many times she must have pondered his words to *not be afraid. You have favor with God Himself. You will have a son* and *will call Him Jesus!* Mary would have known the scriptures. Could it be God was bringing to fruition what He had promised long ago in her life? Yes, indeed! Isaiah 9:6 says in the Word, "For to us a child is born, to us a son is given, and the government will be on His shoulders. And He will be called Wonderful Counselor, Mighty God, Everlasting Father, Prince of Peace."

Let's Glorify: God, thank you for choosing Mary who was humble in your sight. She is a good example of a godly young woman who was devoted to doing your will. Reading the scriptures, I do not see Mary whining and complaining about what you were doing in her life. Although she was anxious, she trusted you and your sovereign plan. Lord, help me today to trust your sovereign plan in my life. I thank you for the favor, grace and kindness you have richly blessed me with. Thank you for being my Jehovah Jireh, my provider in all things. In Jesus' name, I pray. Amen.

Let's Go! In what areas of your life have you found favor in God? Where in your life do you need more blessing or His favor? Do you think you could have responded as Mary did, without whining or complaining even though God had interrupted her plans?

December 14

Victorious Action: Letting Jesus Reign!

"He will be great and will be called the Son of the Most High. The Lord God will give Him the throne of His father David, and He will reign over Jacob's descendants forever; His kingdom will never end" (Luke 1:32-33).

Let's Talk: Jesus is the Son of the Most High God! El Elyon is another name for Most High God. God is more than able to give Jesus the throne of King David. You can be eternally grateful Jesus holds the keys of life and death for an eternity. His reign and His kingdom will never end. Your salvation is sure and protected by the King of Kings and Lord of Lords!

Let's Glorify: Jesus, your birth was foretold and came to pass just as God said it would. You are the Son of the Most High God. You are the only way to experience heaven and salvation after death here on earth. Salvation is found in none other! How I praise you and thank you for your precious and pure life! Lord, I am praying for the people who have not believed who you are. Lord, knock on their hearts. Thank you for your patience, not wanting anyone to perish, but you want everyone to come to repentance (2 Pet. 3:9). Let me be ready and willing to be one cog in the wheel of their salvation process. Lord, reign in my life today. May my life be lived all to your glory. In Jesus' name, I pray. Amen.

Let's Go! Are you ready with your testimony and plan of Salvation so you can be a cog in the wheel of a family member, a friend or a stranger's salvation? Will you get ready today? Their eternal life is too important for you not to be ready!

December 15

Victorious Action: Knowing the Power of the Holy Spirit!

"How will this be," Mary asked the angel, "since I am a virgin?" The angel answered, "The Holy Spirit will come on you, and the power of the Most High will overshadow you. So the holy one to be born will be called the Son of God" (Luke 1:34-35).

Let's Talk: When you are facing the seemingly impossible, look to Jesus. Remember He is the Master Healer, Teacher and your great Savior! Nothing is impossible with Him (Luke 1:37, paraphrased). You know without a shadow of doubt in your own strength and capability you could not possibly complete a project, make it through your day, or face one more heartache. **You can know the power of the Most High will overshadow you.** As you seek Him and pray, God through the Holy Spirit will develop the skills you need. He will equip you and hold you steady until His glorious completion. As you remember all that He has done for you and brought you through, remember to thank Him, giving Him all the praise, honor and glory that is due!

Let's Glorify: God you are over the top amazing! When I have struggled with something that seemed so huge and overwhelming, you have always been right there to help me. You have never let me down. Why is it Lord, when I start something new, I can so easily forget your power, strength and the fact the Holy Spirit promises to be with me? Lord, I want to remember daily that I have your precious energizing love and life living inside me. You are a deep stream that I can drink freely and fully upon. God, with deep and abiding reverence, I thank you for all of your amazing help and power. In Jesus' mighty name, I pray. Amen.

Let's Go! Are you working on any big projects that seem quite daunting? Are you willing to turn your will and life over to Him and His great power so you can finish it victoriously?

December 16

Victorious Action: Believing No Word from God Will Ever Fail!

"Even Elizabeth your relative is going to have a child in her old age, and she who was said to be unable to conceive is in her sixth month. For no word from God will ever fail." "I am the Lord's servant," Mary answered. "May your word to me be fulfilled" (Luke 1:36-38).

Let's Talk: For no word from God will ever fail! I hope this phrase jumped off the page to you as you read it! When God speaks a word, a whisper from His heart to yours, it is done! He is going to make it happen! Isn't that exciting? First of all, just the fact you heard that word through the Holy Spirit is miraculous! Now, wait upon Him. He will give you the next step, the next set of instructions. He is not finished until He brings His word and goal to fruition. What beautiful fruit that will be displayed in your life as you lean in, listen intently and then act on His time frame! Mary did exactly that. I am sure this is why God chose her to be Jesus' mother.

Let's Glorify: Holy Spirit, thank you for speaking exactly what you hear from God, my Father to me. I do not have to worry about the how, why, or what of your will. You will show me the next step. I can get excited because you have me on a grand adventure! "Lord, I am your servant," just like Mary said (vs. 38). I pray I will wait patiently and listen intently, all to your glory! I surrender my will today to you. In Jesus' name, I pray. Amen.

Let's Go! Do you believe no word from God will ever fail? Why or why not? Have you heard the Holy Spirit speak to your heart? Share with each other your divine experiences.

December 17

Victorious Action: Believe His Promises!

"When Elizabeth heard Mary's greeting, the baby leaped in her womb, and Elizabeth was filled with the Holy Spirit. In a loud voice she exclaimed: "Blessed are you among women, and blessed is the child you will bear! But why am I so favored, that the mother of my Lord should come to me? As soon as the sound of your greeting reached my ears, the baby in my womb leaped for joy. Blessed is she who has believed that the Lord would fulfill His promises to her" (Luke 1:41-45).

Let's Talk: What great faith both of these precious women exhibited! Both were having miracle babies! Elizabeth was well past bearing children and Mary was a virgin. Elizabeth recognized the baby her cousin Mary carried was the Son of God. How reassuring and comforting Elizabeth must have been to Mary. What a special visit! She recognized Mary's great faith by exclaiming, **"Blessed is she who has believed that the Lord would fulfill His promises to her"** (vs. 45, emphasis mine).

Let's Glorify: Lord Jesus, thank you for my precious daughters and special girlfriends. They have enriched my life in so many ways and helped me to believe that the Lord will indeed fulfill His promises! Thank you for their loving support and encouragement and "Atta girls" when I did not think I had the expertise to do what you have asked me to do. They have blessed me beyond measure. What fabulous gifts these precious women are to me. Thank you for the fun, laughter and even tears. We are knit together because we are bonded in your precious love and grace. In Jesus' loving and sweet name, I pray. Amen.

Let's Go! Thank God for the special women in your life. Do you believe the Lord will fulfill His precious promises to you? Why or why not? Discuss with your special girlfriend.

December 18

Victorious Action: Glorifying the Lord with Your Soul and Spirit!

And Mary said: "My soul glorifies the Lord and my spirit rejoices in God my Savior, for He has been mindful of the humble state of His servant. From now on all generations will call me blessed, for the Mighty One has done great things for me—holy is His name" (Luke 1:46-49).

Let's Talk: I just love these scriptures! Mary recognized God's blessing and favor upon her in her precious song of praise. She knew the road in front of her was not going to be easy, but because He would be with her, she could rejoice! Biblical scholars tell us Mary was about thirteen or fourteen when she was pledged to be married to Joseph. Then the totally unexpected happened. She was divinely with child! Mary was able to say in the midst of her trial and turmoil and the hushed whispers as she passed by, "From now on all generations will call me blessed, for the Mighty One has done great things for me—holy is His name" (vs. 49). Mary remained humble throughout Jesus' life and stuck by Him even in the agony of His death on the cross.

Let's Glorify: Lord God, thank you for seeing Mary your humble servant. Scriptures give me such a window into your loving and caring heart through Mary's story. I know you see me when I am in turmoil. I know you have and will continue to do great things for me as I seek you, remain humble and repent. Even when I make a mess of my life, you are eager to forgive me. Thank you for your loving grace and mercy, even to women in Mary's time. Holy is your name! In Jesus' name, I pray. Amen.

Let's Go! In the midst of your trials and turmoil is your soul glorifying in the Lord today? Why or why not? Share with each other.

December 19

Victorious Action: Lifted Up When I am Humble!

"His mercy extends to those who fear Him, from generation to generation. He has performed mighty deeds with His arm; He has scattered those who are proud in their inmost thoughts. He has brought down rulers from their thrones but has lifted up the humble. He has filled the hungry with good things but has sent the rich away empty" (Luke 1: 50-53).

Let's Talk: God is still extending mercy and grace today to those who call upon Him reverently! In these scriptures, Mary throws off customary ideas of privilege for the wealthy. She speaks of what God will do for the poor today and in the future. Mary understands what God is doing in her life and in the community of believers in her day and well into the future. God is worthy of your praise because He never stops caring for you or stops loving you. He will help calm your anxious mind and thoughts as you call upon Him. Stop and look around at all of the blessings He has given to you! This is what Mary did. As a result, she was filled with joy and gratitude for who God is and what He was doing in her life.

Let's Glorify: God almighty, thank you for always extending your wonderful mercy and grace to me and my family. Lord, you ask me to be humble inwardly and outwardly. My humbleness begins with a reverent attitude toward you and how BIG of a God you truly are! Lord, I am nothing without you! I do not want to have any pride in me which will only bring me down. Let me look to you, your greatness and mighty deeds. Thank you, I can count on your mercy every day. In Jesus' perfect name, I pray and boast in. Amen.

Let's Go! "He has scattered those who are proud in their inmost thoughts" (vs. 51). Do you have any pride hiding out in your heart? **Discuss your thoughts and possibly share a moment when your pride has gotten you into quicksand!** Whenever I start to say, "I'd never. . ." or "I'm better than. . ." I know I have pride lurking all around me!

December 20

Victorious Action: In Uncertainty, Sing and Praise Him!

"He has helped His servant Israel, remembering to be merciful to Abraham and his descendants forever, just as He promised our ancestors. Mary stayed with Elizabeth for about three months and then returned home" (Luke 1: 53b-56).

Let's Talk: Luke records **God's promised mercy and care** to Abraham's descendants. Mary was included in these descendants. In a **time of uncertainty, she sang to the Lord praising His holy Name.** Mary showed her faith in her Lord and you can do the same! Then, God provided a much needed respite for Mary. She took it and stayed with her cousin Elizabeth for about three months. I can imagine them laughing and carrying on about the growing baby boys in their tummies! I wonder about their conversations, their hopes and dreams for their divine miracle babies. How wonderful God gave each of us special women to love us, encourage us, hug and celebrate us. How we need their precious support in our times of uncertainties and heartache!

Let's Glorify: Lord God, thank you for keeping your promises to me. You are such a wonderful heavenly Father, provider and friend. How wonderful it is you have blessed me with so many incredible women friends who love me and support me. I pray a blessing and favor over each one today. Lord, please strengthen our friendships in you. Jesus, I pray we will always be bonded and knit together because of our common love and commitment to you. Thank you for blessing me with such dear women. In Jesus' name, I pray and celebrate. Amen.

Let's Go! Plan a special outing together. You have almost finished this yearly devotional. This is something to celebrate! Celebrate each other and your individual uniqueness. Celebrate bonding closer together because of your devotion to Jesus and each other!

December 21

Victorious Action: Believing God is in Control When You Are Not!

"He went there to register with Mary, who was pledged to be married to him and was expecting a child. While they were there, the time came for the baby to be born, and she gave birth to her firstborn, a son. She wrapped Him in cloths and placed Him in a manger, because there was no guest room available for them" (Luke 2:5-7).

Let's Talk: No matter what the situation is, God is in control! His plans will happen just as He says they will! You can count on it. Mary and Joseph did not expect to have baby Jesus in an animal's feeding trough. They had traveled ninety miles by donkey to be part of a census. This census was to be taken by the entire Roman world. They were tired, sore and probably hungry. They did not expect to start their family in a stable where animals were housed. But, God knew. He was quietly at work, and our Messiah's first throne room was a stable. The long awaited promised One of God enters our world through His creation with the animals looking on. What a stark contrast between the Holy One's ordinary birth and His greatness! Jesus was born into humility and yet was a King of Kings! This precious baby grew into your Messiah Savior. Hallelujah!

Let's Glorify: God, I am so glad you are in control when I do not understand what is going on. Your ways are perfect and I can rest and trust in you. "Let all that I am wait quietly before God, for my hope is in Him. He alone is my rock and my salvation" (Ps. 62: 5-6). Thank you for holy baby Jesus who grew into a holy man. He walked faithfully in you all the days of His earthly ministry. Because of Him, I can thank you that my victory and honor come from you alone. In you I can rest in all circumstances.

Lord, thank you for Mary and Joseph and their commitment to be godly parents to Jesus. I pray to be a godly mom pointing my children to you, all the days of their lives. May it be all to your loving glory. In Jesus' name, I pray and ask these things. Amen.

Let's Go! Mary and Joseph did not have control over where baby Jesus would be born. They knew God would protect Jesus and them. Do you have any areas where you are having a power struggle with God? Where do you have fear today?

December 22

Victorious Action: Responding to Jesus' Birth with Joy!

"And there were shepherds living out in the fields nearby, keeping watch over their flocks at night. An angel of the Lord appeared to them, and the glory of the Lord shone around them, and they were terrified. But the angel said to them, "Do not be afraid. I bring you good news that will cause great joy for all the people" (Luke 2:8-10).

Let's Talk: Jesus' birth explodes with bright light, joy, surprise and wonder! All these emotions flow from the experience of the shepherds, who observed these wonders with great amazement! Heaven through angels' loud singing and bright star confesses this precious child's identity. He is royalty! All of Jesus' titles are confessed: He is Savior, Lord, King and Christ! As unbelievable as it may seem, the One with authority over salvation spends His first night's rest not in a palace but in the open air of an animal's stall! Jesus birth fulfills God's promise of salvation. God's concern for all people regardless of their social status or vocation is evidenced in the fact He sent His Son Jesus to be born amongst the shepherds.

Let's Glorify: God, you are holy and your plans are perfect. Thank you that Jesus' holy birth in a lowly environment identifies Him as a humble King for all people. Jesus was not wealthy in His life, but came to set the wealthy free from their idolatry of stuff. Jesus was neither fake nor pretentious. He spoke honestly His Father's truths and yet He spoke in love. Lord, forgive me when my stuff gets in the way of my relationship with you. **Jesus, you are more important than anything I will ever own, wear or eat.** Help me to remain humble and walk closely to you. Thank you for being my humble, yet powerful King of Kings! Thank you for bringing me joy today! In Jesus' name, I pray. Amen.

Let's Go! Has there been a time when your stuff or what you wear or eat has become more important to you than your relationship with Jesus? Discuss with each other. Do you have any Nativity scenes to **remind you of His lowly birth?** I have found some really neat and inexpensive ones at thrift stores. Make sure you have a Nativity that little hands can touch and hold as they reenact the Nativity story each year.

December 23

Victorious Action: Knowing the Messiah Came as a Baby!

"Today in the town of David a Savior has been born to you; He is the Messiah, the Lord. This will be a sign to you: You will find a baby wrapped in cloths and lying in a manger" (Luke 2:11-12).

Let's Talk: How did the shepherds know the baby Jesus would be wrapped in cloths and lying in a manger? The angel of the Lord appeared to them and told them! They were the first people to hear the blessed news and to hear of the Messiah being born. "Christ" means "Messiah." What amazing names for the baby Jesus! The sign the shepherds were told to look for was the baby Jesus would be wrapped in cloths to protect His delicate newborn skin. Even in the practical and seemingly normal, (and yet not so normal) God proves the truth of the angel's message. The shepherds would indeed find the Messiah child wrapped just as the angel said. God's words are faithful and true. They will always come to pass!

Let's Glorify: God, you are awesome, faithful and trustworthy! **Your words always come to pass, just as you say they will.** Thank you for revealing baby Jesus, my Savior and Messiah to the least of these, the shepherds. You show me every person has value and honor in your eyes. Thank you for the joy the shepherds must have experienced knowing you had spoken to them through the angel's words! Lord, when you speak to me I have great joy and wonder, too! Thank you for the precious story of baby Jesus' birth. May it never lose its power in my life. How I love and adore you, Jesus! Amen.

Let's Go! Has the Christmas story lost its meaning and power to you? Talk about it. Pray for each other that Jesus Himself would speak a fresh revelation into your heart. Ask to be joyful in His holy birth this Christmas season.

December 24

Victorious Action: Knowing the Favor Which Rests on You!

"Suddenly a great company of the heavenly host appeared with the angel, praising God and saying, **"Glory to God in the highest heaven, and on earth peace to those on whom His favor rests."** When the angels had left them and gone into heaven, the shepherds said to one another, "Let's go to Bethlehem and see this thing that has happened, which the Lord has told us about" (Luke 2: 13-15).

Let's Talk: The heavenly host of angels appeared to the lowly shepherds, who were the most cast away population in this society. The angels exclaimed to them blessing and honoring their faith, "Glory to God in the highest heaven, and on earth peace to those on whom His favor rests." His favor rests; it pauses and tarries on His believers. You can have peace today because of Jesus and His birth. His favor isn't a fleeting moment. It actually rests upon you as focus on Him, His glory and goodness. Take a deep breath and exhale slowly. Rest and regroup in His strength and love. Christmas Eve is a time to slow down from the hub bub of the entire season. Pause and reflect on what this precious baby has meant to your life. Only a sweet and gentle Savior can give such sweet moments of peace and true tranquility. Lean in and listen to the gentle whisper to your heart. Feel His joy in this moment. A Savior has been born!

Let's Glorify: Lord, thank you for giving your favor to me as a follower of Christ. I love how you shared the joyful news of Jesus' birth to the lowliest of people, the shepherds. Lord, you show me how much you love each person. All people are valuable in your kingdom! God, just as the shepherds went and checked out Jesus when they heard the good news, let me keep seeking Him, my holy Lord and Savior. I am so blessed to be a part of your holy family! In Jesus' name, I pray and ask these things. Amen.

Let's Go! What are your family's traditions on Christmas Eve? **Will you take a moment to reflect on what this precious baby has meant to your life?**

December 25

Victorious Action: Glorifying and Praising God!

"So they hurried off and found Mary and Joseph, and the baby, who was lying in the manger. When they had seen Him, they spread the word concerning what had been told them about this child, and all who heard it were amazed at what the shepherds said to them. **But Mary treasured up all these things and pondered them in her heart.** The shepherds returned, **glorifying and praising God** for all the things they had heard and seen, which were just as they had been told" (Luke 2: 16-20, emphasis mine).

Let's Talk: When you encounter the living God, spread the word about His salvation! This is what the shepherds did. They saw baby Jesus firsthand and praised and glorified God the Father for sending Him. **What is your response when you have a fresh encounter with Jesus?** Do you have a jaded response or are you grateful once again, willing to share with others His love and life? Mary treasured up all these things and pondered them in her heart. I am sure deep within her soul she was glorifying the Lord for His goodness and choosing her to give birth to this precious and holy baby. On this Christmas morning, are you treasuring your Lord and Savior?

Let's Glorify: God, thank you for your precious life giving Son, Jesus! He came to the world for everyone and desires that all would open up His free gift of salvation. Lord, I want my faith to be alive and growing. Please help me to have a fresh revelation of Jesus as I seek Him so I will want to go and share Him with others. Thank you for this wonderful time of year to stop and reflect on the miraculous birth of your Son, Jesus. Merry Christmas to my Savior! Amen.

Let's Go! What is your response to the best gift you will ever receive? Is it glorifying and praising God or treasuring up all these things and pondering them in your heart? Share with each other. Share a fun memory of a Christmas past.

December 26

Victorious Action: Calling on the Name of Jesus!

"On the eighth day, when it was time to circumcise the child, He was named Jesus, the name the angel had given Him before He was conceived" (Luke 2: 21).

Let's Talk: The name of Jesus! It has quite a ring to it, doesn't it? God had His name picked out even before He was conceived. He existed before time began in the Trinity. His name contains all power and authority. Jesus' name signifies a Savior. He is your mediator and He brings salvation to our dying world. Remember His Name when you do not know which way to turn. Remember His name when you need endurance, courage and strength to continue in your never ending day. Say His name out loud. Believe He is with you even now. Pour your heart out to Him.

Let's Glorify: Thank you Jesus for being my Savior. I am so grateful your name contains all power and authority to protect me, guide me and keep my salvation sure until you come back for me. Your name is all comfort and guides me into your peace. Your name brings emotional and physical healing. Your name helps me break through my limitations. Knowing your name and your loving presence is better than life itself. Thank you for being my Savior! In Jesus' name, I pray. Amen.

Let's Go! How does calling on Jesus' name bring you comfort, peace, protection and love? Do you call on Him regularly? Why or why not?

December 27

Victorious Action: Holding the Baby Jesus!

"Now there was a man in Jerusalem called Simeon, who was righteous and devout. He was waiting for the consolation of Israel, and **the Holy Spirit was on him**. It had been revealed to him by the Holy Spirit that he would not die before he had seen the Lord's Messiah. Moved by the Spirit, he went into the temple courts" (Luke 2: 25-27).

Let's Talk: What is the Holy Spirit revealing to you today? Do you realize God is looking to and fro throughout the earth looking for sold out hearts and minds? He is searching for those folks who want to do His will whole-heartedly and are listening to the Holy Spirit. He is looking for someone to bless just as He did Simeon. Simeon was described as righteous and devout in the Bible for generations to read. He had the opportunity to hold the consolation of Israel, the comforter, as the baby Jesus in his arms.

Let's Glorify: Oh Lord, thank you for the precious baby Jesus! Who does not like to hold and cuddle a precious baby? I just start to relax when I hold and embrace a baby. And yet, this is exactly what Jesus, my Messiah does for me. He holds and comforts me. He loves me through some really tough moments. He gives me strength and endurance to finish His work. He changes me for the better and transforms me unto His image. Slowly but surely I become like Him as I listen to the Holy Spirit's whisper and wisdom. Lord God, thank you for all that you do for me! I receive you now. Forgive me of my sins and let me walk closer to you today. In Jesus my Messiah, I pray. Amen.

Let's Go! During the Christmas season, will you continue to look to Jesus, your comforter? Will you hold the baby Jesus in your arms and

December

let Him hold you in return? If you'll do so, you will have peace, joy and contentment knowing He is with you! Discuss with your mom, daughter or special friend the first time you held a (your) new born baby.

December 28

Victorious Action: Knowing His Light and Healing!

"Simeon took Him in his arms and praised God, saying: "Sovereign Lord, as you have promised, you may now dismiss your servant in peace. For my eyes have seen your salvation, which you have prepared in the sight of all nations: a light for revelation to the Gentiles, and the glory of your people Israel" (Luke 2: 28-32).

Let's Talk: I love how God keeps His promises to you just as He did Simeon! Your eyes have not seen the physical baby Jesus, but your heart has! God gave Jesus for all people, so they could know Him in a beautiful loving relationship and partake of His salvation. Salvation, eternal life is for Gentiles and Jews alike. Jesus is the light of the world! His light never changes. "He is light; in Him there is no darkness at all" (1 Jn. 1:5b). Jesus' light is spread through the Holy Spirit illuminating His truths in your heart and mind.

Let's Glorify: Jesus, you are the light of the world! In you there are no darkness, no hidden agendas; just pure light and pure love. Thank you for the light of your hope and salvation. Thank you that you are a God who keeps His promises. I can count on you at all times. You will always be with me because of the loving Holy Spirit of truth living inside me. Illuminate your truths and wisdom I need today. Help me to make godly decisions. Let me live in your Spirit and truth, not my own will. In Jesus' name, I pray. Amen.

Let's Go! Do you have any dark areas in your life that need exposing to Jesus' healing light? Let them go to Him. Confess to each other. Pray for each other. Jesus is just waiting to bring His precious transformational heart healing to your life!

December 29

Victorious Action: Knowing His Majestic Character!

"To the only God our Savior be glory, majesty, power and authority, through Jesus Christ our Lord, before all ages, now and forevermore! Amen" (Jude 25).

Let's Talk: Jude reminds his readers of God's power to preserve the faithful from falling away from Him. Jude ends, as does Revelation, by emphasizing that believers will meet Jesus Christ in heaven. What a glorious moment that will be! He is expressing confidence in God's power to preserve His people till Jesus comes back for them. Jude accentuates God's eternal greatness in His "glory, majesty, dominion, and authority." "Majesty" is God's sovereign power, authority or dignity. Majestic is God's character, His greatness or splendor.

Let's Glorify: God, you are the Eternal One. All glory, majesty, power and authority are yours before all time, and in the present and beyond all time! How I look forward to meeting your Son Jesus in heaven! Thank you that He will keep me and His followers from falling away. Thank you for the Holy Spirit guiding me and correcting me. In your majestic name, I pray. Amen.

Let's Go! What character of God and Jesus do you relate to the most? Is it glory, majesty, power, Savior or authority? Maybe you have another one? Have a conversation about God and Jesus' majestic character.

December 30

Victorious Action: Give Jesus All the Glory, Honor and Power!

"You are worthy, our Lord and God, to receive glory and honor and power, for you created all things, and by your will they were created and have their being" (Rev. 4:11).

Let's Talk: God is so worthy to receive all the glory, honor and power! He has created all things and He is pleased with what He has made! This includes you! He has even blessed you with sweet success and enabled you to wear a crown of victory! You and I will lay our crowns down at Jesus' feet just as the twenty four elders do in ceaseless praise and worship of the Great I AM. When you get to heaven you will praise Him out of a heart filled with love and gratitude for saving you from a life of darkness. Ps. 35:3 promises, "I will give you victory!"

Let's Glorify: God, you are the Great I AM! How I look forward to praising you in heaven someday soon. Along with singing your praises in heaven, I will have jobs to do. I know these will be meaningful and satisfying. I look forward to serving you, my King! In Jesus' name, I pray. Amen.

Let's Go! As you studied these scriptures all year long, have you developed a sense of distinction of where you are today from where you have come from? Discuss with your mom, daughter or special friend how you have seen them change and develop their walk in Christ.

December 31

Victorious Action: Blessings and a Happy New You!

"The Lord make His face shine on you and be gracious to you; the Lord turn His face toward you and give you peace" (Num. 6:25-26).

Let's Talk: The Lord will bless you in this New Year! Let this past year go with all of its blessings and even hard moments. **God has a new dream for you to dream!** He will look upon you and bless you with His gracious favor, joy and peace as you trust in Him! He has a Happy New Year for you filled with loving promises and new beginnings. Rest in Him as you wait patiently and courageously for His dreams and desires to be fulfilled. Your dream and desire was put in your heart by God Himself as you walk closely with Him! Be blessed!

Let's Glorify: Dear God, you are my dream maker! Lord, I want to dream the big dreams you have placed into my heart. Let me move courageously into the dreams you have for me, not worrying about *whether I can make them happen or not!* You are the Great I AM and you will cause my dreams to come to fruition as you desire. I can surely wait and rest in you. Thank you for this past year. Lord, help me to grow into the image of your Son Jesus as I walk closer and closer to you. In Jesus' wonderful name, I pray. Amen.

Let's Go! What dreams has God placed in your heart for the New Year? Share with each other and commit to pray for these dreams in the New Year.

CPSIA information can be obtained
at www.ICGtesting.com
Printed in the USA
LVOW12s1108011116
511172LV00001B/41/P